LOVE STORIES

CHARLES MEE

Charles Mee's work has been made possible by the support of Richard B. Fisher and Jeanne Donovan Fisher.

INTRODUCTION

B ack in 1999, Michael Dixon, the literary manager of the Actors Theatre of Louisville, phoned me and asked if I would write a play for the next year's "Humana Festival of new American plays," which they thought should be a festival celebrating the new millennium.

I said of course, I'd love to, but then I thought: I don't think I can write a science fiction play about how life is going to be in the next millennium. But maybe I could go back to the oldest play in the western world and see if it still speaks to us today.

So, I got hold of Aeschylus's *Danaids*, a trilogy about the fifty daughters of Danaus who were pledged by their father to marry the fifty sons of Danaus's twin brother Aegyptus. It was once thought to be the oldest play in the west, but recent scholarship has decided *The Persians* is Aeschylus's first play. But I couldn't resist doing a version of the *Danaids*, set in the world today. It turns out the *Danaids* is the first play of a trilogy called *The Suppliants*, of which the second two plays are lost. So, the play I wrote is the story of those two lost plays.

Of course, the fifty sisters didn't want to marry the fifty brothers, so they got on a boat and sailed away to a foreign country to avoid marriage. And then the fifty brothers got on a boat to go and find them. It is a story about men and women, gender, refugees, whether an unknown stranger, out of a sense of compassion and social love, will give the women help, and, finally, of falling in love. When the women found no one would help them, and there was no escape, forty-nine of the brides murdered their fiancés, and one of the brides fell in love, about the same odds as today.

So, it is a play about romantic love and social love and civilization.

But, of course, it turns out this is not the only love story from the past several thousand years. The second play in this book is *True Love*, inspired by Euripides's *Hippolytus* and Racine's *Phaedra*. And then there is *First Love*, inspired by a novella by Samuel Beckett. And then *Summertime* and *Wintertime* about the same family in two different seasons, together in their summer house, inspired by *The Winter's Tale* and *The Cherry Orchard* and Moliere and Magritte and *As You Like it* and *Midsummer Night's Dream*. And then there is *Fire Island*, inspired by going to Fire Island and eavesdropping on the lives of friends.

None of the Greeks ever wrote an original play, and neither did Shakespeare. Those we think of as the greatest playwrights of the western world stole all their stories from the past and re-made them to suit life in their own times. And now when we go to school to learn playwriting, we are taught how to write original plays, which is to say, not to steal from old stories but to steal from our wives and friends and strangers on the street and do and say in our plays what we have seen them do and say. So, three of the plays here are stolen from the past, two are stolen half from the past and half from the present, and one is completely "original." The truth is, I love them all, stories that are, whether that was the original intention or not, stories of all the complications and joys and terrors of what it is to be a human being, stories of human love.

THE PLAYS IN THIS
VOLUME

Big Love

Fifty brides flee their fifty grooms and seek refuge in a villa on the coast of Italy in this modern re-making of one of the western world's oldest plays, *The Danaids* by Aeschylus. And, in this villa on the Italian coast, the fifty grooms catch up with the brides, and mayhem ensues: the grooms arriving by helicopter in their flight suits, women throwing themselves over and over again to the ground, pop songs and romantic dances, and, finally, unable to escape their forced marriages, 49 of the brides murder 49 of the grooms-and one bride falls in love. About the same odds as today. [9 actors]

First Love

Two people in their seventies fall in love—for the first time in their lives. And, as they work their way toward one another through the accumulated baggage of their lives, they move in fits and starts toward sabotaging the last chance for love they'll ever have. [3 actors]

True Love

Based on Euripides' *Hippolytus* and Racine's *Phaedra*—but placed in America's trailer trash world, in which Phaedra does not restrain herself from sleeping with her fourteen-year-old stepson, and all the townspeople sit around the gas station talking about the extraordinary relationships they have had or known of, living in their normal world—each of them as true a love as human beings are capable of. [11 actors]

Summertime

A sweet, dreamy, romantic comedy from the world of *As You Like It* and *Midsummer Night's Dream* and *The Cherry Orchard* and Moliere and Magritte. This play is a companion piece to *Wintertime*, which has the same characters and setting, set in another season. [13 actors]

Wintertime

A sweet, dreamy, romantic comedy from the world

of *The Winter's Tale* and *The Cherry Orchard* and Moliere and Magritte. This play is a companion piece to *Summertime*, which has the same characters and setting, set in another season. [13 actors]

Fire Island

A young couple gets on the ferry on Friday evening to go to Fire Island, and, after they get there, there are 758 love affairs in the summer house, on the beach, on the porch, in the bedroom and kitchen and living room, and then the couple gets back on the ferry on Sunday evening to go back to work on Monday. [10-20 actors]

BIG LOVE

CAST OF CHARACTERS

Lydia
Olympia
Thyona
Bella/Eleanor
Piero/Leo
Giuliano
Constantine
Oed
Nikos

Blackout.

Full volume: wedding processional music:
the triumphant music at the end of Scene 13, Act III,
of Mozart's Marriage of Figaro.

Lydia walks up the aisle,
looking somewhat disoriented,
carrying a wedding bouquet,
in a white wedding dress that is disheveled,
a little torn in places, dirty in spots.

She steps up onto the stage,
goes to the bathtub,
drops the bouquet on the floor,
takes off all her clothes,
or simply walks out of them,
steps into the tub,
leans her head back against the rim, exhausted,
and closes her eyes,
her arms thrown back out of the tub as though she
were crucified,
as we listen to the music finish playing.

Now, quietly, sweetly, restfully,
Pachelbel's Canon in D
is heard,
and Giuliano steps onto the stage,
a glass of wine in his hand.

He is a young Italian man, handsome, agreeable,
weak and useless.
He seems a little surprised to see Lydia there
apparently napping in the tub.

This is Italy:
rose and white.

If Emanuel Ungaro had a villa on the west coast of

Italy, this would be it:
we are outdoors,
on the terrace or in the garden,
facing the ocean:

wrought iron
white muslin
flowers
a tree
an arbor
an outdoor dinner table with chairs for six
a white marble balustrade
elegant
simple
basic
eternal.

But the setting for the piece should not be real, or naturalistic. It should not be a set for the piece to play within but rather something against which the piece can resonate: something on the order of a bathtub, 100 olive trees, and 300 wine glasses half-full of red wine.

More an installation than a set.

It is midsummer evening—the long, long golden twilight.

Giuliano and Lydia speak, quietly, and with many silences between their words, as the music continues under the dialogue.

[Note: there are lots of Italians in this play,
but I don't think the actors should speak in Italian
accents—
with the sole exception of Bella—
any more than they would if they were doing
Romeo and Juliet
or the Merchant of Venice.
Except for Bella, these are English-speaking
international travelers.]

GIULIANO
Hello.

[she opens her eyes]

LYDIA
Hello.

GIULIANO
I'm Giuliano.

LYDIA
Hello, Giuliano.

GIULIANO
And you are....

LYDIA
Lydia.

GIULIANO
Lydia.
I don't think we've met.

LYDIA
No.

GIULIANO
You've just—arrived.

LYDIA
Yes.

GIULIANO
That's your boat offshore?

LYDIA
Yes.

GIULIANO
A big boat.

LYDIA
Well...it belongs to my family.

GIULIANO
You've come for the weekend?

LYDIA
Yes, oh, yes, at least.

GIULIANO
You're friends of my sister.

LYDIA
Your sister?

GIULIANO
My uncle?

LYDIA
Your uncle?

[silence]

GIULIANO
I don't mean to be rude, but...

[with a smile]

who was it invited you?

LYDIA
Invited us?

GIULIANO
You didn't come to the party?
You mean: you're not a guest.

LYDIA
Oh, you mean, this is your home.
I'm in your home.

GIULIANO
Yes.
Well, it's my uncle's house.

LYDIA
It's so big.
I thought it was a hotel.

GIULIANO
We have a big family.

LYDIA
I'm sorry I just...

GIULIANO
It's OK.

Where do you come from?

LYDIA
Greece.

GIULIANO
Greece. You mean
just now?

LYDIA
Yes.

My sisters and I.
We were to be married to our cousins, and
well, we didn't want to, but
we had to, so
when the wedding day came
we just got on our boat and left
so
here we are.

GIULIANO
Just like that.

LYDIA
Yes.

GIULIANO
Just walked away from the altar
and sailed away from Greece.

LYDIA
Yes.
Where are we?

GIULIANO
Italy.
This is Italy.

LYDIA
Oh. Italy.
I love Italy.

GIULIANO
It's...well...yes. So do I.

And your sisters are still on the boat?

LYDIA
Yes, most of them.
We came....
[looking around]
at least, some of us came ashore.

There are fifty of us all together.

GIULIANO
Fifteen?

LYDIA
Fifty.
Fifty sisters.

GIULIANO [laughing awkwardly]
I...
I don't think even I know anyone who has fifty sisters.

And you were all to get married to your cousins?

LYDIA
Yes.

GIULIANO
To your cousins?

LYDIA
Yes.

We're looking for asylum.
We want to be taken in here
so we don't have to marry our cousins.

GIULIANO
You want to be taken in as immigrants?

LYDIA
As refugees.

GIULIANO
Refugees.

LYDIA
Yes.

GIULIANO
From...

LYDIA
From Greece.

GIULIANO
I mean, from, you know:
political oppression, or war....

LYDIA
Or kidnapping. Or rape.

GIULIANO
From rape.

LYDIA
By our cousins.

GIULIANO
Well, marriage really.

LYDIA
Not if we can help it.

[silence]

GIULIANO
I see.

LYDIA
You seem like a good person, Giuliano.
We need your help.

[silence]

GIULIANO
I think you should talk to my uncle.
Piero, he has...connections.
Just stay right here.
If you'll wait here,
I'll bring him out.

LYDIA
Thank you.

[the conversation ends just a few moments
before the end of the 4:58 of the Pachelbel Canon
in D;
Giuliano leaves, and she weeps and weeps while
the music finishes.

Suddenly, Clarke's Trumpet Voluntary announces
the entrance
of two more young women in wedding dresses:
OLYMPIA and THYONA.

Their wedding dresses, too, are of course white,
but in different styles,
and in varying states of disrepair—
torn or dirty or wrinkled.
Olympia carries the broken heel of a high-heeled
shoe,
and she walks, up and down, in a single shoe.

The women enter without ceremony,
dragging in a huge steamer trunk,
struggling with it.
Or else they have a matching set of luggage,
eight pieces or more, that they wrestle onto the
stage,
and they peel off, one by one, exhausted or
exasperated with the luggage,
giving up on it.

Olympia goes to the bathtub,
pulls up her dress and sits on the edge
with her feet in the tub

as Clarke's Trumpet Voluntary segues into the intro
for "You Don't Own Me,"
and, Olympia sings with all her heart.

Thyona meanwhile, unpacks wedding gifts from
the trunk—
plates and glasses and cups and saucers,
and—to set the scene for what kind of a play this is,
that it is not a text with brief dances and other
physical activities added to it, but rather a piece in
which
the physical activities and the text are equally
important to the experience—she hurls the plates
and cups and glasses with all her force against the
wall shattering them into a million bits.

Lydia joins in singing with Olympia on the choruses;
Finally, Thyona joins in the singing, too.

BELLA, an old Italian woman in black dress and
babushka
with a basket of tomatoes, comes out before the
song ends;
she drags out a simple wooden chair and a folding
card table with her, which she sets up noisily]

BELLA
Scusi, eh?

[and she sits and starts sorting through her
tomatoes,
putting the nice ones to one side,
shining them a bit first on her apron.

Bella looks up at the young women]

BELLA
So.
This is your wedding day?

LYDIA
No.

BELLA
You are trying on your dresses
because your wedding day is coming soon.

LYDIA
No.

THYONA
No, we're not getting married.

BELLA
You have been married already.

OLYMPIA
No.

BELLA
So, it's none of my business.

And yet, I can tell you
marriage is a wonderful thing.

Imagine that:
No husbands.
At your age.

And children.

When I was your age already I had three sons.
Now, I have thirteen sons.

LYDIA
Thirteen sons.

BELLA
My oldest, that's Piero,
he stays home here with his mother.
He's a good boy.

[she puts one polished tomato carefully, lovingly to one side, as though it were her own baby]

But too old for you.

LYDIA
We were hoping to meet Piero. We wanted to....

BELLA [ignoring Lydia, continuing]
My second son, Paolo,
he lives just next door
a doctor
he takes good care of people here in town

[another polished tomato placed lovingly to one side]

Married.
Five children.
A good boy.
Paolo, he is Giuliano's father.
You met Giuliano?

LYDIA
Yes, and he said we might be able to meet....

BELLA [ignoring Lydia, continuing]
My third son, he's in business here in the town,
visits me every week
every Sunday without fail
a good boy.
Also married,
four children.

[another polished tomato tenderly to one side]

LYDIA
Excuse me, but....

BELLA
My fourth son
he was a sweet child
cherubic
such little cheeks
such a tender boy
a sunny disposition

[she puts another tomato to one side,
but too close to the edge so that it
"accidentally" rolls off the table to the ground,
where it splats;]

LYDIA
Oh.

BELLA
he joined the church

[she looks at the splatted tomato for a moment,
then resumes]

My fifth son
he also went into business here in town

[she starts to put the polished tomato carefully to
one side]

but then he got involved with certain business
associates. . .

[she moves her hand out over open space,
pauses a moment,
then drops the tomato with a splat to the ground]

My sixth son
he's married to a German girl.

[splat]

My seventh son
he went to America

[splat]

took his younger brother

[splat]

and then, two years later,
they sent for their brother Guido,
and he went to America, too.

[splat]

My tenth son,
he became a politician.

[she holds the tomato out over the ground for
several moments,
in deep anguish,
then shrugs, and splats it]

LYDIA
Excuse me, but....

BELLA
My eleventh son
he is on television
on a soap opera
with the stories of love affairs
and godknows whatnot

[she starts to drop another tomato to the ground,
thinks better of it,
puts it on the table]

he's not killing people

LYDIA
No.

BELLA
My twelfth son
he's not killing anyone either
but he has his love affairs
he argues all the time with his wife
he keeps her like a tramp

he spends all his money
going here and there for soccer games

[she starts to drop another tomato]

but,
a good man is hard to find

[thinks better of it, starts to put it with the others
she has saved]

OLYMPIA
That's so true.

BELLA
Still, he's always getting into fights
he comes home in the middle of the night

[starts to drop it again]

nobody's perfect

THYONA
No.

BELLA
[she saves the tomato]
he loves his children

[she saves it]

LYDIA
That's a good thing.

BELLA
My youngest son

he likes to ride the motorcycles
he likes to be in Rome
with the young movie actresses
and the parties

[she starts to splat another tomato,
then takes it back and puts it gently on the table]

he's my baby.

LYDIA
I see.

BELLA
So, what do I have left?
Now you see why I love my Piero so much,
and want to protect him,
my first born,
who is too old for you.

[silence]

You're staying for dinner?

LYDIA
We haven't been invited.

[The uncle, Piero, comes out of the house,
a glass of wine in his hand.]

BELLA
Piero,
you should make them stay for dinner.
They're good girls.
[Bella gathers her tomatoes into her apron]

I never had daughters.
Imagine that.

[Bella leaves.]

PIERO
Giuliano,
mi dispiacce, ma....

[Piero shrugs.]

GIULIANO
Si. Fa niente.

[Giuliano picks up a pail and rag
and cleans up the mess Bella has made.

Piero speaks to the young women with great
warmth,
a welcoming manner, relaxed, a sense of playfulness.

There might be music under this scene,
maybe Molloy's Love's Old Sweet Song
or some champagne music from inside the house.]

PIERO
May I offer you something?

LYDIA
No, thank you.

PIERO
A glass of wine?

OLYMPIA AND THYONA
No, thank you.

PIERO
Coffee? Tea?

LYDIA
No thanks.

PIERO
Something to eat?

LYDIA
No, thank you.

OLYMPIA
Actually,
I don't know how to say this,
I don't want to complain
but you don't seem to have a lot of products.

PIERO
Products?

OLYMPIA
Soaps, you know, and creams,
things like,

LYDIA
Olympia....

OLYMPIA
You know, we've been travelling,
and when you've been travelling
you hope at the end of the journey that you might
find
some, like,

Oil of Olay Moisturizing Body Wash
or like
John Freda Sheer Blond Shampoo and Conditioner
for Highlighted Blonds

LYDIA
Olympia....

OLYMPIA
I know this is not a hotel, so you wouldn't have everything,
but maybe some Estee Lauder 24 Karat Color Golden Body Creme with Sunbloc,
or Fetish Go Glitter Body Art in Soiree,

LYDIA
Olympia....

OLYMPIA
or some Prescriptives Uplift Eye Cream, not in the tube: firming,
Mac lip gloss in Pink Poodle
just
some things to make a woman feel
you know
fresh

LYDIA
Olympia....

PIERO
I am afraid I don't know about these things,
but I'll ask Giuliano to go out and see what he can find.

OLYMPIA
Thank you.

LYDIA
Really we were mostly hoping to ask you to just:
take us in.

PIERO
Take you in?

LYDIA
Your nephew Giuliano says you have some
connections.

PIERO
Oh?

LYDIA
And that you can help us.

PIERO
Well, of course, this is a country where people
know one another
and, Giuliano is right, sometimes these connections
can be useful.

If, for example,
you were a member of my family,
certainly, I would just take you in.
But
[he shrugs]
I don't know you.

LYDIA
[thinking quickly]

Oh. But.

We are related.

I mean, you know: in some way.

Our people came from Greece to Sicily a long time ago

and to Siracusa

and from Siracusa to Taormina and to the Golfo di Saint'Eufemia

and from there up the coast of Italy to where we are now.

So we are probably members of the same family you and I.

PIERO [amused]
Descended from Zeus, you mean.

OLYMPIA
Yes. We're all sort of goddesses in a way.

PIERO
Indeed. It's very enticing to recover a family connection to Zeus.

And, where is your father, meanwhile?

Is he not able to take care of you?

LYDIA
Our father signed a wedding contract to give us away.

PIERO
To your cousins from Greece.

THYONA
From America.
They went from Greece to America,
and now they're rich
and they think they can come back
and take whatever they want.

PIERO
And the courts in your country:
they would enforce such a contract?

LYDIA
It's an old contract. It seems they will.
We have nothing against men—

OLYMPIA
Not all of us.

LYDIA
but what these men have in mind is not usual.

THYONA
Or else
all too usual.

[silence]

PIERO
You know, as it happens, I have some houseguests
here for the weekend
and I would be delighted if you would all join us
for dinner,
stay the night if you like
until you get your bearings

but really
as for the difficulties you find yourselves in
disagreeable as they are
and as much as I would like to help
this is not my business.

THYONA
Whose business is it
if not yours?
You're a human being.

OLYMPIA
And a relative.

PIERO
A relative.

THYONA
This is a crisis.

PIERO
And yet...
You know, I am not the Red Cross.

THYONA
And so?

PIERO
So, to be frank,
I can't take in every refugee who comes into my
garden.

OLYMPIA
Why not?

PIERO
Because the next thing I know I would have a
refugee camp here in my home.
I'd have a house full of Kosovars and Ibo and Tootsies
boat people from China and godknows whatall.

OLYMPIA
That would be nice.

PIERO
I don't think I can open my doors to the whole
world.

OLYMPIA
Look at you, you're a rich person.

PIERO
OK. Well, then,
what if I were to say, yes, I can do my part,
in fact, I'm not a bad person entirely,
some people think of me even as a generous person,
and I can help,
but why should I help you?
Shouldn't I rather look around at the world and say:
no, not these people perhaps
but someone else has the greater claim on my
attention.

LYDIA
But we are here.

PIERO
Yes?

LYDIA
We are here on your terrace.
Why do you look for someone else?
Look for someone else, too, if you want,
but we are here.

PIERO
And yet I know nothing about this dispute.
I don't know whether these fellows have some
rights, too.
What shall I do if they come to me
and say you've abducted our women
give us our women
or we'll shoot you?

LYDIA
Shoot you?

PIERO
What do I know?
I don't know what sort of fellows they are.
I should put myself, perhaps my life on the line—
knowing nothing—
and also the life of my nephew
my brother next door
my brother's sons.

I put their lives on the line
for what?
to save you whom
I've never met before
I don't know what this is about
why would I do this?

LYDIA
Because it's right.

PIERO
I understand it may be right,
but one doesn't always go around doing what's right.
I've never heard of such a thing.
The world is a complicated place.

[silence]

OLYMPIA
It's not that no one's never said no to me,
but I don't think I've ever asked a guy to save me
in a situation like this
and had him say no.

THYONA
There is only one question to ask:
do we want to marry them or not?
No, we don't.
Are you going to let them
drag us away from your house
and do whatever they want with us?

Think of it this way:
if you don't take us in,
my sisters and I will hang ourselves here on your
terrace:
fifty dead women hanging in front of your house.

PIERO
Hang yourselves?

THYONA
What choice do we have?

[silence]

LYDIA
Shall we ask your mother what she thinks would be right?

PIERO
You're right.
Of course.
You're right.
I beg your pardon.
Of course, I'll take you in.
I don't know what I was thinking.

LYDIA
Thank you.

PIERO
I beg your pardon, really.
I wasn't quite absorbing what it was you were saying.
I'll tell my mother
you will stay for dinner,
and then we'll talk and see what's to be done.
Please, make yourselves at home.
And if there's anything at all you want, please ask.

[he leaves]

OLYMPIA
Now you see, there are men who are kind and decent.

THYONA
Not so kind and decent
if he's not threatened with some kind of scandal of
dead women hanging off his house.

OLYMPIA
I liked him.
You should give a person the benefit of the doubt.

THYONA
You think you found this man's good side.
Men don't have a good side.

OLYMPIA
I've known men who have a good side, Thyona.

LYDIA
I've known men you could sit with after dinner
in front of the fireplace
and just listen to the way he speaks
and hear the gentleness in his way of speaking
and the carefulness

OLYMPIA
I've known men who think,
oh,
a woman,
I'd like to take care of her
not in any way that he thinks he is superior and has
control
but in the way that he understands
a woman is a different sort of person
and precious because of that

vulernable in certain ways because of that
in ways that he isn't
although he might be vulnerable in other ways
because of his stuff that he has
and that he treasures what a woman has
and thinks, oh, if only I could be close to her
and feel what she feels
and see the world as she sees it
how much richer my life would be
and so, because of that, he thinks,
oh, a woman,
I can really respect her
and love her
for who she really is

THYONA
I know a man who will say I want to take care of you
because he means he wants to use you for a while
and while he's using you
so you don't notice what he's doing
he'll take care of you as if you were a new car
before he decides to trade you in.

LYDIA
I've known men like that, too.
But not all men are necessarily the same.
Sometimes you can hear the whole man just in his
voice
how deep it is or how frightened
where it stops to think
and how complex and supple and sure it is

OLYMPIA
you can hear the strength in it
and you can know that you're safe

THYONA
The male
the male is a biological accident
an incomplete female
the product of a damaged gene
a half-dead lump of flesh
trapped in a twilight zone somewhere between apes and humans
always looking obsessively for some woman

LYDIA
That's maybe a little bit extreme.

THYONA
any woman
because he thinks if he can make some connection with a woman
that will make him a whole human being!
But it won't. It never will.

Boy babies should be flushed down the toilet at birth.

LYDIA
I know how you feel, Thyona.

OLYMPIA
I've felt that way myself sometimes.

LYDIA
Still, this man who doesn't even know us
who owes us nothing
doesn't know what he risks by offering us a place
to stay.

There are places in the world
where refugees are taken in
out of generosity
and often these are men who do the taking in
because people have the capacity for goodness
and there could be a world where people care for
one another

[As the speech goes on,
it is joined by the sound of a helicopter overhead
which grows louder and louder,
drowning out Lydia's words even as she goes on
shouting them
until the helicopter is deafening
and wind is whipping everyone around so they
have to fight to stand up.

Again: the over-the-top extremity of this physical
world,
like Thyona throwing plates just when she enters—
should establish the kind of physical piece this is.]

where men are good to women
and there is not a men's history
and a separate women's history
but a human history

where we are all together
and support one another
nurture one another

[Stanley's Trumpet Tune joins the deafening
helicopter noise.]

honor one another's differences
and learn to live together
in common justice
reconciling our differences in peaceful conversation
reaching out with goodwill towards one another

[A loudspeaker says:
"STAND BACK. STAND BACK.
STAND AWAY FROM THE HELICOPTER."]

not trying to obliterate those who are not as we are
but learning to understand
learning to take deep pleasure
in the enormous variety of creatures

[She is on the ground toward the end of this speech,
her head lifted up to the sky as she shouts her words
until finally, she is hunkered down on stage,
her hands over her head;
the helicopter engine is turned off,
and the noise recedes,
and Stanley's Trumpet Tune concludes;
she lifts her head to see that
three guys have entered: NIKOS, CONSTANTINE,
and OED;
they wear tuxedoes with flowers in their buttonholes

underneath flight suits,
and, as they enter, they are removing their ultra-high-tech flying helmets. Constantine chews gum.]

Oh, Nikos,
you found us.

NIKOS
Lydia, why did you run away from us?

LYDIA
What?

NIKOS
We were waiting for you at the church.

THYONA
You can't force us to marry you, Nikos.

NIKOS
Force you?
We thought you were coming.

OLYMPIA
Why should we come?

OED
Because we were getting married.

THYONA
We never agreed to marry you.

NIKOS
We have a prenuptial agreement, Lydia.

CONSTANTINE
We have a deal.

THYONA
We never had a deal with you, Constantine.

CONSTANTINE
Your father made a deal with my father
before you were born, Thyona.
You are engaged to me,
and I am going to marry you.

THYONA
This is from the Dark Ages.

NIKOS
Well, if there was some misunderstanding....

THYONA
There was no misunderstanding.
We are not marrying you.

CONSTANTINE
There is a contract involved here.

NIKOS
My brothers and I, we've counted on this all our lives.
And, plus, I thought it would be kind of neat:
a big wedding, fifty brides and fifty grooms,
a real event.

CONSTANTINE
And we never agreed to release you from your
promise.

THYONA
Why not?

CONSTANTINE
Because I am a traditional person, Thyona.
I want a traditional marriage,
a traditional wife.
That's the way it is.

THYONA
It's a different world now, Constantine.
You can't just marry someone against their will
because there's been some kind of family
understanding.

CONSTANTINE
What do you think?
You think you live in a world nowadays where
you can throw out a promise
just because you don't feel like keeping it?
Just because
drugs are rife
gambling is legal
medicine is euthanasia
birth is abortion
homosexuality is the norm
pornography is piped into everybody's home on
the internet
now you think you can do whatever you want
whenever you want to do it
no matter what the law might say?

I don't accept that.

Sometimes I like to lie down at night
with my arms around someone
and KNOW she is there for me
know this gives her pleasure—
my arms around her
her back to me
my stomach pressed against her back
my face buried in her hair
one hand on her stomach
feeling at peace.

That's my plan
to have that.
I'll have my bride.
If I have to have her arms tied behind her back
and dragged to me
I'll have her back.

What is it you women want
you want to be strung up with hoods and gags and
blindfolds
stretched out on a board with weights on your chest
you want me to sew your legs to the bed
and pour gasoline on you
and light you on fire
is that what I have to do to keep you?

[silence]

NIKOS
Lydia,
isn't this your wedding dress?

LYDIA
Yes.

NIKOS
It seems you were ready to get married.

CONSTANTINE
The future is going to happen, Thyona,
whether you like it or not.
You say, you don't want to be taken against your
will.
People are taken against their will every day.
Do you want tomorrow to come?
Do you want to live in the future?
Never mind. You can't stop the clock.
Tomorrow will take today by force
whether you like it or not.
Time itself is an act of rape.
Life is rape.
No one asks to be born.
No one asks to die.
We are all taken by force, all the time.
You make the best of it.
You do what you have to do.

OLYMPIA
We have an uncle here, Constantine.
and he is going to take care of us.

CONSTANTINE
I am an American now, Olympia.
I'm not afraid of your uncle.

Do you watch television?
Do you see what happens when Americans want something?

[the uncle has entered]

PIERO
Excuse me.
I am Piero. This is my home.
And you would be the cousins of these young women?

NIKOS
We're engaged to be married.

PIERO
I understand the women are no longer interested.

CONSTANTINE
We are not here to negotiate.

PIERO
That's a forthright position.
I like to know where I stand when I deal with a man.
But, before we talk, let me welcome you properly.
Why don't you come into the house with me,
and have a glass of something.

What's your favorite cigar?

Do you like a Cuban?
A Vegas Robaina?
A Partagas?
Is it...?

CONSTANTINE
Constantine.

PIERO
Constantine. And you are...?

OED
Oed.

PIERO
And. . .

NIKOS
Nikos.

PIERO
Nikos. Come with me.
We'll have a glass of something,
have a smoke,
get things sorted out.

NIKOS
I'd like that.

PIERO
Excuse us, ladies.
Come with me.

[He leads them out.]

THYONA
That bastard!
What did I tell you?

OLYMPIA
He's going to solve it peacefully.

THYONA
He's giving in, don't you get it?
These men and their deals.

LYDIA
Right.
You could be right.

OLYMPIA
I don't think he would do that.

THYONA
Sometimes a person can talk a good game,
but when push comes to shove, they're weak right
to the core.

OLYMPIA
Except for Constantine.

THYONA
And except for me.
I haven't given in either.
This game isn't over till someone lies on the ground
with the flesh pulled off their bones.

Men.
You think you can do whatever you want with me,
think again.
you think that I'm so delicate?
you think you have to care for me?
You throw me to the ground
you think I break?

[she throws herself to the ground]

you think I can't get up again?
you think I can't get up again?

[she gets up]

you think I need a man to save my life?

[she throws herself to the ground again]

I don't need a man!
I don't need a man!

[she gets up and throws herself to the ground again
and again as she yells]

These men can fuck themselves!
these men are leeches
these men are parasites
these rapists,
these politicians,
these Breadwinners,

[she is throwing herself to the ground over and over,
letting her loose limbs hit the ground with the
rattle of a skeleton's bones,
her head lolling over and hitting the ground with
a thwack,
rolling over, bones banging the ground,
back to her feet,
and throwing herself to the ground again in the
same way over and over

music kicks in over this—
maybe J.S. Bach's "Sleepers Awake! " from Cantata

No. 140
and, as she hits the ground over and over,
repeating her same litany as she does,
Olympia watches her
and then she joins in,
and starts throwing herself to the ground
synchronously
so that it is a choreographed piece
of the two women throwing themselves to the
ground,
rolling around, flailing on the ground,
banging angrily on the ground,
rising again and again]

THYONA [yelling simultaneously with Olympia]
these cheap pikers,
these welchers,
these liars,
these double dealers,
flim-flam artists,
litterbugs,
psychiatrists!

[And now Olympia starts to yell, too,
simultaneously with Thyona, on top of her words,
as both of them continue to throw themselves to
the ground over and over.]

OLYMPIA
These men!
These men!
All I wanted was a man who could be gentle

a man who likes to cuddle
a man who likes to talk
a man who likes to listen

THYONA
Men who speak when they have nothing to say!
These men should be eliminated!
These men should be snuffed out!
Who needs a man?
Who needs a man?
I'll make it on my own.
I'm an autonomous person!
I'm an independent person!
I can do what I want!
I can be who I am!

OLYMPIA [still yelling simultaneously with Thyona]
And I don't think it's wrong
to lie in the bath
and curl my hair
and paint my nails
to like my clothes
and think they're sexy
and wear short skirts
that blow up in the wind
I don't think it's wrong
for a man to love me
to like to touch me
and listen to me
and talk to me
and write me notes

and give me flowers
because I like men
I like men
And, I like to be submissive.

[and, finally, Lydia joins in, too,
until all three women are yelling their words
over the loud music
and throwing themselves to the ground over and
over]

ALL THREE WOMEN TOGETHER
Why can't a man
be more like a woman?

LYDIA
Plainspoken and forthright.
Honest and clear.
Able to process.
To deal with his feelings.
To speak from the heart
to say what he means.
Because if he can
I don't have a grudge
or something against him
we couldn't work out.
I think it's wrong
to make sweeping judgments
write off a whole sex
the way men do to women
we could talk to each other
person to person

get along with each other
then we could go deep
to what a man or a woman
really can be
deep down to the mysteries
of being alive
of knowing ourselves
to know what it is
to live life on earth

[the women work themselves, still in choreographed sync,
to a state of total exhaustion
until one by one, they sprawl on chairs, panting.

Giuliano comes in with a cart piled high with wedding gifts.
Bella enters with him, also carrying gifts.]

GIULIANO
The wedding presents have come
now that everyone knows where to find you.
Frankly, I've never seen so many gifts
so much silver
so many white things
so much satin ribbon.
Do you think
we could save the ribbon?
Because
I wouldn't mind having the ribbon
I haven't taken any yet
I was going to ask you

if you don't want it
because I have a collection of Barbies and Kens
and this ribbon would go with the whole ensemble
so perfectly
this ensemble that I have
they are all arrayed together with their hands up
in the air
because they are doing the firewalking ceremony
and Barbie has her pink feather boa
and her lime green outfit with the flowers at
the waist
and the gold bow at the bodice
and Ken is doing the Lambada
so of course they all have mai tais
and they're just having a wonderful time
and their convertible is parked nearby
so you know they can take off to see the sunset any
time they want
and when people come over and see my collection
they just say wow
because
because they can't believe I've just done it
but I think if that's who you are
you should just be who you are
whatever that is
just do who you are
because that's why we're here
and if it's you
it can't be wrong.
Some people like to be taken forcibly.

If that's what they like, then that's okay.
And if not, then not.
I myself happen to like it.
To have somebody grab me.
Hold me down.
To know they have to have me
no matter what.
It's not everyone's cup of tea.
Everyone should be free to choose for themselves

OLYMPIA
[picking up one of the wedding gifts]
Plus some of these things are nice.
Can we keep them?

THYONA
No, Olympia.
Not if you aren't getting married.

OLYMPIA
Maybe we should think about it.
Some people go on honeymoons, too.

LYDIA
Olympia.

OLYMPIA
They go to places where there are hammocks and
white sand
and people hold them by the waist
and lift them up out of the water
splashing and laughing
and they dive underwater

without the tops to their swimming suits
and the sun sets
and people drink things through straws

LYDIA
Olympia....

OLYMPIA
and they listen to the waves
and even make love in the afternoon
and even like Giuliano says to be submissive
because, to me,
submission is giving up your body,
and your mind and your emotions
and everything
to a someone who can accept all the responsibilities
that go with that.
And I myself enjoy the freedom that submission
gives me.
I like to be tickled and tortured
and I like to scream and scream
and feel helpless
and be totally controlled
and see how good that makes someone else feel.
It is for me the most natural high.
It is so much better than taking drugs.
You can just relax and enjoy yourself
and feel alive and free inside.

LYDIA
I think we're losing the point.

Like
shouldn't we be leaving?

THYONA
You don't think they'll follow us wherever we go?

BELLA
I had a man once
I was walking along the Appia Antica
and he came along on his motor scooter
and offered me a ride.
A skinny, ugly fellow with dark hair and big ears
and skin so sleek and smooth
I wanted to put my hands on it.
I got on the back of his motor scooter
and ten minutes later
we were in bed together at his mother's house
and I married him
and we had our boys.
All his life he worked
giving the gift of his labor to me
and to our children
he died of a heart attack
while he was out among the trees
harvesting the olives

and
if he came along now
I would get on the scooter again just like the first time.

[Bella plumps down the wedding gifts she was
carrying and goes out.

By this time Giuliano is sitting at the piano
and he plays and sings:]

After one whole quart of brandy
like a daisy I'll awake
with no bromo seltzer handy
I don't even shake
Men are not a new sensation
I've done pretty well I think
but this half pint imitation
put me on the blink.

I'm wild again
beguiled again
a simpering, whimpering child again
bewitched, bothered and bewildered
am I

couldn't sleep
and wouldn't sleep
when love came and told me I shouldn't sleep
bewitched, bothered and bewildered
am I

[Two more house guests enter,
Eleanor and Leo,
with arms full of wedding gifts.
She is English; he is Italian.]

ELEANOR
Look, we have more presents.
Are these things for you girls?

THYONA
We're not accepting gifts.

ELEANOR
Not accepting gifts?
Whoever heard of such a thing?
Oh, Leo, these girls!
I suppose they're nervous before the wedding!

LYDIA
We are not nervous.
It's like Thyona says.
We don't want wedding presents!

OLYMPIA
Yet.

ELEANOR
Oh, darling, don't say that.
There are so few occasions
when people give you things
and things are good!

LEO
A bottle of champagne.
Good food.

ELEANOR
A handsome man.
A sunny day.
Life's pleasures,
you can't have too many really.

LEO
When you are young, you think nothing of it.
But the older you get
the more you think: oh, god, let me have more pleasures!

ELEANOR
Don't take me away from the blessed earth
and all its joys.
A swim in the afternoon.
Sex.
A man with a nice nose
a good pair of shoulders
sky blue eyes—

[remembering Leo]

or chocolate brown eyes!

THYONA
Who are you?

ELEANOR
House guests, dear.
Guests of Piero. Eleanor and Leo.
And you're the brides?

THYONA
No.

OLYMPIA
We're still sort of thinking about it.

ELEANOR
How exciting for Piero to have a wedding for us.
To me, it just makes a perfect weekend.

LEO
I always say:
you need to embrace life.

ELEANOR
You need to let it in through every pore.

LEO
We come this way but once
this brief, brief time on earth
we need to suck it in.
The key thing is
you'll be wanting to let go of fear

ELEANOR
throw yourself into life

LEO
put all your fears and pain in a garbage can
and attach the garbage can to a yellow balloon
filled with helium
and let it go!

Love,
love touches,
love fondles,
love listens to its own needs.

THYONA
What is it with you Italian guys?

You spout this kind of bullshit
and all you're ever thinking is,
if I keep up this line of chatter,
can I pinch some woman's butt?

ELEANOR
Isn't that the truth?
And if you smile
or simply return a look with a look
you find you've sealed your fate
you've fallen into life way over your head
nothing is held back
like a Roman fountain
all splash and burble
and you find yourself carried off
or even to walk through a crowd
you're in constant contact
with all sorts of elbows and knees
and souls and buttocks
touching and rubbing
everything that in another minute will all be naked.

I just think everything is shocking in Italy,
and I'm not a puritan
I mean, of course, I am a puritan,
but that's what I love about Italy,
because here, I am not a puritan.
I am alive. I love life. I take it in,
its tomatoes, its sunshine,

LEO
its olive oil,

ELEANOR
its paintings, its men

LEO
everything is as though a giant mother
were squashing you to her breast.

ELEANOR
In Italy, to go out
is to come home.

OLYMPIA
I'd like to take it in.
You know, I wouldn't mind, like,
going swimming even.
Plus guys.
I don't have a problem with guys.

THYONA
I don't have a problem with guys either.
This is not about sunshine and olive oil.
This is about guys hauling you off to their cave.

LYDIA [to Leo]
Still.
You remind me of my father.
So kind and gentle.
So full of enthusiasm.

[Music.
Handel's Air from Water Music, Suite No. 1.

Lydia and Leo dance,
a long, long, slow, intimate, heartbreaking father/

daughter dance.

The others are all silent,
respectful of the moment.
They stand watching.

And when the dance is ended,
and the music stops,
there is a moment of silence before Giuliano speaks
meditatively—
or, if it seems good, Giuliano can start speaking
while they are still dancing.]

GIULIANO
I knew a man once
so kind and generous.
I was a boy
I was on a train going to Brindisi
and he said, I'm going to marry you.
He asked how far I was going.
To Rome, I said.
No, no, he said,
you can't get off so soon,
you need to go with me to Bologna.
He wouldn't hear of my getting off in Rome
or he would get off, too, and meet my family.
He gave me a pocket watch
and a silk scarf
and a little statue of a saint
he had picked up in Morocco.
He quoted Dante to me
and sang bits of Verdi and Puccini.

He was trying everything he knew
to make me laugh and enjoy myself.
But, finally,
he seemed so insistent
that I grew frightened of him.
He never touched me,
but he made me promise, finally,
that I would come to Bologna in two weeks' time
after I had seen my family.
I promised him,
because I thought he might not let me get off the
train
unless I promised.
He gave me his address, which of course I threw
away,
and I gave a false address to him.
And when I got off the train,
I saw that he was weeping.
And I've often thought,
oh, well,
maybe he really did love me
maybe that was my chance
and I ran away from it
because
I didn't know it at the time.

OLYMPIA
I think,
for me,
there's nothing quite like it
when you know a person is attracted to you

and you look into his eyes and see your own reflection
through the tears of joy in his eyes,
as you've always wanted to see yourself,
and never have since you were a child
just sharing the daily things with another person
knowing you can count on him.
And I know he loves me all the time,
hugging me all day
treating me as though I were precious.

THYONA
You are a twit.

OLYMPIA
I am not.

THYONA
I'll tell you something, Olympia.
You're the kind of person
who ends up in the bottom of a ravine somewhere
with your underpants over your head.
I'm trying to save your neck
and you don't even get it!

OLYMPIA
Oh!
What did I say wrong?

THYONA
Do you think I like feeling this way?
do you think it feels good to feel bad all the time
do you think I wouldn't rather just be a nice, happy

well-adjusted seeming person
who can just take it as it comes and like it?
But I can't just not be honest.
Do you think that makes me happy?
To spend my whole life on earth
the only life I'm going to have
feeling angry?

[she turns and runs out]

OLYMPIA
Thyona!

[she runs after Thyona;

Nikos enters, shyly, stands to one side.

Eleanor and Leo hold a moment, seeing Nikos and
Lydia looking at each other.]

ELEANOR
Come, Leo.
Let's leave them alone.

[Eleanor and Leo leave.]

NIKOS
I'm sorry
for the way Constantine seemed a little rude.
Well,
I shouldn't put it all on him.
I'm sorry for the way that we've behaved.

LYDIA
Thank you for saying so, Nikos.

NIKOS
I thought,
I've always liked you, Lydia
seeing you with your sisters
sometimes in the summers
when our families would get together at the beach.
I thought you were fun, and funny
and really good at volleyball

LYDIA
Volleyball?

NIKOS
which I thought showed you have a
well,
a natural grace
and beauty
and a lot of energy.

LYDIA
Oh.

NIKOS
And it's not that I thought I fell in love with you at
the time
or that I've been like a stalker or something in the
background
all these years.

LYDIA
No, I never....

NIKOS
But really, over the years,
I've thought back from time to time
how good it felt just to be around you.

LYDIA
Oh.

NIKOS
And so I thought: well, maybe this is an okay way
to have a marriage

LYDIA
A marriage.

NIKOS
to start out
not in a romantic way, but
as a friendship

LYDIA
Oh.

NIKOS
because I admire you

and I thought perhaps this might grow
into something deeper
and longer lasting

LYDIA
Oh.

NIKOS
but maybe this isn't quite the thing you want

and really I don't want to force myself on you
you should be free to choose
I mean: obviously.

LYDIA
Thank you.

NIKOS
Although I think I should say
what began as friendship for me
and a sort of distant, even inattentive regard
has grown into a passion already

LYDIA
A passion.

NIKOS
I don't know how
or where it came from, or when
but somehow the more I felt this admiration
and, well, pleasure in you

LYDIA
Pleasure.

NIKOS
seeing you become the person that you are
I think a thoughtful person and smart
and it seems to me funny and warm

LYDIA
Funny.

NIKOS
and passionate, I mean about the things
I heard you talk about in school
a movie or playing the piano
I saw you one night at a cafe by the harbor
drinking almond nectar
and I saw that happiness made you raucous.
And I myself don't want to have a relationship
that's cool or distant
I want a love really that's all-consuming
that consumes my whole life

LYDIA
Your whole life.

NIKOS
and the longer the sense of you has lived with me
the more it has grown into a longing for you
so I wish you'd consider
maybe not marriage
because it's true you hardly know me
but a kind of courtship

LYDIA
A courtship.

NIKOS
or, maybe you'd just I don't know
go sailing with me or see a movie

LYDIA
Gee, Nikos,
you seem to talk a lot.

NIKOS
I talk too much.
I'm sorry.

LYDIA
Sometimes it seems to me
men get all caught up
in what they're doing
and they forget to take a moment
and look around
and see what effect they're having
on other people.

NIKOS
That's true.

LYDIA
They get on a roll.

NIKOS
I do that sometimes.
I wish I didn't.
But I get started on a sentence,
and that leads to another sentence,
and then, the first thing I know,
I'm just trying to work it through,
the logic of it,
follow it through to the end
because I think,
if I stop,
or if I don't get through to the end
before someone interrupts me
they won't understand what I'm saying

and what I'm saying isn't necessarily wrong—
it might be, but not necessarily,
and if it is, I'll be glad to be corrected,
or change my mind—
but if I get stopped along the way
I get confused
I don't remember where I was
or how to get back to the end of what I was saying.

LYDIA
I understand.

NIKOS
And I think sometimes I scare people
because of it
they think I'm so, like determined
just barging ahead—
not really a sensitive person,
whereas, in truth,
I am.

LYDIA
I know.

Do you know about dreams?

NIKOS
Well, I have dreams.

LYDIA
But do you know what they mean?

NIKOS
I don't know. Maybe.

LYDIA
I had this dream
I was going to a wedding
of these old friends of mine
and part of the wedding—uh, sort of event—
was an enormous pond that they had built,
and I was late getting to the wedding
so I got someone to airlift me in,
and I dove into the pond but,
when I landed in the water,
the walls of the pond collapsed and it drained out
and 1500 fish died,
and everyone was looking for survivors
but I had to leave to take Yeltsin to the Museum of
Modern Art,
because I had to get to the gym.

So, when I took him in to one of the exhibits
and turned around to hug him goodbye,
he turned to my mother and said,
"Wow, look at that Julian Schnabel bridge."
There was an enormous sterling silver bridge
designed by Julian Schnabel.
So I walked my mother into the water to say
goodbye to her,
and this immense 25-story high tidal wave crashed
over me
and threw me up over the Julian Schnabel bridge
and then I was completely alone in the middle of
the ocean
until I realized:

I had the cell phone tucked into my undies.
So I phoned Olympia to come and get me,
and she said, oh, perfect, I'll send Chopin—
which is the name of her dog—
I'll send Chopin over in the car,
and then would you take him for a walk
and leave the car on 8th avenue?

What do you think of that?

NIKOS
Well,
I think things happen so suddenly sometimes.

LYDIA
Sometimes people don't want to fall in love.
Because when you love someone
it's too late to set conditions.
You can't say
I'll love you if you do this
or I'll love you if you change that
because you can't help yourself
and then you have to live
with whoever it is you fall in love with
however they are
and just put up with the difficulties you've made
for yourself
because true love has no conditions.
That's why it's so awful to fall in love.

[The heartbreaking music of the Largo
from Bach's "Air on the G-string"

and after a moment,
Lydia and Nikos dance—a long, long, sweet dance.

And then, when they stop at last:]

LYDIA
What would you like to do with me?

NIKOS
I'd like to kiss you.

LYDIA
Kiss you? But I don't even know you.

NIKOS
Well, if you'd kiss me, then you'd know me.

[they kiss; they part;
she looks at him,

and then she turns and runs out.]

NIKOS
Oh.
God.
God.
Goddammit.

[he throws himself to the ground]

Goddammit!

[he gets up;

Constantine enters, sees Nikos;

Nikos whirls and throws himself to the ground again]

NIKOS
Goddammit.

CONSTANTINE
Goddammit.

[Nikos gets up;

Constantine saunters over to stand next to Nikos.]

CONSTANTINE
This is how it is.

NIKOS
Yes, this is how it is.
Goddammit!

[Nikos throws himself to the ground again;

Constantine hesitates a moment; then throws himself to the ground, too,

in imitation of Nikos—not that he, Constantine, has any particular agenda about it.

Music.

Marc-Antoine Charpentier's Prelude to Te Deum at full volume
so that hardly any of the following words can be heard.

Oed enters.

he sees Nikos and Constantine
and stands watching them out of curiosity.

Nikos and Constantine continue to throw
themselves to the ground over and over as they
talk/shout.]

NIKOS
When I was a boy I thought
I had it made.
My coach said to me
you could be good.

CONSTANTINE
damned good

NIKOS
I had the instincts.
I could hit the ball.

CONSTANTINE
I could hit the ball.

NIKOS
I could run.

CONSTANTINE
I could run

NIKOS
My dad played football.

CONSTANTINE
My dad played football.

[working along at this kind of rhythm
Constantine repeats the words of Nikos that are
underlined;
and sometimes he can take just one thought, such
as "jerk" or "big man" and keep yelling it over and
over while Nikos goes on with the rest of what he
is saying;
or sometimes he says it simultaneously or nearly
simultaneously with Nikos;

and, pretty soon,
Oed joins in,
yelling out the words and phrases that are
underlined
sometimes simultaneously with Nikos and
Constantine,
or at different moments,
so it is a chaos of three talking at once,
but we can hear it because it is the same phrase
repeated]

Then everybody told me
you're just a jerk
this macho stuff
big man
bullshit
and then I thought
my instincts are off
my instincts are all off

[he's starting to cry now]

I thought: girls will like this
but they didn't
so I hung out with these guys
it wasn't what I had in mind
and all the fun had gone
pretty soon I couldn't hit
I couldn't catch
I was slowing down

[as he continues
and as he and Constantine continue to throw
themselves to the ground in synch,
Oed joins them;
now all three men are throwing themselves to the
ground
over and over and over
in synchronization,
while they yell the dialogue,
now Constantine and Nikos picking up phrases
from Oed to repeat;

although, with the music deafening now,
we can't hear more than occasional words or
phrases]

OED[shouting, as the action continues]
You should have gone to your dad
you think no one could understand
but you can talk about these things
to other men
because, these men,
they understand

because this is what it is to be a man
men know about this
because they have gone through it
and they remember
they know the pain,
they don't want to talk about it
they try to hide it
but if you open up to them
they'll open up right back

[Oed rips off his shirt and throws it to the floor, picks up circular saw blades, one after another, from a pile of saw blades, and hurls them across the stage so they stick in the side of another building that has been wheeled into place, yelling, for no good reason other than that he has gotten himself worked up; he is hopping mad, throwing a saw blade, then jumping into the air and stomping back down on the ground and yelling.

Constantine cuts out of the synchronized collapsing and starts jumping up in the air and landing with apparent full force on Nikos's splayed body, as Nikos rolls over and over on the stage, and Constantine yells, on top of the other yelling:]

CONSTANTINE
Girls are socialized
so they want a man to be older
take charge
have money
have status

while they play hard to get
and boys are taught to feel stupid
feel inferior
not as smart as girls
then hormones happen
a boy wants a girl
she plays hard to get
so a boy learns to
talk big
develop a line
take all the risk
hit on women
not take the answer no
look for younger women
go for status jobs
how do the women
handle men like this?
they get more hostile
more aloof
they wear high heels
they diet too much
they hate themselves
they blame the men
the men hate them
it's a vicious circle
it's a vicious circle
so fuck these women
fuck these women

NIKOS   [continuing   simultaneously   with
Constantine, as the action continues]

I said to my dad
I don't want to do this
this isn't me
I felt so ashamed
He said, what do you mean?
your friends out there
they're doing it
they like it
just get in there
don't be afraid
you can't get hurt
if you get hurt
it doesn't matter
that's how it is
you pick yourself up get on with it
what do you care
because you belong
but I never did belong
it never was for me
Little League never was for me

[The music is drowning out all the speech
and finally, it comes to an end.

Silence.

The men stand panting, embarrassed, looking at
one another.
Constantine and Nikos are weeping.

Oed snatches up his shirt from the ground and
struts out in a huff.

Constantine kicks the ground over and over—
releasing the last spasms of rage, like little
aftershocks, to finally settle down.

Nikos watches him.

Finally, Constantine speaks very quietly.]

CONSTANTINE
People think
it's hard to be a woman;
but it's not easy
to be a man,
the expectations people have
that a man should be a civilized person
of course I think everyone should be civilized
men and women both
but when push comes to shove
say you have some bad people
who are invading your country
raping your own wives and daughters
and now we see:
this happens all the time
all around the world
and then a person wants a man
who can defend his home

you can say, yes, it was men who started this
there's no such thing as good guys and bad guys
only guys
and they kill people
but if you are a man who doesn't want to be a bad guy

and you try not to be a bad guy
it doesn't matter
because even if it is possible to be good
and you are good
when push comes to shove
and people need defending
then no one wants a good guy any more

then they want a man who can fuck someone up
who can go to his target like a bullet
burst all bonds
his blood hot
howling up the bank
rage in his heart
screaming
with every urge to vomit
the ground moving beneath his feet
the earth alive with pounding
the cry hammering in his heart
like tanked up motors turned loose
with no brakes to hold them

this noxious world

and then when it's over
suddenly
when this impulse isn't called for any longer
a man is expected to put it away
carry on with life
as though he didn't have such impulses
or to know that, if he does
he is a despicable person

and so it may be that when a man turns this
violence on a woman
in her bedroom
or in the midst of war
slamming her down, hitting her,
he should be esteemed for this
for informing her
about what it is that civilization really contains
the impulse to hurt side by side with the gentleness
the use of force as well as tenderness
the presence of coercion and necessity
because it has just been a luxury for her really
not to have to act on this impulse or even feel it
to let a man do it for her
so that she can stand aside and deplore it
whereas in reality
it is an inextricable part of the civilization in which
she lives
on which she depends
that provides her a long life, longer usually than
her husband,
and food and clothes
dining out in restaurants
and going on vacations to the oceanside
so that when a man turns it against her
he is showing her a different sort of civilized
behavior really
that she should know and feel intimately
as he does
to know the truth of how it is to live on earth

to know this is part not just of him
but also of her life
not go through life denying it
pretending it belongs to another
rather knowing it as her own
feeling it as her own
feeling it as a part of life as intense as love
as lovely in its way as kindness
because to know this pain
is to know the whole of life
before we die
and not just some pretty piece of it
to know who we are
both of us together
this is a gift that a man can give a woman.

[Constantine finally leaves—pushing Nikos on his
way out.
Nikos hustles to catch up to Constantine, and gives
him a shove.
Constantine shoves back.
They leave shoving one another back and forth.

Eleanor enters, with Olympia helping her,
carrying a huge wedding cake.]

ELEANOR
Let's put it here, dear,
over here.

OLYMPIA
Does it have candles?

ELEANOR
No, dear, no.
Usually it has a little bride and groom on top
but this time we need fifty little brides and fifty
little grooms
so we will have them all around on all the different
tiers
and it will be like a huge party
like Carnival.

OLYMPIA
I would like candles.

ELEANOR
Oh, candles. You want candles. Yes.
Of course, love. Think nothing of it.
You'll have candles if you want them.

[Thyona enters.]

THYONA
We don't want a cake.
What are you doing, Olympia,
helping with this cake?

LYDIA
Did someone order a cake?

ELEANOR
It was delivered to the house.

LYDIA
I thought there were some conversations to be had.

THYONA
What's going on?

LYDIA
Things are moving awfully fast.

PIERO [entering with a glass of brandy in hand]
I ordered the cake.

Thank you, Eleanor.

ELEANOR
Any time, dear.
I'm just going to get some candles for the cake.

[she leaves]

THYONA
So.
You gave in to them, didn't you?

PIERO
I thought I might be able to strike an accommodation
with your cousins.

THYONA
An accommodation?

PIERO
In the world I come from
it's not always all or nothing.
Men learn to compromise all the time.
After all we have to go on living in the same world
together.

THYONA
So you get up every morning and say
who can I compromise with today?
Surely there's a sociopath somewhere who wants to
make a deal.

PIERO [ignoring her]
Frankly, I could see why you wouldn't want to accept
the proposal of your cousins
50 grooms for 50 brides
in its entirety.
But it seemed to me that this young man Nikos,
was not such a bad a fellow after all.

THYONA
They're all the same
just different manners.

PIERO [ignoring her still]
And I thought it might be
that there could be one or two others like Nikos,
and, that, if one were to find them,
there might be some room to negotiate.

THYONA
To negotiate?

PIERO
To see whether there might be one or two natural
alliances.

OLYMPIA
I'd like to love the person that I marry.

PIERO
Yes, we all would. To be sure.
And sometimes we do—at first.
Sometimes it lasts a little bit.

OLYMPIA
I know people who have loved one another
all their lives.

PIERO
I do, too.
And yet, it's very rare.
For the rest of us,
we make do.

THYONA
Maybe some of us don't want to be married at all.

PIERO
I thought that could be an option, too.
And yet,
for some of you—
having a family is something you might long for as
much as I do.
To be close for all your lives
to another human being
and to the children that you have together
coming through pleasures and pain over the years
that bring you closer together
closer to knowing the deepest truth of life
that life is nothing for us
but an experience that we share with others.

And, if we want our experience of life to be deep
and passionate,
to have a sense of its unfolding over many years
to be in touch with the whole of it
as we grow old,
a lifelong marriage some of us will welcome.

THYONA
What are you saying?

PIERO
It seemed to me
you might say to these fellows,
look, the deal as a whole is no good,
but we'll take 50% of you
or 10%.

THYONA
What?

PIERO
Of the fifty of you young women,
I felt sure there must be some
who still wished to be married to these young men.

And that was the accommodation I tried to arrange.

THYONA
Take 50%. Take 10%.
This is insane.
What is this?
We'll make some package deal?

LYDIA
Is Nikos part of this?

THYONA
And what about Constantine?
Is he part of the deal?
Am I part of the deal or not?

PIERO
We didn't get that far.

THYONA
Didn't get that far?
How long does it take to get that far?
These men think they can do anything.

OLYMPIA
I'm not afraid of men, Thyona.
In fact, I kind of like them.

THYONA
So?

OLYMPIA
Maybe you think I shouldn't play their game, but
I think I'm not a helpless victim.
When I put on a short skirt and paint my toe nails
and dye my hair
I don't think that I'm a twit.
I think men know what I'm doing
and they think it's fun
and I think it's fun, too,
and I think I'm an equal

in the game we play.
I wouldn't mind some sort of negotiation.

THYONA
We don't accept your deal.
You can tell these men we don't accept it.
What we would accept is
if these men like
they can come to us one by one
and beg us to marry them
give each one of us time to make up our minds
postpone the wedding day
let us consider and reconsider
let us think about it when we are on our own
ground
when we are strong and they are weak
let us come to them one by one
and say freely if we want to marry them
otherwise there's nothing to be said

OLYMPIA
Except....

THYONA
Nothing.
We reject your offer.

LYDIA
Thyona....

THYONA
I speak for all of us.

LYDIA
Thyona....

PIERO
I'm sorry to tell you
what I have been saying,
this is only the accommodation I was trying to
work out.
In fact, Constantine won't have it either,
and he speaks for all your cousins.
Your cousins will marry you
whether you want to marry them or not.
None of you has a choice.

[silence]

LYDIA
And Nikos?
What did Nikos have to say?

PIERO
He let his brother speak for him.

LYDIA
Oh.

THYONA
Isn't this just what I said?

LYDIA
Yes.

[silence;
then, defeated, to Piero]

Well, this is why we came to you.
Thank God
we were lucky enough to come here.
Thank God we found you.

PIERO
I wish, in fact, you had found someone else.
Because I can't protect you.
I can't put my home at risk
my home and my family.
My nephew.
The daughters of my brother.
I can't do it.
I'm sorry.
For me, that never was an option.

The wedding will take place today.
The arrangements have been made.

[He leaves;

silence.]

OLYMPIA
Who am I supposed to marry, then?
This is no different than it would be
if we were lying in our beds
and soldiers came through the door
and took whoever it was they wanted.

I'm not going to do this.

LYDIA
What else can you do?

THYONA
What else can you do
if your father won't protect you
your country won't defend you
you flee to another country
and no one there will take care of you
what is left?

Nothing except to take care of yourself.

[silence]

We have no country.
We have become our own country now
where we make the laws ourselves.

LYDIA
Right.

OLYMPIA
Right.

THYONA
And when these men take us to bed
on our wedding night
these men who left us no alternative
these men who force themselves on us,
we will meet force with force
and we will kill them
one by one.

LYDIA
What?

OLYMPIA
Kill them?

LYDIA
Kill them?

OLYMPIA
I can't kill them.
Are you crazy?

THYONA
Would you kill them if they were soldiers
coming through your bedroom door?

OLYMPIA
Of course I would.
But to kill them.

LYDIA
We can't kill them.

THYONA
What choice did they give you
but to stop them
the only way they ever will be stopped.
All these men understand is force.

LYDIA
But to kill them?

At the least maybe we don't want to kill them all.

OLYMPIA
Maybe some of them are good.

THYONA
None of them are good.

LYDIA
How can you say that?

THYONA
Here's how you can tell:
none of them objected to Constantine,
not one of them stood up against him and said:
No, Constantine,
let's take this deal,
or let's at least negotiate,
let's talk to these sisters and see if one or two of them
wants to marry us
and let the rest go free
let those go free who don't want to marry.
Take the risk that some of us will be rejected.

No, no one stood up against him.
All his brothers are his silent partners.

Would you want to live with someone
who just gives in like this?
Would you ever be safe with a person as weak as
this?

[silence]

LYDIA
No.

THYONA
They have all gone along with this.

They have made their decision.
The only question is:
Will you defend yourself
and defend your sisters?

[silence]

OLYMPIA
Lydia?

Lydia?

LYDIA
Yes.

THYONA
Olympia?

OLYMPIA
Yes.

THYONA
We have a pact then.
Not one groom will live through his wedding night,
not one.
Are we agreed?

LYDIA
Yes.

OLYMPIA
Yes.

[Eleanor enters.]

ELEANOR
I'm going to help you girls get dressed
for the wedding.

[through the following,
Eleanor helps the women get into their petticoats
and dresses,
veils and garters and shoes
and powder and lipstick and rouge.

As the brides dress to kill,
sweet music plays,
J.S. Bach's Air on the G string, from Orchestral
Suite No. 3 in D,
while Giuliano,
who at first has helped Eleanor bring in clothes for
the brides,
goes off on his own transvestite solo dance]

LYDIA
Sometimes I feel as though I'm standing on a
thousand dinner plates
on the side of a muddy hill
and my job is to keep from sliding down the hill!

OLYMPIA
Nothing seems to be working out.
I was hoping for a wedding dress from Monique
Lhuillier,
but back home in Greece,
all I could find was an Alvina Valenta,
not even a Vera Wang

and I'd been planning all my life
or most of it
for something with little spaghetti straps
and some lace right on the bodice
and little lace flowers just where the straps join
the bodice
and people said sometimes you just have to settle
but I don't want to
I don't think I have to settle
I don't see why
at least on my wedding day
I can't have things exactly the way I want them!

ELEANOR
Never mind, dear.
You're going to love the way you look
by the time we're finished.

What lovely faces you all have
I think myself
if I'd had such a complexion
I'd have been married seven times by now.

What I always say is:
if both of you are physically fit
you should lie face downward on the bed
legs hanging over the edge
and let him help you raise your legs
and wrap them around his waist or shoulders
or if you like
you can start on the floor
and let him lift your ankles

while you walk around the floor on your hands
because I think you'll find
this makes for very deep penetration—
some say the very deepest.

LYDIA
Probably this is how people feel when they're
drowning!

ELEANOR
Now, I suppose you might be saying to yourselves
before we make the final decision,
let's ask ourselves:
Do we have similar backgrounds?
Do we agree on our religious beliefs?
Do we have the same ideals and standards and
tastes?
Are we real friends?
Do we have a real happiness in being together,
talking, or just doing nothing together?
Do we have a feeling of paired unity?
[The wedding music begins at full volume:
Wagner's "Wedding March" from Lohengrin.

In stately fashion
the grooms enter in a line, wearing tuxedoes:
50 grooms (or a few more grooms, in the economical
production),
led by Constantine and Nikos.

And our three brides take their places
and they are followed by their

47 (or several more) sisters, all in wedding dresses,
who enter in a stately manner.
Finally,
Eleanor cuts the wedding cake
and hands a piece of cake to Olympia
who feeds it to Oed,
crushing it playfully into his mouth;
he smiles at this,
takes her in his arms
and dances with her.

Lydia does the same with the cake with Nikos,
and they dance.
Thyona does the same,
but mashing the whole piece of cake all over
Constantine's face.

Constantine retaliates by picking Thyona up
and shoving her head-first into the wedding cake.
She recovers and wrestles him head-first into the
cake.

He takes off his jacket
as though to start a real fight with her.

She pulls up her wedding dress
to show her bare butt to him
and to do a seductive-hostile butt dance
while she faces upstage.

The music segues into the exuberant party music
of Handel's "Arrival of the Queen of Sheba " from
Solomon.

Constantine, taking Thyona's dance as a seductive challenge,
undoes his tie,
unbuttons his shirt,
and joins the dance with Thyona.

As her dance gets increasingly lewd and hostile
he takes off his shirt
and then his shoes
and then his pants
until he is doing a complete, abandoned striptease

while the others have moved into throwing themselves to the floor
and throwing themselves down on top of one another
or throwing one another to the floor
and them jumping on the one who lies there

—as the music segues into the wild, violent, dionysian
Widor's "Toccata " from Organ Symphony No. 5—

and, of all the brides and grooms, some are

burning themselves with cigarettes

lighting their hands on fire and standing with their hands burning

throwing plates and smashing them

throwing kitchen knives

taking huge bites of food

and having to spit it out at once, vomiting

Not these things necessarily, but things like these,
things as extreme as these:
one groom lying across two chairs—his head on
one, his feet on the other, dropping bowling balls
on his stomach and letting them roll onto the floor

one groom on his back on the ground,
a board filled with nails resting on his naked chest;
another groom putting an anvil on the board,
and then hammering the anvil with a sledgehammer

one groom with his feet locked into moon boots
nailed to the ground
and he is rocking violently back and forth

one bride slamming her head repeatedly in a door

Eleanor screaming, running from side to side, and
smashing plates and cups

Some of the wedding guests are enjoying
themselves;
so that, as at any wedding reception,
there is also joy, and warm sentiment, and
sentimentality,
people happy,
young people in love,
quiet conversations, laughter,
older people remembering happy times.

If there is a cast of hundreds,
Leo can re-appear as a character now

and dance with the brides, one after another,
as though he is their father.

It may be that Constantine is the groom who should
have his feet in the moon boots
so that he is naked now, rocking back and forth
violently,
when Thyona
comes to him with a kitchen knife
and stabs him in the heart
so that blood floods over his chest and stomach
and onto her white dress

and the other brides pull out kitchen knives
and murder their husbands, one by one,
all of them splashing their white wedding dresses
with blood

and one of them circling round and round the stage
holding his crotch
and he, too, bleeds and bleeds,
circling dizzily,
finally coming to his knees,
continuing on his knees.

And, all this while,
Lydia and Nikos are off to one side
making love.

(NOTE:
while the Widor may be the best music for the large
cast, a small cast production might need a more
controlled music to go with the more ritualized

murders, so we might think of having Bella singing
Ave Maria or Handel's "Pena tiranna"; from Amadigi.)

A little before the music ends,
all the violent action on stage has subsided.

Thyona drags Constantine's body downstage
and throws it into the orchestra pit
(or else, a trap door opens, she dumps him in the hole,
and the trap door accommodatingly closes again).

People lie or sprawl, exhausted.

Only Lydia and Nikos are moving, gently,
with one another.

Piero enters — with Guiliano —
a cup of espresso in his hand,
and walks among the bodies,
in shock and dismay.

Bella enters from the other side.
People begin to stir.]

PIERO
Guiliano, mi dispiacce, ma . . .
(he gestures to the carnage.)

GUILIANO
Si, si. Lascia me.
(he starts to pick things up.)

BELLA
Piero
you should have stopped this.

PIERO
What,
what could I have done?

BELLA
Piero....

THYONA
Lydia!
Lydia!
Who is that with you?

[all eyes turn to Lydia and Nikos]

LYDIA
This is Nikos,
my husband.

THYONA
Your husband?

LYDIA
Yes.

THYONA
You didn't kill him?

LYDIA
I love him, Thyona.

OLYMPIA
You broke your word?

LYDIA
I couldn't do it.

THYONA
We all agreed what we were going to do!

LYDIA
I love him!

THYONA
You love him?

LYDIA
I'm sorry, Thyona,
I couldn't help myself.

THYONA
You go behind our backs.
You break your promise.
You betray your sisters,
and you're sorry?
In any civilized society
you would be put on trial.
And hanged probably.
Or electrocuted.

PIERO
Now. Now. Let's just stop where we are.

THYONA
We are not finished here.

PIERO
Let's just slow things down.
Everyone deserves a fair trial, after all.

THYONA
Oh! Right! Right! OK.
We'll put Lydia on trial.
And we will be the jury.

PIERO
You'll be the jury?

BELLA
And I will be the judge.

(silence)

PIERO
The judge?

THYONA
You?

BELLA
Yes.
Who else?
[to Piero]
You want to put it in the hands of some judge
chosen by the business associates of your brother?
I don't think so.
I will be the judge.
Is that okay with you?

LYDIA
Yes. Good. I agree to that.

OLYMPIA
I agree to that, too.

THYONA
All right, then.
Betrayal is the charge.
What Lydia did, in any other country,
would be treason.

LYDIA
I love him.
I have nothing more to say.
Olympia, how could you just kill someone
You're just a girl.

OLYMPIA
I was confused.

LYDIA
How could you be confused?

OLYMPIA
I thought you said it was a good idea, Lydia.
Remember, you said you agreed?

LYDIA
I had to agree with the argument the way Thyona
put it,
But if we live in a world where it is not possible
to love another person
I don't want to live.

THYONA
All this talk of love.
In the real world,
if there is no justice

there can be no love
because there can be no love
that is not freely offered
and it cannot be free
unless every person has equal standing.

[What follows is not a reasoned argument
but a rush of judgment
that pours out faster than she can think about it.]

First comes justice,
and if there is no justice
then those who are being taken advantage of
have every right
to take their oppressors
to take those who stand in their way
and drive them across the fields
like frightened horses
to set fire to their houses
to ruin everything that comes to hand
to hurl their corpses into wells
where once there were houses
to leave rubble
smoldering woodpiles
to leave shattered stones,
empty streets,
and silence
no living thing
no bird, no animal
no dogs,
no children,

not one stone left standing on another,
rather a wilderness of stones
and see if finally then
a lesson has been learned.
Because there are times
when this is justified
there are times, though you may not like it,
when this is all that human beings may rightly do
and to shrink from it
is to be less than human.

LYDIA
You know, everything you say may be right, Thyona
but I have to ask myself,
if it is
then why don't I feel good about it?
I have to somehow go on my gut instincts
because sometimes
you can convince yourself in your mind
about the rightness of a thing
and you try to find fault with your reasoning
but you can't
because
no matter how you turn it over in your mind
it comes out right
and so you think:
I know it's right but I don't think it is
or I think it's right but I know it isn't
and you could end up thinking
you're just a moron
or some sort of deficient sort of thing

but really there are some things
when you want to know the truth of them
you have to use not just your mind or even your
mind and your feelings
but your neurons or your cells or whatever
to make some decisions
because they are too complicated
they need to be considered in some larger way
and in the largest way of all
I know I have to go with my whole being
when it says I love him and he loves me
and nothing else matters
even if other things do matter even quite a lot
even if I'm doing this in the midst of everyone
getting killed
I can't help myself
and I don't think I should.
Probably this is how people end up marrying Nazis
but I can't help it.

THYONA
You should.
You should.

LYDIA
I couldn't!

OLYMPIA
Lydia!
If I'd known it was okay to do what you did,
I might have loved someone, too.
I was just

I know everyone says this
but the truth is
I was just following orders in a way.
I should kill myself probably
now that I see the kind of person that I am.

BELLA
That's enough now.
That's enough.
I'm ready with my verdict.
This is what I have to say.

[silence]

You did a dreadful thing, you women, when you
killed these men.
What could be worse than to take another's life?

And yet,
you came to us,
to my family and to me,
to help you, and we failed you.
We share the blame with you.

What else could you have done?
You women made your own laws because you had
no others to protect you.
This was your social contract.
And Lydia, in her betrayal of your pact,
imperiled all of you.
I understand what you say.

And yet,

you can't condemn your sister.
No matter what.

She chose love.
She reached out
she found another person—
and she embraced him.

[Thyona turns her back
and takes several steps to the side, facing away.
Bella continues her argument, to persuade Thyona
and Olympia.]

She couldn't know
when she did
whether all the hopes of her childhood for true
love and tenderness
for a soulmate for all her life
were destined for disillusion.

Still, she reached out.

And, if we cannot embrace another
what hope do we have of life?
What hope is there to survive at all?

[spoken out, as though from a judge's bench]

This is why: love trumps all.
Love is the highest law.

It can be bound by no other.
Love of another human being—
man or woman—
it cannot be wrong.

Does this mean every woman must get married?
Not at all.
A woman might want another woman;
sometimes a man prefers a man.
But to love:
this cannot be wrong.

So Lydia: she cannot be condemned.
And that's the end of it.

And as for you,
there will be no punishment for you either,
even though you may have done wrong,
there will be no justice.

For the sake of healing
for life to go on
there will be no justice.

Now, Piero, it will be your job
to keep all this out of the hands of courts and judges.
That much you can do.

And now,
you girls,
alone in the world,
what will you do?

I have to tell you, I wish you would stay on here with me.
I would take you in and care for you
as my own daughters.

That would make me happy.

[Thyona turns back to face her,
and she speaks to Thyona]

I like a strong woman.

[and then to Olympia]

And I like a woman who sticks with her sister.
You'll see,
one day you'll find a good man.
Or not.

A woman doesn't always need a man.
I myself, I no longer need a man—
except, of course, my son Piero,
who stays with me forever,
and Giuliano, who takes such good care of me.

For we all live together
and come to embrace
the splendid variety of life on earth
good and bad
sweet and sour
take it for what it is: the glory of life.

This is why at weddings
everybody cries
out of happiness and sorrow
regret and hope combined.

Because, in the end,
of all human qualities, the greatest is sympathy—

GIULIANO
for clouds even

BELLA
or snow

GIULIANO
for meadows
for the banks of ditches

BELLA
for turf bogs
or rotten wood
for wet ravines

GIULIANO
silk stockings
buttons

BELLA
birds nests
hummingbirds

GIULIANO
prisms

BELLA
jasmine

GIULIANO
orange flower water

BELLA
lessons for the flute

GIULIANO
a quill pen

BELLA
a red umbrella

GIULIANO
some faded thing

BELLA
handkerchiefs made of lawn

GIULIANO
of cambric

BELLA
of Irish linen

GIULIANO
of Chinese silk

BELLA
dog's blood

GIULIANO
the dung beetle

BELLA
goat dung

GIULIANO
a mouse cut in two

BELLA
In spring the dawn.
In summer the nights.

In autumn the evenings

GIULIANO
In winter the early mornings
the burning firewood
piles of white ashes
the ground white with frost

BELLA
spring water welling up

GIULIANO
the hum of the insects
the human voice

BELLA
piano virtuosos
orchestras

GIULIANO
the pear tree

BELLA
The sunlight you see in water as you pour it from a
pitcher into a bowl.

GIULIANO
The earth itself.

BELLA
Dirt.

[Here comes, immediately, at full volume,
Mendelssohn's "Wedding March" from Midsummer
Night's Dream.

Lydia and Nikos kiss
and a hundred flashbulbs go off for a wedding
picture.

A receiving line
is instantly constituted,
and Lydia and Nikos make their way down the
line—
all the guests kissing the bride and shaking the
groom's hand
and talking among themselves and fussing with
their clothes.

Nikos stops for an earnest conversation with
Piero—
which we cannot hear at all over the music—
about how sometimes men don't even want to get
married
because they find it hard enough getting through
the day on their own
all by themselves, and the burdens of life are so
heavy and the demands so great
they think: how can I take on the responsibility of
someone else, too,
not that they would take on the responsibility
entirely, but to the extent they do,
because they have made a promise to see life
through together
and sometimes a man could just cry, things seem
so hard,
but when you fall in love, what choice do you have?

At the last moment,
everyone turns front,
a hundred flash cameras go off again,
the family photo is taken.]

OLYMPIA
Lydia! Lydia! Throw your bouquet!

[Lydia throws her bouquet into the audience.

Booming music.]

OLYMPIA
And your garter! Your garter!

[Lydia pulls up her dress.
Nikos takes her garter
and throws that into the audience.

Everyone throws rice.

Lydia and Nikos, the bride and groom,
exit up the center aisle to the music.

Nikos's clothing is disheveled,
and he looks sheepish and uncertain,
even frightened, maybe even filled with
foreboding—
in fact, they both look shell-shocked and
devastated—
as Nikos exits up the aisle with Lydia.

Fireworks.]

THE END

NOTE:

Big Love is inspired by what some believe to be the earliest surviving play of the western world, *The Suppliant Women* by Aeschylus.

Big Love is also inspired by, or takes texts from, Klaus Theweleit, Leo Buscaglia, Gerald G. Jampolsky, Valerie Solanus, Maureen Stanton, Lisa St Aubin de Teran, Sei Shonagon, Eleanor Clark, Barbara Grizzuti Harrison, Kate Simon, and Laurie Williams, among others.

FIRST LOVE

[We are indoors and out at the same time.

This is the world of Magritte.

There is a tree, perhaps with a bright yellow summer dress hanging from a branch.

A piano.

We hear birds singing.

Harold, in his seventies,
lies napping on a stone bench.

After a few moments, Edith, in her seventies, enters.]

EDITH
Shove up.

HAROLD [awakened from sleeping -still half-asleep, disoriented]
What?

EDITH
Shove up I said shove up.

HAROLD
What what?

EDITH
I want to sit down here.

HAROLD
Goddam it to hell, this is my God Damn bench.
Can't you see I am sleeping here?

EDITH
This is not your God Damn bench.
This is a common bench
and I said:
[shrieking]
shove up!!!

HAROLD [shouting]
Can't you see
I am trying to sleep in peace?

EDITH
You want peace?
You want peace?
Go someplace else.

HAROLD
I did go someplace else.

This is where I went.

EDITH
I am going to explain this to you:
I am not the sort of person who looks at a man
and thinks
oh, I could take him on
make a project out of him
fix him up
he looks okay to me
not too disgusting
I am going to reason with the sonofabitch.
No.
This is not who I am.
I am the sort of person who says shove up
or
[she starts trying to kick him]
I will kick you black and blue,
because I am tired of walking around!

HAROLD
Okay, okay, sit.

[he makes room for her on the bench]

EDITH
Thank you.

HAROLD
Do we know each other?

EDITH
No. No, we do not.

[she rummages through her stuff,
brings out a bottle]

Sherry?

HAROLD
What?

EDITH
Would you like a little nip of sherry?

No hard feelings.

HAROLD
Well.
Yes.
Okay.
Thank you.
Very kind of you.

[he takes a drink;
then, talking too loud]

You can't get this any more on your Medicaid card
the bastards.

EDITH
You never could.

HAROLD
Never could what?

EDITH
Get sherry on your Medicaid card.

HAROLD
How the hell do you think I got it then?

EDITH
How the hell should I know?
Maybe you had a credit card.

HAROLD [shouting]
Credit card, that's what I said.
You can't get the stuff on a goddam credit card any more.

EDITH
Are you hard of hearing?

HAROLD
What?

EDITH
Can't you hear too well?

HAROLD [shouting]
What does that have to do with it?
I don't enjoy the opera any more, if that's what you mean.
Or the symphony.
I used to go to Ravinia.
Do you know Ravinia?

EDITH
Ravinia.

HAROLD
Outdoors, in the summertime

every Friday night.
Fritz Reiner conducting.
You remember Fritz Reiner?

EDITH
Of course I remember Fritz Reiner.

HAROLD
That was lovely.
You know, lying out on the lawn listening to
the music.
Mozart, all those fellows.
Like the Grand Canyon, you know,
a marvel of nature, that's all,
a complete breakthrough of the divine
or whatever, you know,
if you believe in that sort of thing.

EDITH
I don't.

HAROLD
Well, then, a breakthrough of the human.
But that's all gone
now that I can't hear a thing
you know there's a lot you can't enjoy any more.
When you get down to it, at my age,
I don't see so well either.

EDITH
Well, it's the end of an era.

HAROLD
That's for sure.
The end of a way of life.

EDITH
An entire way of life.

HAROLD
The end of poetry.

EDITH
Of the book itself.

HAROLD
Yes, well....

EDITH
Don't go gentle into that good night!

HAROLD
No. No. Right you are.

EDITH
We lost a lot when we lost communism.

HAROLD
Isn't that the truth?

EDITH
Where's the opposition anymore?
I never said I loved Stalin
but where is the inhibition any more
if the bastards know you have nowhere else to turn

HAROLD
Castro! Castro!

EDITH
Castro!
Che!

HAROLD
Che!

EDITH
Danny the Red!

HAROLD
Abby Hoffmann!
Jerry Rubin!

EDITH
Jerry Rubin:
There's a flash in the pan if ever there was one.

HAROLD
Allen Ginsberg.

EDITH
Gregory Corso!

HAROLD
Ferlinghetti!
These are the heroes!
All gone!

EDITH
Trotsky!

HAROLD
Trotsky!

EDITH
The Red Brigades!

HAROLD
The Catholic Workers!

EDITH
Gandhi!

HAROLD
Mao!

EDITH
Lenny Bruce!

HAROLD
Lenny Bruce goddammit. Goddammit it to hell.

Where is everyone when you need them?
Where is the threat if the bastards don't deliver?
Something to say:
the way things are
is not the way they have always been

EDITH
or the only way they can be.

HAROLD
These sons of bitches:
Just like they say themselves:
all they understand is force!

[they begin to cry and yell with frustration through
the rest of this;

speaking on top of one another in a confused babble, a steady crescendo]

EDITH
You could die from neglect

HAROLD
die from it

EDITH
I mean it

HAROLD
I'm not kidding around

EDITH
people are dying from neglect

HAROLD
and indifference

EDITH
and indifference

HAROLD
sheer—indifferent indifference

EDITH [declaiming]
Ah, Carl Solomon!
I'm with you in Rockland
where you're madder than I am
Do you know this poem?

HAROLD
Do I know this poem?

I'm with you in Rockland
where you bang on the catatonic piano the soul
is innocent and immortal it should never die
ungodly in an armed madhouse

EDITH
I'm with you in Rockland
where you scream in a straightjacket that you're
losing the game of the actual Ping-Pong of the
abyss

HAROLD   EDITH ALMOST TOGETHER
I'm with you in Rockland
where there are twenty-five-thousand mad
comrades all together
singing the final stanzas of the Internationale

[they are both spent from this, exhausted;
Edith fiddles with the knobs on the radio,
and we hear one of the Bach cello solos
or the Adagio from Alessandro Marcello's
Concerto for oboe, strings, and continuo in D
minor,
while they sit and weep;
Harold reaches out and takes her hand;
they sit, holding hands;
and then, when they are composed again,
he speaks]

HAROLD
You know, you go through life.
There were certain things I wanted to do

certain ambitions
some things that had to do with politics and the
world
things I thought when I was a boy
what I wanted to be when I grew up
and so I pursued it
worked at it
it preoccupied me
I did it with more or less success
and then it turns out really
all life comes to be about is
I miss my kids.
I think, well, I threw away a lot of time on my career
worked nights and weekends
neglected my family and friends
end up all these years later
and I just wonder where my kids are

EDITH
Well, we all have a history.

I knew Ginsberg as a matter of fact.
Patti Smith
and Kerouac
Kathy Acker.
I've been on the stage.

HAROLD
On the edge?

EDITH
On the stage!

HAROLD
Yes, I can believe it.

EDITH
It was a community then.
Everyone knew each other.

HAROLD
Like the Cedar Tavern.

EDITH
Exactly.

HAROLD
I met John Simon once.
Do you know John Simon?

EDITH
John Simon?

HAROLD
Yes.

EDITH
There's a jerk if ever there was one
a real jerk.

I was there when Joe Chaikin tried to throw an ice
cream cone at him
in the Theatre de Lys
and missed him and hit some innocent bystander
in the face
and then he had to apologize
and that shit Simon got off free.

What a prick.
Opinionated little prick.
Stupid, opinionated little shithook that fucking creep.

HAROLD
I knew David Rattray.

[silence]

EDITH
Who was that?

HAROLD
Poet.

EDITH
A poet.

HAROLD
Wonderful, wonderful poet.
Not well known, but a wonderful poet.
New York School.

EDITH
No.

HAROLD
Good friends with Herbert Huncke.
Huncke used to stay with him in New York.
Very
sort of
fucked up.
He's gone now.

Paris '68.

EDITH
What's that?

HAROLD
He was in Paris in '68.

EDITH
I was in Paris in '68.

HAROLD
That's where I wanted to be
but
I had a job.

EDITH
Well, I've had a life.
My friends and I
we went places, you know.
Nicaragua.
We were active.

HAROLD
Yes, I can see that in you.

EDITH
We were in bed
my husband and I one time
this was in Nicaragua
making love in the daylight
there were sounds of voices and movements around
the house
but I was not so attentive to them

I heard him whisper in my ear
-teasing me-
to come again
but this time
be very quiet.

And then
it was as if
a box of matches
had been struck by a hammer.

I heard no sound
but the glass was shattered on the floor.

I took a deep breath and then
I noticed that
the side of my own body
was on fire.

HAROLD
My first wife was holding our son in her arms,
standing on the bus,
this was in Washington, D.C.
when we all rode the busses
when a young woman in front of her said, "Please
take this seat."
They were just changing places
when all of a sudden there was a strange sound.

All at once it was dark
and before she knew it,
it seemed she had just jumped outside.
She was outside the bus on the grass

and fragments of glass had lodged themselves in
our son's head.
Of course, he didn't know what had happened.
And soon after that
he died.

EDITH
I'm sorry.

Imagine:
There was a time
when a person came indoors from the fields
they would expect to see
traces of human occupation everywhere;
fires still burning in the fireplaces
because someone meant to come right back;
a book lying face down on the window seat;
a paint box
and beside it
a glass
full of cloudy water;
flowers in a cut glass vase;
an unfinished game of solitaire;
a piece of cross-stitching
with a needle and thread stuck in it;
building blocks
or lead soldiers
in the middle of the library floor;
lights left burning in empty rooms.
This was the inner life.

HAROLD
That was another time.

EDITH
We miss it.

[a waitress enters,
coming right through a wall by magic]

WAITRESS
Now then, who was having the raspberry tart?

HAROLD
I was having a lemon tart.

WAITRESS
The lemon tart is finish.

HAROLD
Oh.

WAITRESS
So you are having the raspberry tart.

HAROLD
No, thank you. Perhaps I will have the cookies.

WAITRESS
I have brought you the raspberry tart.

HAROLD
I think I'd rather have the cookies.

WAITRESS
You can have the cookies tomorrow.

HAROLD
No. I'd like the cookies today.

WAITRESS
You can't have cookies every day.

HAROLD
I'll have something else tomorrow.

WAITRESS
What will you have tomorrow?

HAROLD
Well, I don't know. Perhaps I'll have the chocolate cake tomorrow.

WAITRESS
We don't have the chocolate cake tomorrow.

HAROLD
Well, look, then today I'll have the-what?
What was I having?

WAITRESS
The raspberry tart.

HAROLD
I don't want the goddam raspberry tart.

WAITRESS
Look at yourself.
Sitting in a cafe, not a care in the world.
Other people are dying everywhere or starving, sick and starving
and you are in a snit over a raspberry tart.
Aren't you ashamed of yourself?

HAROLD
Yes. Yes, I am.
Give me the tart and I just won't eat it.

WAITRESS
You're going to let it go to waste?

HAROLD
Okay, I'll eat it. I'll eat it.

WAITRESS
Sometimes in life
you have to be happy with what you get.

[the waitress leaves through a wall]

EDITH
Perhaps you would think of coming home with me.

HAROLD [startled]
Come home with you.

Well, I think of myself as an outdoorsman really.

[A couch appears.]

HAROLD
This is a nice place.
I've always liked the coziness of a basement.
Close to the furnace.

EDITH
I was lucky to find it.

HAROLD
Very nice.

EDITH
I'll tell you what you do.
You throw these on the floor.

[she picks up some magazines from the couch]

We'll do a little rearranging.

[she hands him a stack of magazines from the couch]

HAROLD
Well, you don't want them on the floor.

EDITH
Put them on the floor.

HAROLD
You don't want people to trip on them.

[he takes the magazines, goes to the easy chair that has appeared,
puts them there,
and, as he returns to get another stack of magazines from the couch,
she takes the magazines out of the chair and puts them on the floor]

EDITH
Who's going to trip on them?

HAROLD
Unsuspecting people!

EDITH
There's no one here but us!

[he returns, gets another stack, brings it to the chair,
where she, meanwhile, has put the magazines on
the floor;
he puts more magazines in the chair,
returns to the couch for another stack of magazines,
takes them to chair;
she has removed the magazines and put them on
the floor;
he puts stack of magazines on the chair,
picks up a stack from floor and puts it on chair,
and returns to the couch for another stack of
magazines
while she is putting the magazines from the chair
on the floor;
and so forth around and around
while they say:]

HAROLD
Oh. Right.
You say come home
you invite me to set up housekeeping with you
make a home together

EDITH
What?

HAROLD
And the next thing you know
you don't think of it as our home.
All I am saying is:
You might have unexpected guests.
You never know.

EDITH
I know! I know!
I have no unsuspecting people in my life.

Put them on the floor.
Just put them on the floor.

HAROLD
Exactly.
The trouble is:
you wouldn't welcome my children into our lives.

EDITH
What lives?

HAROLD
That's how it is with a woman
you want to start with a tabula rasa
as though there were no history.
We are all the creatures of our histories!
We don't come naked into the world again every day
born anew.
I have a past.

[by this time, he has found an electrical appliance
that he picks up]

EDITH
Of course you do. I know you do.

HAROLD
So,
are my children free to come and go or not?

[absently, he starts to fix the appliance]

EDITH
What children?
Of course they are.
They should phone ahead.
There are certain days I like to be alone.

HAROLD
There you are.
Just as I said:
but you see, if you need to phone ahead,
this isn't any longer home
home is where you don't need permission to
come to
and I don't think any place that isn't home to my
children
can be home to me.

EDITH
Why do you make a problem out of nowhere
when everything was going so well.

HAROLD
Yes.
[yelling]
Everything is going well if you never talk about
anything
but the moment you want to deal with the real
issues
of how real people are going to get along with each
other
then things aren't going quite so well!
[the appliance blows up in his face,

exploding sparks and shooting flames;
silence;
he turns to her, amazed, speechless,
his hands out in a gesture of innocence]

EDITH
It doesn't matter.
I have another one somewhere.

HAROLD
I thought I could fix it.

EDITH
It was good of you to try.

[silence]

HAROLD
That's kind of you to say.

EDITH
It's nothing but the truth.

The fact is:
I've never been in love before
I thought I was
but I never felt like this

HAROLD
What?

EDITH
And I'm thinking: at my age
how can this be your first time

HAROLD
Right.

EDITH
The truth is
I'm not a baby.

HAROLD
No.

EDITH
I've had a whole life
I've had other relationships in my lifetime
and other things, not even relationships
and people I've cared about

HAROLD
Yes, indeed.
So you've said.

EDITH
cared about deeply
people, in fact, I thought I loved
but it wasn't as though I looked at them
and felt at once I had to cry
because I felt such closeness

HAROLD
Empathy.

EDITH
Empathy.
Exactly.
Immediate empathy.

I looked at you
I almost fell on the floor.

HAROLD
Things happen so suddenly sometimes.

EDITH
Do you believe in love at first sight?

HAROLD
No.

EDITH
Neither do I.
And yet there it is: I'd just like to kiss you.

HAROLD
Oh.

EDITH
I think for me it took so long to be able to love
another person
such a long time to grow up
get rid of all my self-involvement
all my worrying whether or not I measured up

HAROLD
Yes.

EDITH
or on the other hand
the feeling that perhaps other people were just
getting in my way
wondering if they were what I wanted

or what I deserved
didn't I deserve more than this
to be happier
is this all there is

HAROLD
Right.

EDITH
Or I thought
I need to postpone gratification
and so I did
and I got so good at it
I forgot how to seize the moment

HAROLD
breaking hearts along the way if someone else *was*
capable of love
at that earlier age when you weren't

EDITH
exactly
and now I think: what's the point of living a long
time
if not to become tolerant of other people's
idiosyncrasies

HAROLD
Or imperfections.

EDITH
you know damn well you're not going to find the
perfect mate

HAROLD
someone you always agree with or even like

EDITH
and now you know that
you should be able to get along with someone who's
in the same ball park

HAROLD
a human being

EDITH
another human being

HAROLD
because we are lonely people

EDITH
we like a little companionship

HAROLD
just a cup of tea with another person
what's the big deal

EDITH
you don't need a lot

HAROLD
you'd settle for very little

EDITH
very very little when it comes down to it

HAROLD
very little
and that would feel good

EDITH
a little hello, good morning, how are you today

HAROLD
I'm going to the park
OK, have a nice time
I'll see you there for lunch

EDITH
can I bring you anything

HAROLD
a sandwich in a bag?

EDITH
no problem
I'll have lunch with you in the park

HAROLD
we'll have a picnic
and afterwards
I tell you a few lines of poetry I remember
from when I was a kid in school
what I had to memorize

EDITH
and after that a nap or godknows whatall

HAROLD
and to bed

EDITH
you don't even have to touch each other
sure, what

a little touch wouldn't be bad

HAROLD
you don't have to be Don Juan
have some perfect technique

EDITH
just a touch, simple as that

HAROLD
an intimate touch?

EDITH
fine. nice. so much the better.

HAROLD
that's all: just a touch
that feels good

EDITH
OK, goodnight, that's all

HAROLD
I'd go for that.

EDITH
I'd like that.

HAROLD
I'd like that just fine.

EDITH
I'd call that a happy life

HAROLD
as happy as it needs to get for me

EDITH
Sometimes in life
you just get one chance.
Romeo and Juliet
They meet, they fall in love, they die.
That's the truth of life
you have one great love
You're born, you die
in between, if you're lucky
you have one great love
not two, not three,
just one.
It can last for years or for a moment
and then
it can be years later or a moment later
you die
and that's how it is to be human
that's what the great poets and dramatists have
known
you see Romeo and Juliet
you think: how young they were
they didn't know
there's more than one pebble on the beach
but no.
There's only one pebble on the beach.
Sometimes not even one.

[Harold sits down at the piano and plays a medley
of romantic songs, which he sings as well as plays -
or, if he can't play the piano, then the waitress
returns as a pianist and plays

while he sings -
maybe Cole Porter, Gershwin,
maybe some of these songs:]

I love you
for sentimental reasons
I hope you do believe me
I'll give you my heart

I love you
and you alone were meant for me
please give your loving heart to me
and say we'll never part

I think of you every morning
dream of you every night
darling I'm never lonely
whenever you're in sight

I love you
for sentimental reasons
I hope you do believe me
I've given you my heart

Edith sits on the piano and sings:

I'm wild again
beguiled again
a simpering whimpering child again
Bewitched bothered and bewildered
am I

couldn't sleep
and wouldn't sleep

when love came and told me I shouldn't sleep
bewitched bothered and bewildered
am I

lost my heart
but what of it
he is calm
I agree
he can laugh
but I love it
although the laugh's on me
I'll sing to him
each spring to him
and long for the day when I'll cling to him
bewitched bothered and bewildered
am I

They sing a duet:

Oh it's a long long while
from May to December
but the days grow short
when you reach September
when the autumn weather
turn leaves to flame
one hasn't got time
for the waiting game
oh the days dwindle down
to a precious few
September
November
and these few precious days

I'll spend with you
these precious days
I'll spend with you

EDITH
I was thinking of changing into a little something else.
What do you think?

HAROLD
Yes. Good. Excellent.

EDITH
What should I wear?

HAROLD
I don't know. What are my options?

EDITH
I have a basic black.

[taking it from a rack of clothes that has appeared, holding it up]

How do you like it?

HAROLD
Very nice.

EDITH
Nice? It's very nice?

HAROLD
I mean it's lovely. Very elegant.

EDITH
But it's not good on me?

You don't really like it?

HAROLD
I have to admit I had been thinking of something
with a little color.

EDITH
Something like this?

HAROLD
That's beautiful.

EDITH
Or something in red?

HAROLD
Or something in red.
I always love red.

[as she looks through the rack of clothes,
he continues]

It's such a mysterious thing.
People try to make a connection
but why is it one person is attracted to another
person in particular?

EDITH
I know what you mean.

HAROLD
You can say
well, it's where she comes from
or how she was brought up

EDITH
her relationship with her mother or her father

HAROLD
but, as it turns out, that explains nothing

EDITH
No.

HAROLD
that a person wears her hair in a certain way
or puts her hand to her cheek in a certain way
and you find it irresistible
otherwise in every other way she could be an
numbskull
or you could be an numbskull
but you can't resist her
and she can't resist you
where does this come from?
These are mysteries buried so deep inside a person
you can never understand them.

EDITH
How is this?

HAROLD
Lovely.

EDITH
Should I have some jewelry?

HAROLD
A necklace.

And then,
you put two people together
each with these idiosyncrasies
that are so particular

EDITH
so odd

HAROLD
so pointless

EDITH
and yet so crucial
because these are the connections people have
to one another's strangest aspects

HAROLD
what seems hot to them

EDITH
the reason they make a particular choice
and not just a general one

HAROLD
not any man or woman
but this unique person

EDITH
responding to something unfathomable

HAROLD
the particularity of it

EDITH
the mystery of two people finding their way to the
same particularity

HAROLD
it seems hard enough all the neurons working in
one brain
but then all the neurons in two brains together
getting along
plus the hormones and whatnot.

EDITH
It is so fragile.

HAROLD
And so strong.

EDITH
And so fragile.

HAROLD
This is what it is to love another person.

EDITH
How is this?

HAROLD
Good. I like the necklace.
I don't think I'd wear the bracelet.

[as she looks again at the necklace]

There are people
who simply need to have ants crawling on their
stomachs
or across their chests
before they can think of having some sort of
relationship

or even friendship with another person
and I make no judgments

EDITH
No.

HAROLD
I make no judgments.

EDITH
Neither do I.

HAROLD
People are unique, each one of them.

I knew a fellow
who used to go to a bar in Oregon
where he knew a couple of women
who were willing
to go up to his hotel room with him
watch him strip naked,
get into a tub of bath water,
and walk back and forth.
His only request was that the women
would throw oranges at his buttocks
as he walked back and forth.
Then he would get out,
pick up the oranges,
put them in a paper bag,
get dressed,
and leave.
That's simply how it was for him
how he was able to connect to another human being

in an affectionate way.
This went on for some years
this relationship among the three of them.
In a sense, you might say,
this is the way in which they were able to constitute
a human society
in which they felt comfortable.
Freud never explained that.

EDITH
People are like that.

HAROLD
Some people.

EDITH
Some people are.

[while Harold continues talking
he finds his way over to the barbecue
where he puts coals on the grill
and pours kerosene over the coals]

HAROLD
It's not my taste as it happens.
And yet it can't be wrong
if that is the only way they can reach out to another
and have a relationship that is rewarding for them
both
because, as Aristotle said,
man is a social animal.

EDITH
And woman, too.

HAROLD
And woman, too.
We are ourselves only in our relationships.
We are human only in our societies.
And this is how it is to be human
whether your love is erotic love for another
individual person
what the Greeks called erotike
or it takes the form of friendship
which the Greeks called senike
or was that heteraike

EDITH
What's that?

HAROLD
What the Greeks called friendship

EDITH
How would I know?

HAROLD
Is that how you pronounce it?

EDITH
I wouldn't know.

HAROLD
In any case
that's what the Greeks knew
that love is not just an agreeable option
love is the glue of human society
we can't live without it

EDITH
Peculiar as it may sometimes seem to us

HAROLD
the forms that it may take
that may seem objectionable or wrong to one
person or another

EDITH
nonetheless without it the world just comes apart.

HAROLD
There was a woman in Milwaukee
who could only have sex in the back yard.
She needed to be in a public place.
She tried parks and other outdoor places
but none of them were any good,
only her own back yard,
and never in the house.

[silence]

And I myself, I have to say,
it may sound strange
but I just like to rub my buttocks on someone else's
buttocks.
I like to kiss someone's buttocks, too,
or just,
fondle them,
but mostly I just love to rub buttocks.

[silence]

EDITH
There was a fellow
who was arrested in Syracuse
for sexual abuse
because he was going around and knocking down
girls and young women
and taking off their shoes
and sucking on their toes.
And I have to say,
I can understand that
because
I like feet.

I myself I used to go into bars in Alberta
every Friday night during rodeo season
and challenge the cowboys to leg wrestle
clear the tables and chairs and lie down in the
middle of the barroom
and bet these guys I could beat them, which I could
and you might say after that
that I should spend my Saturdays praying for
forgiveness
bon a Friday night in Alberta?

[Harold turns around from the barbecue;
his hands are on fire;
he holds his arms bent at the elbows,
his hands up in front of his face,
looking at his burning hands]

EDITH
Your hands are on fire.

HAROLD
Yes.
Yes. They are.

[they both watch his hands burn;
he is wearing asbestos gloves]

I'm afraid I won't be able to cook dinner now.

EDITH
I think I have something in the refrigerator for dinner.

[she goes to the refrigerator
and gets out two tuna fish sandwiches in their wrappers;
they go to sit by the edge of the plastic swimming pool,
their feet in the pool;
she unwraps the sandwiches;
he sits next to her;
they sit side by side,
their feet in the water, while his hands burn out
and then they eat their sandwiches;

she picks up a magazine]

EDITH
OK, let's see how you do on this quiz.
When I'm feeling stressed out or anxious, I usually prefer:
a) closeness
b) solitude

c) doing something, like gardening, playing a sport, or getting on the computer for a few hours

d) daydreaming, hiking, or just taking off on a long walk.

HAROLD
Mm-hmmm.
I would say c) gardening, or playing a sport.

EDITH
I think of myself as:
a) sharing and emotionally available
b) agreeable and cooperative
c) fun-loving and creative
d) rational and well-organized

HAROLD
Mmmmm.
That's a hard choice.
I'd like to, you know, choose them all.

EDITH
Right.

HAROLD
I guess I'd have to say sharing and emotionally available.

EDITH
When it comes to sex, I usually:
a) initiate
b) wait to be invited
c) schedule sex
d) am a spur-of-the-moment type

HAROLD
I'm an initiator, I'd say, definitely an initiator.

EDITH
When my romantic relationships end, I tend to be
the one who:
a) leaves
b) is left
c) has a plan worked out
d) has another lover in the wings

[silence]

HAROLD
Leaves. I'd say: the one who leaves.

EDITH
Do you want me to tie you up and dominate you?

HAROLD
I don't know.
I don't know if I want to be dominated.

EDITH
I'd like to dominate someone sometime.

HAROLD
Well, sure, so would I, I suppose.
I'd never thought about it.

[Edith reaches over, turns on the radio,
then gets up and starts to do a seductive dance to
the music -
not too graceful, a little unruly, raunchy, and fun.

He turns and just looks at her.
As she moves upstage, dancing as she goes,
she pulls her skirt half-way down her butt
and continues dancing.

He then joins in the dancing,
doing his solo at a distance from her.
After a few moments, he unbuttons his shirt,
then slowly strips it off,
twirls it above his head and throws it across
the stage.

As she continues to dance, into her own world,
he does a complete striptease,
doing something wildly suggestive with each piece
of clothing -
beyond sexy and on into Dionysian.

When he is naked,
she grabs him,
and throws him down on the couch
and jumps on top of him,
and has her way with him for 17 seconds,
and then kicks him onto the floor,
and the music stops.

They are both embarrassed.
Neither speaks.
She arranges her clothes.
He goes around picking up bits of clothing from
the floor,
hiding his nakedness as he does so,

awkwardly trying to get back into his trousers,
putting on his shirt and leaving it unbuttoned.
Some minutes pass before they speak again.]

HAROLD
You kicked me out of bed?
Did you kick me out of bed?

EDITH
I might have.

HAROLD
What is that supposed to mean?

EDITH
I've had enough.

HAROLD
You've had enough?
What is that supposed to mean?

[no answer]

Well.
You never know where you stand with a woman,
do you?
Whatever you do is wrong.
One day they call you a satyr,
the next day an impotent idiot.
And then women will complain about physical
satisfaction!
A man would rather die before he complained.
Or gossip to his friends about her.
He would consider it a betrayal of her trust,

her privacy.
It never occurs to a woman to think a man
might have miscalculated about her!
Might have second thoughts about her -
in giving her what she needs to feel secure,
having given away himself
no longer *possesses* himself
so that he no longer knows who he is
or if he even exists any longer!

And then she turns right around and invites you
to dinner.

EDITH
What are you saying:
You can't have dinner with me?

HAROLD
You know, this is too much. I can't....

EDITH
Dinner? You're saying you can't have dinner?
Just dinner. Nothing more.

HAROLD
You say so, and then you'll just want me to stay on
after dinner.
In a word, a man is an object to be used, that's all.
One of a number of equally acceptable items
taken down from the shelf, used, put back,
never valued for himself, no,
but only for what can be gotten out of him.

EDITH
How can you talk like this?

HAROLD
I hope we're not going to argue
and then you're going to try to cajole me,
you don't let me leave, you don't leave,
I begin to feel cornered.

EDITH
This is crazy talk.

HAROLD
Next thing you know you think
there's no reason I shouldn't spend the night....

EDITH
Well, sure, just sleep together,
just sleep in the same bed, that's all, nothing more

HAROLD
And then [yelling] when you fall asleep
I'll look at you
and I'll see how ugly you are when you're relaxed.

EDITH
What?

HAROLD
Probably that's when you're at your ugliest,
when you're asleep so that I can't stand it.

EDITH
When I'm asleep I'm ugly, that's what you're saying?

How can you say such a thing?

HAROLD
Or really any time after twelve o' clock: old and ugly

EDITH
Every night? Are you saying every night?

HAROLD
Almost every night probably.
Ugly and repulsive.
Like another person altogether.
So that I would hardly recognize you
except I would say to myself:
right, yes,
there you are again
the way you really are.
I would wake up with palpitations
and a pain in my head and I would think:
right, there you are again,
attacking me in the middle of the night
when I'm defenseless.

EDITH
Attacking you!

HAROLD
Trying to hypnotize me while I was asleep,
setting my nerves on edge
so I would have to hit you in the face
to get you to stop,
and then you would make some remark probably
like how you are being eaten alive by worms.

EDITH
Worms! Worms?
You crazy sonofabitch!

HAROLD
What are you saying?
What are you saying to me?

EDITH
What does it matter? You never hear a word I say.

HAROLD
I hang on every stupid word you ever say!

EDITH
Every stupid word I say!
You are stupid.
Stupider than ever.
And black and venomous.
Poisonous poisonous,
more poisonous now than ever.

HAROLD
Ever before when?
Before you gave me that filth at dinner
 -on purpose, on purpose -
so that it made me shiver?
Before that?
Before you would seek some intimacy with me,
force yourself on me,
demanding I make love to you....

EDITH
Excuse me, would this be after you turned your
back on me?

HAROLD
Excuse me, I think it was you who turned your
back on me.

EDITH
No. No, I don't think so.
If I remember correctly
it is you you who turned your back on me,
as probably you always would,
always.
So that I am supposed to pursue you I suppose,
put my arms around you
so that I am always in the position of the suitor,
and you can be always cool,
no, cold,
and I would be the beggar the suppliant
and then, if I *had* to turn over
because my arm had gone to sleep
and my shoulder felt broken
and I had a pain in my head,
and I turned over because
I couldn't bear the pain of holding you in my arms,
then would you ever, ever, ever once,
would you ever a single fucking time
turn over and hold me the way I held you?
No.
Would you ever pursue me the way I pursued you?
No.

HAROLD
I have pursued you.
I have pursued you.
It's you who have never pursued me.

EDITH
When did you?
When did you ever?

[silence]

HAROLD
I don't remember.
But it seems to me I did.

EDITH
You just got finished saying
I made you come over to dinner and try to stay the
night.
Is this not pursuing you?

HAROLD
Oh, sure! Now! Now! Now it's too late!

EDITH
Too late?

HAROLD
Because I woke up this afternoon
in the middle of the afternoon
with women's voices in the apartment below
and I thought I had come to live finally
in a home invaded by sluts!

EDITH
What!?

HAROLD
And I began to cry!
I'm a man, and I began to cry!

EDITH
What?

HAROLD
I can't take this bullshit forever!
What kind of person do you think I am?
Do you know why the earth has governments and dictators
and none of the other planets do?

EDITH
Where does this come from?

HAROLD
Because this is the only planet
where all the inhabitants do not say what they think,
where people lie all the time,
lie and lie and lie all the time,
and I am sick of it.
No, I will not stay for dinner.
No! Just fucking leave me alone!

EDITH
Right! Right! Leave you alone!
I am leaving you alone, you nutcake!

No wonder your family won't speak to you
and every woman you've ever been with has gone
crazy
probably or killed herself.
Did you ever think about that?
It's not them, it's you!
You're like a baby with a switch blade.
So fucking needy
and when you get everything just the way you
want it
you attack who ever gives in to you
for being weak and pathetic and worthless.

[she exits]

HAROLD
Who told you this?
You don't know this about me.

[she enters]

EDITH
Nobody needs to tell me.
It's written all over you, you crazy fucker!
You make me crazy.
You drive me down into the pit of my own craziness
till I'm begging for mercy
you hunt me down
you throw me down the stairs
you rip off all my hinges
till my ears are flying in every direction
I can't understand a thought I'm having

my mind is a million bits of shattered glass on the
kitchen floor
and you stand there calmly yelling at me
go ahead and die, go ahead and die
you don't think I have inside me a capacity for
misery?

[she exits;
she enters]

I'm off the edge of the world here!
I'm into the abyss
where is your helping hand?
are you a human being?
You are making me crazy!
I'm begging you!
Who could live with you?
Who needs you?
Now that a person sees how you are,
who would want you?

[she exits;

he half follows her to the edge of the stage,
yelling after her]

HAROLD
Who would want you?
You crazy needy person
grabbing grabbing whatever you see
a bottomless pit of wishes and longings
a man could work and work and give you all he has
and you would be asking what's next what's more

and all the while telling him he is clumsy and ignorant
withdrawn graceless brutal insensitive confused
This is why men drive naked women into a pit with bayonets

[she enters]

EDITH
And this is why women want to shoot men on sight
This is why they flush boy babies down the toilet at birth

[she exits for good;

he yells after her]

HAROLD
This is why
everywhere a man finds a house
he will leave rubble
smoldering woodpiles.

[she is not coming back]

This is why a man will smash his way into crowds of women
raging and beating and hunting;
drive them across the fields
like frightened horses;
set fire to their houses;
hurl their corpses into wells.
This is why a man pulls the hair out of his head
and hopes to die of a heart attack

[he realizes she is never coming back]

weeping
always weeping
with his head in his hands
his knees around his shoulders.

[quietly now]

They say
there are places in the world today
where the houses are all collapsed as far as the eye
can see
the father of one family standing outside his door
almost naked
his skin peeling off the upper half of his body
and hanging down from his fingertips
standing outside the door
looking for his family.

It can take generations to recover.
And sometimes you never recover.

You feel the chill in the countryside,
the low-lying white mist,
shards of farmhouses in the haze,
shattered stones,
empty streets,
and silence
no living thing
no bird, no animal breaks the silence
no dogs,
no children,

not one stone left standing on another,
rather a wilderness of stones.

[He goes to one side
where he begins to slam a door over and over
and over.
And, after a while, he notices the hinge needs
fixing,
and he sets to work on fixing it.

After a few moments,
Edith enters again, and,
in a fit of insane rage,
she throws 100 dishes against the walls and to the
floor,
dish after dish after dish,
singly and in gobs,
and smashes them.

The two of them sit, exhausted, looking at the floor.]

HAROLD
I'm sorry.

EDITH
What?

HAROLD
I'm sorry.

[silence]

EDITH
How could a person be like this?

[A flower seller
with a bouquet of roses
appears at a window
or else she enters, steps to a microphone,
and sings a Frank Sinatra song.

Or else,
the flower seller comes up miraculously from a
trap door,
sings,
and descends again.

Or she emerges from a steamer trunk
and disappears back into it.

In any case, she sings Sinatra:

song lyrics song lyrics
and more song lyrics
song lyrics song lyrics
and more song lyrics
song lyrics song lyrics
and more song lyrics
song lyrics song lyrics
and more song lyrics
song lyrics song lyrics
and more song lyrics
song lyrics song lyrics
and more song lyrics
song lyrics song lyrics
and more song lyrics
song lyrics song lyrics

and more song lyrics
song lyrics song lyrics
and more song lyrics
song lyrics song lyrics
and more song lyrics

Harold remains distracted by the flower seller after
she leaves,
looking after her, in the direction she has
disappeared.]

EDITH
I think
what brings people together
is their common humanity
and what pulls them apart
is their separate histories.

HAROLD
Oh, yes.
I'd have to agree with that.

EDITH
Life is a strange thing.

Nowadays, everyone lives alone.
You get up in the morning
you have to know
when you got up
to know if you are right on schedule.
6 AM
And then recite
briefly

the main goal
getting fit
10 exercises
at one time it might have been
running
chin-ups, pushups
the indoor track
the weight machines
nowadays it would be
ten times swinging of the head
ten winks
ten nose-ups.
A good workout.

Then.
Washing.
Eau de Portugal
left temple, armpits,
face upwards. Nose.

Dressing toward the north.
Feng shui
dress in parallel, first right, then left,
doing it in order also
so that you don't forget to dress
one side or the other.

8 o'clock.
Hand practice -working out the kinks
42 glasses of water.

And then, with the other folks in the park,
remember:

Be sociable!
Droll stories. Anecdotes.
Unforgettable characters.
And so forth. And so on.

Later. Back home. Supper alone.
Eat soup in silence.
Dear little right finger plays at tasting.
Sit towards the right.
(don't cross left foot)
remember the circulation.

In the evening hours:
sofa -prone exercises.
make a little poem.
enjoy colors.

And then,
to bed at 8 o'clock
bed in northerly direction, head better towards the
east.
Feng shui.

[she stops, thinks]

Shui Feng.
Eye exercises: glossy spots, bright spots, distance.
Rest towards southeast.
Estimate star,
weather glimpse.
10 glimpses through the room (left, right, above).
Remember Beckett.

Ten o'clock.

Midnight.

One.

Day's end.
Fetal position.
Left hand sideways.
Rectum.
Left ass cheek.

Four o'clock. Night's end.
Another day.

[he reaches out and puts his hand on her;
they sit with his hand on her, in sympathy]

EDITH
There needs to be love in the world.

HAROLD
Oh, yes.
Yes.
There does.
And where does that start?
I don't know.
I've come to feel very close to you.

EDITH
I feel it, too.
I feel such warmth and
comfort.

HAROLD
I feel so at ease
we have become such good friends

EDITH
I feel it in my entire body.
I feel so at peace, and so light.

HAROLD
Such a sense of wellbeing.

EDITH
Such happiness.

HAROLD
I would call it
even
joy.

[silence]

EDITH
What makes us start singing, do you think
if it isn't making love?

HAROLD
Well, yes.
And why do we make wine?

Indeed, why do we set sail on the high seas?

These are the mysteries of life.

EDITH
Among the mysteries.

HAROLD
Among the mysteries.
To be sure.

EDITH
When you think
how we used to live in the ocean
in the salt water
you think:
we don't live there anymore.
but really, in fact, we just took the ocean with us
when we came on land.
The womb is an ocean really,
babies begin in an ocean,
and human blood has the same concentration of
salt
as sea water.
And no matter where we are
on top of a mountain
or in the middle of a desert,
when we cry or sweat,
we cry or sweat sea water.

HAROLD
What you're saying is:
humanity, the earth
the great thing of life itself.

EDITH
Precisely.

HAROLD
I know what you mean.

I listen to your voice, I think
I could nestle right into it,
I could crawl right up inside it
you take me to a world that frankly
seems not altogether rational to me
more a world of tarot cards and chakras and the I
Ching
mystical stories and folk tales
I guess I'm saying stories from the heart
I could get happily lost in your world
just letting go of my mind
and feeling your sweetness and your vulnerability
your tenderness and frankly your generosity
your lack of judgment of me
even though
or even at the same time really
that you were raking me over the coals
at the same time not holding it against me
as though it were some final judgment
sending me to hell
but just speaking the truth
that seems so generous to me and ultimately loving
in the deepest and truest sense
that I have to say
I've come to think of you almost as a mountain.

EDITH
A mountain.

HAROLD
Like a mountain rising up from a lake

smooth and soft
covered with fuzzy fir trees
but solid rock underneath
strong and everlasting
the valleys and crevices
the swelling softness
the little village on the shore
nestled into the mountainside
secure, protected
settled there for eternity
on the breast of the earth.
I look at you, I think
Mother Earth.

[silence as she considers whether or not to call him on the
over-the-top stupidity of what he has just said, and
then decides not to]

EDITH
No one's ever talked to me like this before.

HAROLD
I think there are qualities you have that are so sweet
they are beyond the beyond really
qualities to cherish really
I cherish them.
If you want to know the truth
I cherish you.
I cherish you.

[silence

church bells ring]

EDITH
Well, we've gone some places together.

HAROLD
Why do you say that?

EDITH
Because it's the truth.
We've been places, you and I,
that other people haven't gone to,
shared things.
In life, it's not just that you meet and fall in love
but the experiences you share
that either drive you apart
or bring you closer together.
Sometimes even difficult experiences,
bad things,
even tragedies that you share
deepen your love for one another.

HAROLD
That could be true.

EDITH
Of course it's true.
Why do you say could be.

HAROLD
Well, things are not always the same
under every circumstance.
Sometimes tragedies deepen your love

sometimes they don't
and sometimes you might not even feel as though
you've shared them
at all.

EDITH
I mean, if you are together.

HAROLD
If you are together, even so,
sometimes people live lives apart
even when they are together.

EDITH
Well, then they wouldn't be together.
I was talking about things that you share when you
are together.

HAROLD
And what I am saying is that sometimes
you are apart when you are together.

EDITH
That's very sad.

HAROLD
Very sad.
You feel even lonelier
being together with someone and feeling apart
as though who you are, for example, is not
being loved
or even acknowledged
your essential self is not appreciated

for instance, a person doesn't think your jokes are funny
or your advice is worth listening to
or a person doesn't feel excited or interested just to be in the room with you
then you feel every moment you are together
you are being injured
by disdain or scorn or indifference
you feel even more alone than ever
and so what you share together is a sense of being alone
and you could shoot yourself.

EDITH
Have you felt this way?

HAROLD
Yes, I have. In the past.
I've felt that way.

EDITH
I'm sorry.

HAROLD
Thank you.
You've never felt that way?

EDITH
Oh, yes. Very often.

HAROLD
Or a person might be subject to fits
or sudden rages

that have nothing to do with you necessarily
it's just the way they are made
suddenly they explode
a love is destroyed
and it can never be regained

EDITH
This is a sad thing.

HAROLD
Very sad.

[A beautiful young woman,
a high wire walker
(whom we recognize as having been the waitress
and the flower seller),
walks through the air
from one side to another,
holding a crimson umbrella.

Or she walks down a board
(hidden by all the other set pieces so she seems to
walk on air)
from high on one side
to the floor level on the other side
with her crimson umbrella.

In any case, as Edith speaks,
Harold is distracted by the wire walker.]

EDITH
And yet I think: what difference would it make
whether I was a professor

or a shopkeeper
as long as somehow I had a time sitting by a lake
in the late afternoon
watching the light soften and change
the church bells ring
no matter whether they ring three times or four
or five
so long as I can hear them ring
and the weather is not too cold
or not too cold all the time
I've had a time on earth
and if I can add some years of love to that
why, I'd rather have this than heaven
because I am having such joy
and I am still alive on top of it all
if I could be with you the rest of the years of my life
wake up in the morning
have a cup of coffee
do a little work in the garden
a light lunch, napping in the afternoon
music, reading in the evening
and holding you the whole night
what more would I wish for
I love you
I love you like life itself
I don't understand how I can be so happy.

I wonder if you've ever thought of marriage.

[silence]

HAROLD
Marriage.

Well, yes, I suppose I have.
You mean, marriage again.

EDITH
Marriage to me.

HAROLD
Now.

EDITH
Yes.

HAROLD
Well, no.
Well, yes.
I mean, of course I have.
One always thinks of these things.
But then I think: I've been married before.
I haven't perhaps been gifted at marriage.

EDITH
Or you haven't found the right person.

HAROLD
That, too.
That's a possibility.

EDITH
And now you have.

Some people say
there is something frightening
about the branches of the camphor tree,
about the way they are so tangled.

And yet,
it's because of that
that poets will sometimes use the image of the tree
to refer to people in love.

[silence]

HAROLD
I feel that.

EDITH
You feel that?

HAROLD
Yes, I feel that.

EDITH
You only feel it?

HAROLD
How do you mean?

EDITH
For example, I know it.
And you only feel it?

HAROLD
Oh, I see.
Yes. Yes, I know it, too.

EDITH
Because I wouldn't want to be making a mistake.
We're talking marriage here
for the rest of our lives.

And I don't think of marriage just because everyone
does.
I mean, who cares?
At my age especially.
It's an old convention, stupid really. Pointless.
A way of doing things that we've discarded
gotten past to new ways of doing things.
But, it signifies a commitment.
And that feels good to me. And specific.
I think we ought to be specific.

HAROLD
I don't know if I'm quite ready to be exactly specific.
Things are moving very quickly it seems to me.

EDITH
I see.

Shall we see if we can't imagine how it might be
and see how we feel about it.

HAROLD
Yes. Yes. Good idea.

EDITH
Let's say,
we get married,
and let's say, how would you like to do it,
with a justice of the peace,
or in a church for example?

HAROLD
Right, okay.

EDITH
So, in a church.

HAROLD
A church?

EDITH
You don't like a church?

HAROLD
Well, okay, a church.
Yes, a church.

EDITH
A large wedding or small?

HAROLD
Well. Whatever you like.

EDITH
Say just the two of us?

HAROLD
Say just the two of us.

EDITH
And then where shall we live?

[silence]

HAROLD
I'm afraid I've fallen in love with someone else.

EDITH
What do you mean?

HAROLD
I don't know. Just
I've fallen in love.

EDITH
How is that possible?
Who else do you know?
Do I know this person?

HAROLD
No.
I hardly know her myself.

EDITH
Then how can you say you are in love?

HAROLD
Do you know the way you fell in love with me?

EDITH
So suddenly you mean?

HAROLD
Yes. Well. At first sight it seemed.

EDITH
Yes, I do.

HAROLD
That's how I've fallen in love,
except with someone else.

EDITH
Who is she?

HAROLD
The flower seller.

EDITH
The flower seller?

HAROLD
Yes.

EDITH
You don't even know her.

HAROLD
I've gotten to know her a little bit
in a way.

EDITH
What do you know about her
except maybe her measurements?

HAROLD
Her what?

EDITH
Her proportions of bust to waist to hip.
It turns out it's true what the scientists have been
saying
a man is just a sucker for certain measurements
as though a man had no brains
only biological instincts.

HAROLD
That may be true.

EDITH
Of course it's true, you idiot.
How could you do this to me?

HAROLD
I don't think of it as doing it to you.

EDITH
What does it matter
who's done what
when you've lost someone
there's no bottom to it
your life is over
there's nothing to look forward to
but darkness till you die
your pleasures are all behind you
the afternoons lying in your arms
the glass of wine in the evening
the feeling of being known
and loved
of having a home
in your heart
for all that I feel
so that it matters
what I feel resides somewhere
it's not just a passing daydream
forgotten in a moment
it rests on the earth
in the heart of the one I love
I am not alone
and then, all at once, it seems

I am alone
my thoughts and feelings have no place
there is the present moment
and there is the end
and nothing in between that I can bear
and I wish the interval would pass
as quickly as it can
so I can find a place of rest again for my soul.

HAROLD
Do you think forgiveness is possible?
In general, I mean, in life.

EDITH
No.

HAROLD
Ever.

EDITH
No, never.

HAROLD
Sometimes people forgive the worst things
I know someone whose little boy rode his bicycle
out into the street
and a car came along and killed him
and the mother forgave the driver of the car
immediately
they fell into each other's arms and cried

EDITH
That's not how it is going to be for us.

HAROLD
Why not?

EDITH
Because you hurt me and I hate you.
I hate you.

HAROLD
How can you hate me?

EDITH
You've ruined my life.
I fell in love with you,
you were the only love of my life
you changed my life completely
completely
and now you're going to dump me
for what?
on a whim
to run off with someone
something that will last three months if you're lucky

HAROLD
Oh, I don't....

EDITH
Or a year, so what?
For a year's happiness you ruin my life
when I love you
I love you so much
I would care for you forever
you think love is so cheap
you think it comes and goes
but it doesn't

and you could have had love for the rest of your life
and now you will end up with a fling
and then nothing
you will be lonely
you will die alone and lonely
when you could have been with me
no one has ever loved you as I do
and you could be happy with me
you think you don't love me
the way you love this bimbo
because she is blond
and you think
you need some hot sex before you die
because you never had enough sex in your life
but you would end up loving me so much
because you would see
you couldn't resist me after a while
when a person loves you so much
finally you can't resist you end up loving them
like crazy

[Harold is standing in the wading pool,
fixing the radio
which blows up in his face,
and he turns around,
his hands and face blackened,
looking hopeless]

HAROLD
I'm sorry.

Sometimes you can't help it
where your heart takes you.

You see what's happening
you think, oh, no,
I don't think this is good
this could be so wrong
I think this might be shortsighted thinking
or worse
some damage will be done
and that sense of emptiness in the pit of your stomach
when you realize you've made a mistake
in your life
when I think I've gone down a road
and there is no turning back
and this is the only life I have to live
and I don't have that much time left anyhow
but time enough to live some years regretting it
getting up each morning
and feeling first
before I feel anything else at all
that I would like to weep
nonetheless
I can't help myself from doing it
because my heart takes me there
and I can't live a life that isn't true to my heart
no matter how wrong my heart might be
and how devastating my life might become.

I'm sorry.

EDITH
We could try again.
We could start from the beginning.

I could say shove up.
You could say what what?
We could begin again.
Because I think what we felt
was precious
not something to throw away
something this good
you don't just walk away from it
without making another attempt.
I love you.
You are my first love ever
and my last.

[silence]

Go ahead.
Get out.
I have a life without you, you know.
Before you, I had a happy life.
I'm the kind of person who doesn't need another person.
I'm an autonomous person.
I don't need you.
I don't want you.
Get out.
Get out.

HAROLD
Right.

[He gathers up his clothes and leaves;

she curls up on the bench alone;

while we hear a soprano sing a piece from Alessandro Marcello's 17th century opera *La Lontananza*, "Lontananza, crudel lontananza/ch'a me togli l'amato tesoro...."

all the set pieces ascend to heaven,

leaving her alone on the bench on a bare stage

along with a refugee's suitcase tied with rope.

While we hear the soprano, the English translation is projected in supertitles:

"Separation, cruel separation
which robs me of my beloved treasure
tell me when my suffering will end.

"For if with sweet hope
you do not soon offer me balm
my heart will only find death.

"For one who is too long apart
from her beloved must end her love
or die."

As the music continues,
Harold returns,
lies down on the bench with Edith,
taking her in his arms,
her back against his stomach,
embracing her,

and, with one hand, she takes his hand,
and the lights fade slowly to darkness.]

TRUE LOVE

Lights come up on Edward's bed,
set in front of an abandoned gas station.

Surrounded wall to wall by red clay stained with
oil and gas.

A bright orange and yellow gas pump,
surreally supremely beautiful.

Nearby, a motel, the "Mo el Aph it ".

A kids' inflatable plastic swimming pool is to
one side.

To one side, an abandoned Lincoln Town Car
that just broke down and was left there,
its hood up, its wheels off, splattered with dried
mud.

A keyboard.
An electric guitar with amp.
A set of drums.
A microphone on a stand.

Elsewhere, a dog house.
A chain, with a dog no longer there.

We hear a love song on the radio.

Edward, age 13 or 14—or the youngest possible legal age
for the youngest-possible-looking actor to play this role—
is roller blading around his bed,
lost in the music and the pleasure of movement,
luxuriating in his cool moves,
naked from the waist up.
He is a handsome WASP adolescent
with the coolest rollerblades and the best athletic clothes.

Polly, age 34, enters—as though with a purpose,
but then stops, and, standing silently, watches him.
She wears Armani, with some rips and stains.

Edward doesn't notice her;
and they don't speak.
She watches him.
She doesn't move.

This opening moment of the piece—
first Edward alone on stage,

then Polly watching him,
is meant to establish the two principals of the piece,
and their relationship,
so that this relationship—and plotline—
is stated clearly enough at the top of the piece
that we have noted it, attached our attention to it,
and can track it through the confusion that follows.

The song ends.
He sits on the bed to adjust his rollerblades.

RADIO TALK SHOW HOST
That was SINGER, with NAME OF SONG.
And we were talking about love
with our guest Bobby Beausoleil.
What is love, Bobby?

BOBBY ON THE RADIO
That's what I'd like to know, Tim.

[they both laugh]

But I mean, basically,
I guess you'd have to say
that the Greeks, pretty much anticipated everything
western folks have thought and felt for 25 centuries.

HOST
Well, I'd have to agree with that.

[JIM enters, looks at Edward, looks at Polly,
looks back at Edward,
turns,

lifts the hood of the Lincoln Town Car,
and goes to work on it.]

BOBBY
You'd be talking here,
for instance,
about love as friendship,
which the Greeks called *philia*,
benevolence towards guests
which would be *senike*,
the mutual attraction of friends,
or *hetairike*,
and then sensual love of course,
or *erotike*.

HOST
Let's talk about that.

BOBBY
Fundamentally,
what the Greeks thought
was that love is not just a sentiment
but is actually the physical principle of the
universe itself
the very stuff that unifies the universe
you know, binds the universe together.

[PHIL enters, carrying a wrench and a rag,
looks at Polly, at Edward,
back at Polly,
drags a garbage bag full of something to the edge
of the stage,

stands,
looks,
hesitates,
throws the garbage bag off the edge of the stage
and then joins Jim at work on the Lincoln.]

HOST
Unh-hunh.

[silence;

Bonnie, a nasty, slatternly girl, enters,
looks at Edward, at Polly,
back at Edward,
takes a lunch box, hands it to Phil,
takes out a magazine and reads.]

2ND TALK SHOW GUEST
You know, I have to say, as an Italian,
I grew up in a family where people just hugged
each other all the time.
All the time.
If you were Italian you'd know what I mean.

HOST
I know what you mean.
I know what you mean.

2ND TALK SHOW GUEST
I don't think you do.
Of course you do.
But I don't think you do.
I mean, the other night I went to this cocktail party,

and someone handed me this glass of gorgeous
ruby red wine.
And I'm, you know, something of a wine freak.

HOST
I don't mind a glass of wine myself.

2ND TALK SHOW GUEST
And just as I put out my hand to take the glass,
someone came up behind me and shouted
"Leo!"
and grabbed me.

[Shirley, a librarian, enters,
checks out the others present,
looks confused.]

HOST
People do that all the time.

2ND TALK SHOW GUEST
Right. And the wine flew into the air.

HOST
God.

2ND TALK SHOW GUEST
And everyone screamed,
even though, in fact, the wine landed only on me.
And I said what the Italians always say when you
spill wine.

HOST
What?

BOBBY
What does this have to do with love?

2ND TALK SHOW GUEST
You want to know what I said?

HOST
Sure. Sure.

2ND TALK SHOW GUEST
I said: Allegria!

HOST
Right.

2ND TALK SHOW GUEST
which means
joy!

[Edward rises to test his rollerblades,
sits to fix them again.]

Because what I saw,
which I have to say I don't think any of the others
really saw;
was that the wine added color to my evening!

HOST
Right.

2ND TALK SHOW GUEST
And this is how it is to be human.

HOST
Right.

2ND TALK SHOW GUEST
I mean you have to bump into walls.

HOST
Don't I know it?

2ND TALK SHOW GUEST
You have to celebrate your craziness and your humanness.

HOST
That is so true.

[Red Dicks enters;
she is a transvestite, accordion-playing hairdresser.
S/he goes straight to Bonnie,
and begins to fix her hair
using Coke cans as rollers.

Shirley still looks confused,
finally sits on a crate.

They are all motionless,
listening to the radio.

CASTING NOTE:
Ideally, Phil, Jim, and Jim all play musical instruments
and have formed a garage band.
And/or Shirley and/or Bonnie might fill in or play with the band
depending on their musical talents.

Red Dicks will play the accordion.

Polly will sing.

The garage band will have a number of opportunities to play
at various points during the piece—either the entire band
or a single instrumentalist with a singer.

Shirley takes out her cell phone and dials.]

2ND GUEST
Because, the fact is,
we're dying of loneliness,
all of us.
Just dying of it.

HOST
Well, now. we have a caller here on line one.
Hello, there, you're on the air.

SHIRLEY
Hello?

HOST
Hello, you're on the air.

SHIRLEY
Hello?

HOST
Hi, doll.
What's your name?

SHIRLEY
Shirley. My name is Shirley.

HOST
OK! Well, it's your nickel, Shirley!
What'd you want to say?

SHIRLEY
Well, what I wanted to say is
what I think is—what love is:
Love is how you relate to people
or, if your love is channeled in some other way
it is how you are cold or indifferent or hurtful
to another person.
And so love is who you are
and how you are
what kind of person you are
it's the most factual thing about how you are.
You can't talk your way around it,
make it come out some other way.
It remains the deepest fact about you.
I mean, you can say,
oh, I'm really a nice sensitive person
I treat people with dignity.
But the only way you really know how you relate to
other human beings
is in the most secret, secret place
where you are most vulnerable
most open to your private self
when you are making love
you don't even know what you're doing
until you're doing it
and then you see what sort of person you are
whether you are making love with someone else

or you are the president of the united states passing
a welfare bill
then you've done it
it's not talk any more
you've acted out your most private deepest self
and lodged it in the flesh of another human being
so that another person feels pain or pleasure
and then you know:
this is who I am.
This is what I do.
And who I am
what I want to do
what feels hot to me
the person or the behavior I can't keep myself from
is so strange
so idiosyncratic
is so odd
so that usually I repress it
if I find myself drawn irresistibly to a man
with bushy eyebrows
or a comforting voice
or something even stranger
muscular thighs
or hair on his chest
or a certain weakness
a vulnerability
so that I sense I can hurt him in a certain way
and then take him to me like a wounded animal
and comfort him
if these are the things that make me weak and
shaky with desire

I know this is my truest self
what makes me break out in a sweat.
the kind of thing that makes me a little sick to
my stomach
it feels so incredible to me
and of course, I feel embarrassed by it
because people will think I am a sick person
and I am a sick person

and you think: I don't even know where this
comes from.
You think back through your childhood:
could it have been this or that?
But the thing that makes you crazy with desire
is too exact and too
strange
to have come from anything you can remember.
You have touched the real mystery of human beings
the thing beyond any knowing
the thing that comes from so deep down
no one can tell you where it comes from

This has nothing to do with sex.
Of course, I am talking about sex
about having sex with another person
but it has nothing to do with sex
it has to do with who I am
at such a deep and secret place
no one could explain it.

And this is why people don't want to talk about sex
or think about it

because if they do
they see so deep down into themselves
they see such a strange creature
such a hungry animal
so uncivilized
they don't want to hear about it.

And so they repress the thing that is deepest in
them
and most unique
I, for instance,
I might become a person who thinks
I am attracted to nice, gentlemanly men
or men who are well-groomed and considerate
I try to forget who I really am
by loving some approximation of what I hope for
or, even worse, by loving someone who has nothing
of what I want.
Because I want to think I am a good person.
I think:
what is it to be really, freely who I am
would that be just to follow my urges
and not repress them
or is that just to become enslaved to my urge
and not be free at all
Am I free only when I repress what I freely feel?

And then I think:
well, finally, none of us is free.
We all repress what is most deeply true about us
otherwise we can't go on.

[silence]

RADIO HOST
Right.
Well.
No one could disagree with that.

2ND TALK SHOW GUEST
I don't know.
Frankly I think I could disagree with it.
I mean, when you're talking about
civilization and....

[Edward turns off the radio
and roller blades on out.

Polly, riveted by him, watches him go,
looks after him for a few moments.

Shirley, confused, turns off her cell phone
and puts it away.

One of the mechanics riffs on his electric guitar,
taking off on the love song we heard at the top of
the piece,
through the following dialogue.]

POLLY
Oh.

[She moves slowly downstage,
in a reverie.]

POLLY
Oh.

[She pulls a chair up next to the kids' plastic
swimming pool,
puts her feet into it.
Red Dicks eventually comes over and gives her a
pedicure
while she sits with her feet in the pool.]

Oh.

RED DICKS
So.
He's at loose ends, I think.

POLLY
Edward.

RED DICKS
Yes.

POLLY
Oh. Well.
He's just a boy.

RED DICKS
At his age, a boy needs his father.

POLLY
Yes.

RED DICKS
I don't say he doesn't need his mother.

SHIRLEY
Or his step-mother.

RED DICKS
Or his step-mother, right, sure.

JIM
It's true, you can talk all you want about mother love,
but for a boy, really, he needs his father.

BONNIE
[with some rancor]
And maybe not, by the way, a man who just takes off
when the car breaks down,
leaves his wife and son wherever they happen to be
because he has business.

POLLY [in a reverie still]
He'll be back
when he's finished.

BONNIE
Isn't that just what he would say?
I mean:
what kind of man would just leave his wife wherever
his car broke down?

SHIRLEY
And no mechanic for 50 miles.

PHIL
A woman like you
stranded in the boondocks.

BONNIE
And what he really had in mind probably was to cat around with some woman in Utica!

POLLY
Excuse me?

BONNIE
Or not.
Or not.

SHIRLEY
Doesn't he love his son?

RED DICKS
Men should ask themselves:
What about all these images of fathers and sons and other men and boys as pals and buddies?
Why are they so popular in books and movies?
Why are they encouraged in Boy Scouts and Big Brothers.
Maybe boys and men need this.

BONNIE
Especially during puberty.

RED DICKS
When a boy is entering the grown-up world,
maybe a boy needs a sense of apprenticeship,
or just going fishing,
and a lot more gentle touching from a father figure.

SHIRLEY
Or you might ask yourself:

is it dangerous for men to have a role in the socialization of boys?
Will men just teach boys to be pigs?

BONNIE
But women can't do this all by themselves.
Boys have testicles and ejaculation and beards and erections,
and women can't be expected to understand these things as well as men!

RED DICKS
We need to recognize there's nothing wrong with this.

SHIRLEY
What the women should be doing
is directing their efforts toward advocating
anti-sexist socialization
within the existing man/boy and woman/girl relationship model,
while continuing to encourage cross-sex interactions as well.
Because love is not just a thing
that has to do with men
or men and women.
Love is a whole weltanschauung.
Or gestalt.
And you can't leave all this to boy scout leaders.

BONNIE
Because what you have now are jerks.

SHIRLEY
The way it is now:
dogs are better than men.

BONNIE
For sure.
At least dogs miss you when you're gone.

SHIRLEY
Dogs look at your eyes.

BONNIE
And they feel guilty when they've done something
wrong.

SHIRLEY
You can force a dog to take a bath.

BONNIE
Dogs mean it when they kiss you.

SHIRLEY
Dogs understand if some of their friends can't
come inside.

BONNIE
Dogs are already in touch with their inner puppies.

SHIRLEY
How can you tell a man's sexually excited?

BONNIE
He's breathing.

SHIRLEY
What should you give a man who has everything?

BONNIE
A woman to show him how to work it.

SHIRLEY
What do men have in common with floor tiles?

BONNIE
If you lay them right the first time,
you can walk all over them forever.

SHIRLEY
What is a man, really?

BONNIE
A man is a vibrator with a wallet.
A man is an unresponsive lump of flesh
obsessed with screwing,
incapable of empathy,
love,
friendship,
affection,
or tenderness—
a half-dead isolated unit that will swim a river
of snot,
wade nostril-deep through a mile of vomit
if he thinks there'll be a friendly cunt waiting for him
at the other end.
A man
is a creature who will fuck mud if he can.

JIM
Oh.

Oh.

And then these women wonder why
a man would prefer masturbation to marriage.

PHIL
I know some guys who like electronic masturbation.

JIM
What?

PHIL
You know, you take some electrodes
and some low-power, carefully controlled electric
current,
run that through your genitals
and you'll get some very interesting tingling and
throbbing sensations.

JIM
And why do you want to do that
when you can masturbate with your hand?

PHIL
You ask that because you've never done it.
You'll get something very different with electronic
stimulation.
You get yourself a stereo audio amplifier,
with 1 to 5 watts per channel of output power.
A tone generator of some sort.
An electronic music synthesizer like Casio or
Yamaha.
You don't want to use an electric guitar,

which could put a current through your whole torso.

You set the amp control to MINIMUM.

Set your tone source to produce a continuous tone of about 440 Hz:

that's the "A" above "middle C" on a musical keyboard.

Insert the small loop electrode just inside your urethra.

SLOWLY turn up the amplifier's volume control.

Then you can play the "A above middle C" on the left channel,

and play the "A" an octave lower on the right channel.

Or play "C" on one channel

and the adjacent "C sharp" on the other channel.

Play a steady

tone on the left channel

and do a downward "glissando" on the right channel.

You know: fool around.

It's just like any other kind of sex:

it's not always the same.

[A big macho explosion of a performance piece:

one of the mechanics does a heavy macho drum solo

while the others strut and preen

and behave like guys—

in a performance piece that goes on for several minutes at least

before the guys calm down

with just a few little aftershocks of dirt kicking and bicep inspecting.]

RED DICKS
What do you think caused your heterosexuality?

JIM
What?

RED DICKS
What do you think caused it?
I mean, for example,
when did you decide you were a heterosexual?

JIM
I don't know.

RED DICKS
Or do you think your heterosexuality is just a phase
that you'll grow out of.

JIM
I hadn't thought about it.

RED DICKS
Well, think about it.

Do your parents know you're straight?
What do men and women *do* in bed together?

SHIRLEY
These men
they talk sex
always nothing but sex.

BONNIE
Right.
And I am looking for love.
I am looking for a relationship
with warmth
and soul
and humanness.

PHIL
So am I!
It's not easy!

POLLY
I miss my husband.

I miss having him hold me when we sleep at night

his arms around me
his stomach pressed against my back
his face nestled in my hair

and when I turn in my sleep
I turn within his embrace
his arms around me still
my head on his shoulder
his leg between my legs

For him, making love is the most important thing,
for me, being held.

A mature man—
not a boy,
not a randy young man
who doesn't know yet who he is

or who you are
or how to be together with another person—

holding you in the palm of his hand
keeping you safe
knowing when he holds you
this is where your home is.

A lot of men you think are bad
or
insensitive or cold
are really just suffering from touch deprivation.
You know, touching
is just as important for human beings as eating.
Babies, sometimes, will wither and die if they're
not touched.
You've seen these stories on television.
But men, now,
men are raised to be tough and independent
and taught to avoid touching.
And for many men,
the only time they're touched at all
is when they make love with their wives.
And so they develop a craving to be touched,
that's why it is a man might even touch a child in
the wrong way
but if he does
he can't be blamed for it.
Or he can be blamed
but I understand
just how he feels.

It's like they say
sometimes
you hear people talking on the radio:
Sometimes a woman will see someone, she'll think:
Oh.
Oh.
I could imagine myself being attracted to him.
But no.
You stop yourself
because you think:
this is what it is to be a civilized person.
Not just a creature subject to any kind of urge
but that, as a married woman,
you have made a different choice
of your own free will.

For example,
you could say, the thing about *incest* is,
the reason incest is the only thing forbidden
in every society everywhere—is that the *incest*
prohibition is the step
by which human beings make the transition
from nature to culture.
Because this is what it is to be human,
to make this transition:
Because the human being
is the animal that *became* human.
And how was that?
By denying its animal needs.
The human being is the only animal
who obliterates the very traces of nature as we

leave it.
Because we are sorry we came from life,
from meat,
from a whole warm, bloody mess.
We are *ashamed* of the nature that we come from.

For instance,
for instance, no one would say that excrement
is a substance like any other.
although for animals that is exactly what it is;
and some of these animals will just *eat* excrement
because they just don't care; they just don't think it
is any big deal
or different from any other natural element;
and those animals that don't positively eat excrement
nonetheless, they show no particular revulsion
for it.
But the shame *people* feel for the excremental
orifices
testify to the separation between human beings
and nature
and it is clear, too,
that nothing will prevent this shame
from rubbing off
on the nearby genitals.
This is human nature.
We don't want to hear about it.
We like things to be nice.
We like these things to be full of warm human
compassion,
feeling, soul,

we don't want to talk about excrement
unless we can put it in some human,
psychic context
so that it's not just *pornography*!

And nothing could be more horrifying to a woman
than the love she may feel for someone
she can't resist—
because then she knows
suddenly she's become the unwilling subject
of the uncontrollable,
indiscriminate excitement of just pure animal sex.

And so of course we seek out marriage
where we are able to have sex
and at the same time
we can have the denial of sex
—with those other than our husbands
and sometimes, even, with our husbands, too -
because
nothing is more common
than the *innocent* love a woman has
for a man she is entitled to love,
the infinite sense of peace and wellbeing
that can come of that
the sense of civility
so that at last she may settle down,
and not keep living in the daily fear of the beast
that is settled deeply in her heart.

And so I e-mailed my husband today,
and I said:

[Polly goes to the microphone
and speaks into it.]

Dearest Richard,

Autumn has finally come here.
Less than ten days ago,
it was close to 100 degrees in the afternoon.
Now the house is cold when I wake up in the
morning.

This morning
I had on my pale pink thermal leggings
and a matching long-sleeved shirt,
with tiny buttons up the front.
And when I woke up I was
rubbing myself with one hand without thinking
about it.

I don't think I'll ever get enough of you.

And I began to think
about you loaning your latest tape of me to a couple
of friends,
and I could see them watching it, enjoying it,
admiring me,
and finally having to take their cocks in their hands
while they watched me come.

I thought: well,
I love watching *your* hands—
moving up and down your cock so slowly.
And seeing you come makes me so greedy for you

I feel like screaming.

I imagined you picking up the phone at your office,
and hearing my voice:

"Hi, Richard, are you having a nice day?
Are you busy right now?"

I'd say:
"I'm in bed right now,
and very very naked
and I've been thinking all about you.

Just the sound of my voice
would make your cock start to swell.

Then would you
—without even realizing it—
move your hand down to feel your hardness?

You would hear my breath growing ragged,
as I tried to keep talking to you
my other hand pressing deep inside me,
to come again for you.

Is it okay for me to talk to you like this, Richard?
I like it.
I love you so much.
You make me so crazy,
I hope you never stop.

So. Well.

Enjoy the rest of your day, my love,
my one true, and only love,

you know I'll be thinking about you.

Your,

Polly

[Edward enters again.]

EDWARD
Mother.

POLLY
Oh!
Edward.

You've come back.

EDWARD
Come back?

POLLY
Didn't you just
go out?

EDWARD
Oh.
Right.

POLLY
I didn't know you were coming right back.

EDWARD
I came to play with you.

POLLY
Play with me?

EDWARD
I'm feeling....

SHIRLEY
At a loss.

BONNIE
Without his father.

EDWARD [distracted first by Shirley then by Bonnie]
Yes.

RED DICKS
He needs someone to play with him
the way boys play.

POLLY
I know some games for boys.
I know
Smugglers and Spies.

RED DICKS
Smugglers and Spies?

EDWARD
That's a Cub Scout game.

POLLY
Is it?

EDWARD
Yes.

POLLY
Is that bad?

EDWARD
Mother....

BONNIE
He calls her "mother."

RED DICKS
Why not?

POLLY
You're too old for a Cub Scout game.

EDWARD
Well, yes.

POLLY
What would you like to play?

EDWARD
I don't know.
Some games we play in school.

POLLY
What do you play in school?

EDWARD
I don't know.
Like,
Car Wash.

POLLY
Car Wash?

EDWARD
You know,

one person is the car
and the other person is the car wash.
And the car goes through the car wash.

POLLY
Goes through the car wash?

EDWARD
I'll show you.
You be the car wash.

POLLY
Okay.

POLLY
I'll be the car wash.

EDWARD
And I'll be the car
and I'll go through the car wash.

[Edward gets down on his hands and knees
and moves forward.]

POLLY
Right. OK.

EDWARD
And you wash me and you know
you be the rollers and the stuff in the car wash.

POLLY
OK.

RED DICKS
Don't forget to roll up your windows.

BONNIE
And put it in neutral.

[Edward moves up to Polly,
who begins to lightly pat and rub his back.]

SHIRLEY
Not much of a car wash if you ask me.

EDWARD
But you really have to get into this game,
you know,
you've really got to wash me
if you really want to play the game.

SHIRLEY
This is a school game?

RED DICKS
Not when I was in school.

SHIRLEY
They don't play: spelling contest, or something?

RED DICKS
This is a pathetic game.

[Polly works more vigorously.]

EDWARD
But hey, hey, but no tickling!

POLLY
Tickling is allowed.
Tickling is always allowed.

BONNIE
Especially in this—
[his hands in the air, fingers flailing]
this is the—you know—
that part of the—
where you have all the little, uh—

[She goes for him with hands and arms flying,
to his hair, his ribs, his butt.]

EDWARD
Hey, what are you doing?

POLLY
I can't—
I don't know.

[She puts a hand between his legs—
everyone else is silent and motionless—
and she massages him with pleasure.

Suddenly, she stops.

She stands up.

He stands up uncertainly, slowly—
having enjoyed it.

Then, not knowing what to do about it,
he turns and runs out.

Polly looks stunned.

Silence.

One of the mechanics plays a low, easy saxophone
or keyboard solo.

Shirley stands, turns, walks to the margin, facing
away from the others.
Bonnie, too, turns away, looks off.
Red Dicks works out with free weights
made of a car axle and spare parts.
Phil puts a tire in the kids' plastic swimming pool
and checks it for leaks.
We hear the hissing sounds of the hydraulic hoist,
the thumping, banging sound of the tire machine.
Jim gets a cellophane bag of peanuts, opens it,
pours it into a Dr. Pepper,
and drinks the Dr. Pepper and eats the peanuts at
the same time
one-handed,
leaving the other hand free to scratch.
More awkward silence.]

POLLY
Sometimes you see a man doing something
thinking about nothing else except what he's doing
he's completely unconscious really
maybe he's chopping wood in the backyard
and it just stops you from breathing
and it brings tears to your eyes
he's so beautiful
so much himself
you find him irresistible.
You love him, that's all.

BONNIE
Right. We see how you look at him.

POLLY
Who?

BONNIE
Edward?

POLLY
Just now, you mean?

SHIRLEY
Well. For a while.

POLLY
For a while.
Did I look at him like this before?

[silence]

It's not my fault.

RED DICKS
Nobody's like, blaming you, you know.
It's just,
well:
he's your son.

POLLY
My step-son.

BONNIE
So it begins:
the lying to yourself,

putting a good face on it.
Isn't that just always the way?

PHIL
This is a boy.
You're talking about a boy
who loves you

JIM
and counts on you
to take care of him
whatever your relationship might be
you're the grownup

POLLY
I know that.

SHIRLEY
I need an older man
because I don't know
because I need a man I can count on
I remember when I met my husband
he asked me on a date
and we went out to shoot pool at Mickey's
and when he walked me home
I asked him if he wanted to come in.
So he did, and we had a drink
and then we went to bed
I don't remember how
in those days it was not such a big thing
and I don't remember anything about it
except in the middle I suddenly felt very sick

and I yelled at him to stop
he thought, probably, I was going to say something
like
this is just our first date or something like that
but instead I said, I think I have to throw up,
and he just started laughing
and I thought: oh, he's okay,
he's got a sense of humor
and the rest of the night he just took care of me
which is, you know, a lot more than most people
would do on a first date
so I married him
and I don't think I was wrong
we had a good marriage
and I miss him still
he was good in bed in every way.

RED DICKS
Not all men are bad.

BONNIE
I just needed to be tied up until I learned my place
and this guy I lived with knew that.
Not all men know that.
I just need to be bent to the will
of an insatiable man.
I need shackles, ropes,
stuff to keep me submissive and obedient.
I need leather,
I need it, that's all
and I need to be flogged, pretty hard and pretty
often.

You know,
some people like to be dominated.
Sometimes you would be better off asking a person:
how is it for you?
Because sometimes a person will tell you:
much better than the life of vanilla sex I used
to have!
My husband and I
we just don't do any of that vanilla sex any more.

I need to be alternately fondled and beaten.
And then I need to be cuffed and forced to
masturbate
until I'm completely humiliated by my own
nastiness and
insatiability.
I need my master to comment on what a nasty,
slutty bitch I am.

And then I need relief from my pent-up desires.
That's how it is for me.
I need a man who will hold me and comfort me
and then rub me, and lick me, and finger me
and fuck me to as many orgasms as each of us
can have.
I need to be taken to a state of complete exhaustion.
I'm not saying this is for everyone.
I'm just saying this is how I am.

JIM
Some people like feet
this is simply how they are

or toes
They like to touch them and feel them and kiss
them
they can't be blamed
some people like to suck on someone else's toes,
but they can't just go around doing it all the time.

PHIL
I don't understand it.

JIM
I can understand it.
Like sometimes I like to rub my buttocks on
someone else's buttocks.

BONNIE
I like to strip search a guy,
like make him face the wall with his hands in the
air,
pat him down with my hands on the outside of his
clothes,
make him take everything out of his pockets
and put it on the table,
then take off all his clothes.
I look at everything for drugs,
microfilm, bugging devices, weapons, or sex toys.
He has to stand there all the time,
naked,
with his hands behind his head.
And then I search his body,
I search every opening, very thoroughly,
and then, if he's clean, I release him.

That's all.
I just release him.
To me: that's sex;
that's all there is,
that's how it is for me.
I'd say, a lot of what passes for my sexuality goes on invisibly
inside my head,
and I think it would be safe to put me
in the addicted slut category.

SHIRLEY
Sometimes when you're with a man,
you can cut a hole in a paper plate
and put it over his genitals,
and then
put some lukewarm spaghetti and meatballs on the plate,
and then, when you eat the spaghetti,
you wrap each strand around his penis
and suck it up into your mouth.
I knew someone,
that was the only way she could have sex.

PHIL
There was this guy I heard of once
who shaved the hair from the heads of Barbie dolls
and swallowed their heads to get excited,
and one time he felt sick and went into the hospital,
and the x-rays showed he had six Barbie heads
stuck in his intestines.

JIM
I like to have people put pies in my face.
You know, and smear them around.
In restaurants or parties, wherever.
I'll see some guy I kind of like and I'll go up to him
and ask him to pie me, and, you know,
most men will.

PHIL
Really.

JIM
You get all these feelings of anticipation,
the fear of rejection,
the thrill of acceptance, humiliation...

PHIL
Right.

JIM
the wish that a partner will say
or do something you don't expect...

PHIL
Right.

JIM
sharing an intimacy with someone
who might not otherwise even notice me,
doing something that sexual and unacceptable
right out in public.
I guess maybe I've been pied as many as
150 times a month when I've really been,

you know,
unable to stop.
And sometimes I'll say to a man, you know,
I'd really like it if you'd do it to my crotch.
Sometimes they're scared,
but usually they'll do it.

SHIRLEY
That's incredible.

POLLY
I like to sleep with someone with all my clothes on.
It can be like the olden days,
with a board in between us,
or even with my legs tied together so penetration
isn't possible.
Or we can sleep together naked,
just looking at each other for hours at a time,
letting our eyes go up and down each other
for three or four hours,
taking each other in,
but I can't, you know,
make love any other way.
Mostly I just like to be held and touched and
cared for,
you know,
loved.

RED DICKS
We should all embrace love, because
this is a good thing.
we need to be touched

we need to be felt
we need nurturing
we need some sort of manifestation of love
because life is a process of becoming
and once you are involved in that
you're lost
lost forever
but what a fantastic journey!

Every day is new.
Every flower is new.
Everything in the world!
Every morning of your life!
In Japan, even the running of the water is a ceremony!
You have to ask yourself:
when was the last time you listened to the water?
People take showers and run water in their sinks
every day of their lives
and they never hear it!
You should go home tonight
and turn on the faucet
and listen to the water!
Because:
it's beautiful!

And how many people these days are intimidated
when someone says:
I want to touch you.
Everybody has got to be loved!
Sometimes I have to throw oranges at young people
just to get them to pay attention and listen!

I was talking with a little boy once,
and I said: what can you do, David.
And he said: lots of things.
And I said: like what?
And he said: I can spit.
Yes! He could spit! Can you top that?

I said: what else can you do, David?
And he said: I can put my finger up my nose.
And I said: you bet you can!
Isn't it some sort of miracle
that you can raise your hand whenever you want to
and want to put your finger in your nose
and it gets there!
We should celebrate our wonder!
Everyone!
You've got to have people who are interested in
your tree!
And not the lollipop tree!
And you've got to be interested in their tree!
You've got to say:
show me your tree, Johnny.
Show me your tree,
and then we'll know where we can begin!

BONNIE
You can't blame people for how they are.

JIM
Right.

RED DICKS
I could agree with that.

SHIRLEY
I could agree with that.

PHIL
What's the argument here?

[JIM suddenly begins to sing a song made famous by the castrato Farinelli,
perhaps Handel's "Pena tiranna" from Amadigi.
The others listen to the heartbreaking song.

At the end of the song, there is silence for a moment.
And then:

PHIL
So, you remember when
this teacher stuck the fork in your hiney?

JIM
What?

PHIL
You remember,
you were saying about when she stuck the fork in your hiney?

JIM
Who?

PHIL
What do you mean who?
You told me, when you were in third grade. Or Second grade.
When did she stick a fork in your hiney?

JIM
I don't remember.

PHIL
What did she do to your hiney?

JIM
I forgot.

PHIL
What did she do to your hiney?

[silence]

Did she ever make you kiss her vagina?

JIM
I forgot.

PHIL
Come on.

JIM
I forgot.

PHIL
Did you have to kiss her on the butt?

JIM
I forgot.

PHIL
What did you have to do with the knife?

JIM
Okay, okay, right.

Put the peanut butter on her.

PHIL
And the jelly?

JIM
And the jelly on her mouth and on her eyes.

PHIL
You put jelly on her eyes and her vagina and her mouth.

JIM
On her back, on her socks.

PHIL
This was in second grade?

JIM
First grade.

PHIL
And how did everybody take the peanut butter and jelly off?

JIM
We ate her and licked her all off.

PHIL
You had to lick her off?

JIM
And eat her all up.

PHIL
Was that scary?

JIM
It was fun. I thought it was funny.

[Awkward silence.]

PHIL
Of course, you get into an area like this
it's hard to judge.

[A very quiet, gentle conversation follows.]

I mean:
your daughter was, how old,
nine?

JIM
How do you mean?

PHIL
When you had incest with your daughter.
JIM
Three.

PHIL
She was three?

JIM
From the time she was three
until she was ten.

PHIL
From the time she was three?

BONNIE
Is this true?

Did I know this?
Did everyone know this?

JIM
And, well, it started when she was three.
I was in the bedroom and I was standing in my
shorts and a T-shirt,
and she walked up to me and she pulled the edge
of my
my shorts,
and I just had this overwhelming desire to have sex
with her.
And....

PHIL
And this is your daughter.
She is three years old.
Whatever.
And,
and,
but wouldn't your first instinct be to just move
away and say,
"geez."

JIM
It was.
It was.
But it, it, I, I guess my, my instincts to,
to move against this, to—to guard against that,
to not do that
were just not strong enough.
I had a determination not to

but that,
you know.

PHIL
How did you feel?

JIM
Like a piece of garbage.

Basically.

[silence]

PHIL
And then
when did you do it again?

JIM
It was probably a few weeks later.

PHIL
And this kept going on when she was four?

JIM
Right.

PHIL
And did she ever tell her mom?

JIM
Well, yes, she did.
When she was nine.

PHIL
When she was nine.
And what did your wife say?

JIM
She, uh, she confronted me on it.
And—and I made promises that—

PHIL
Had you thought about
how that moment would be before it happened?

JIM
Oh, sure.
I'd, you know, had visions of the police pulling up
and hauling me off.

PHIL
Did you love your daughter?

JIM
Yes, I—
I love her now.

PHIL
You love her now?

JIM
Of course, yes,
I do.
If—
if I answered your question in the negative,
then I would be in denial,
and I would be in a more dangerous place than I
am by saying,
"Yes, I am."
And, in being aware of that

and having the tools that I have gained in therapy
there are strategies I have for now—
for dealing with that that I did not have before.
There's learning strategies to deal with that.

Sometimes a moment will come in a child's life
when you will realize:
oh, this child loves me;
she
she's beginning to know me,
to recognize me,
to smile every time I come near her;
when I sing songs to her in my terrible voice
she loves to listen to them;
she doesn't cry or pucker up her face when I kiss her;
she stopped crying when I picked her up.
If anything were to threaten her
I would trade my life for hers.

PHIL
Sometimes you think,
oh,
men's lives.

JIM
Right.

PHIL
But then you think:
well, I mean: women's lives, too.

JIM
For sure.

PHIL
But when you think about men
I think part of it is
that men don't like their jobs.

JIM
Unh-hunh.

PHIL
I mean, if you'd ask them,
probably 90% of men would tell you
they are feeling this incredible sense of bitterness
and
and frustration about their wives and families.

JIM
I think this is true.

PHIL
They don't feel appreciated.

JIM
This is so true.

PHIL
It makes a man angry the way everyone just
takes for granted the things his earnings buy
for them
and sort of come to expect it as their due.
And then his kids put him down
for being this materialistic middle class jerk—
and he'd like to tell them,
okay,
okay,

why don't you just get someone else to support you!
But he holds himself back
because
because
he thinks: that's what it is to be a man.

[Silence.

Phil gets an axe and demolishes a wooden crate.

Polly wanders offstage, distracted.

And then JIM begins to throw himself, loose-limbed, to the ground,
over and over again,
collapsing to the ground like a sack of loose bones,
his head lolling over and thumping on the ground,
then rolling over, as though convulsively, several times,
his elbows and knees and head thumping on the ground.

Then he gets up and repeats the action,
gets up and repeats the action.

PHIL joins JIM, synchronously, in the same set of repeated actions.
So, it is a dance for two men.

Then RED DICKS joins the other two,
so the three of them are going through the same repeated actions,
and adding some additional synchronized choreography

with break dancing moves on the ground,
and a sort of ground slam dancing
with spins and twirls and twirling headstands,

and finally a recording of a loudly barking dog
joins in

until everyone hears the barking dog, and gradually
stops dancing.

Polly wanders back in
with a chicken on a leash;
she is in her bathrobe;
she sits at a table and smokes a cigarette,
drinks a cup of coffee,
and does her nails.]

POLLY
I should leave town.

[silence]

Probably—
what?
I should just leave town.
I should go,
you know:
somewhere.
I mean, where no one could find me—
and,
if I were lucky,
I'd forget how to find my way back.
I'd get lost.

[she picks up a dry bagel,
picks it into pieces as she talks,
and, as she talks, tries to choke down the occasional dry piece.
She picks up the newspaper and reads:]

"Wanted: gas station attendant with five to ten years' experience to clean pool in exchange for swimming privileges. Must have own snowplow."

I could do that.

"Wanted: Dark room manager with experience in stripping.
Professional wrestling background preferred."

I could do that.

"Wanted: Chiropractic assistant for night shift. Must play the flute."

I could do that.

You know, they say the reason the Lord's Prayer goes "lead us not into temptation"
is because human beings can't resist temptation.
The prayer is not:
"lead us not into sin."
Just into temptation—that's enough for it to be too late.
That's how bad human beings are.
And then, if you fall in love,
what can you do?

[In frustration,
Polly picks up the chicken,
takes the chicken by the feet and swings it around
violently in circles,
apparently killing it (though really only knocking
it unconscious),
and putting the apparently dead chicken quietly on
the ground.

The garage band pick up their instruments
and launch in to a big love song—
full out—
and Red Dicks goes to the trunk of the Lincoln
Town Car
and gets his accordion out of the trunk and joins in
with vocals and accordion
—and Polly steps up to the microphone
and sings.

At the end of the song,
Alicia enters.
She is 11 years old—or the youngest possible legal
age
for the youngest-possible-looking person to play
this role.

Edward enters at the same moment.
They both stop short,
on opposite sides of the stage.

The grownups all watch.]

ALICIA
Oh.
I'm sorry.
I didn't know you would be here.

EDWARD
That's OK.

[They both move toward his bed at center.]

ALICIA
I know you
just think of me as
a kid.

EDWARD
No.
Well, yes.
But
I think you're pretty grown up for your age.

ALICIA
I'm eleven.

EDWARD
Right.

ALICIA
Almost twelve.

EDWARD
Right.

ALICIA
Probably you're embarrassed to be seen with me.

EDWARD
No. Not at all.

ALICIA
Do you think it's wrong of me?
EDWARD
Wrong?

ALICIA
I mean, do you think I'm bad?

EDWARD
What for?

ALICIA
To be in love with you?

EDWARD
Oh, I don't think you're really....

ALICIA
Yes, I am.
I know.
I think it's wrong.
Probably you think I should be spanked.

EDWARD
No, not at all.

ALICIA
I do.

[she starts almost to weep]

Sometimes I think I'm so evil,
the things I think

[she starts to bite her wrist]

EDWARD
Hey, what are you doing?
What are you...
are you biting yourself?
Don't do that.
Hey.
Hey!
Don't do that.

[he takes hold of her, tries to wrest her forearm out
of her mouth]

Cut it out.
That's crazy.
Hey!

[he pulls her down on the bed on top of himself,
across his lap,
and spanks her;
she stops biting herself.]

That's kind of crazy
you know that?

ALICIA
I feel better now.

EDWARD
I don't think I do.

ALICIA
Did you like spanking me?

[silence]

Well, did you?

EDWARD
I don't know.
I think
probably
I've got to go.

ALICIA
Hey, Edward!
Edward!

[With longing, she watches him go.]

RED DICKS
I guess you have to wonder sometimes
what catches a guy's eye.

ALICIA
Yeah.

PHIL
I think a guy likes a pretty face.

JIM
That's the first thing I always notice.

PHIL
And great hair.

JIM
Great hair, that's true.
Great hair.

PHIL
I don't like a woman with messy hair.

JIM
Or too much spray.
If it looks too stiff, that's not good.

PHIL
Do you like wavy hair?

JIM
Yes.

PHIL
I do.
I'd have to say, probably that's my favorite.
Wavy hair.

JIM
Right.

PHIL
Most guys will like a natural look
or soft
not too much makeup

JIM
a great smile.

PHIL
You know, I think these are the basics.

ALICIA
How can you tell when he's your boyfriend?
I mean, say you've been together, you know,

hanging out
maybe hanging out a lot,
when do you say to your friends, like, "we're together."

BONNIE
Does he call you "kiddo?"

ALICIA
I don't know.
I guess he might.

BONNIE
Right.
That's not a good sign really.

SHIRLEY
Or, if you're going somewhere together,
do you break into a sweat trying to keep up with him?

ALICIA
We haven't exactly gone anywhere together.

[silence]

BONNIE
You know, there are things you can do to get a guy's attention.

[silence]

Like, say you're having a conversation with a guy:
while you're talking to him, you could
put your hand on his knee

SHIRLEY
Lightly.

BONNIE
You could unbutton a button on your sweater

JIM
I don't know.

BONNIE
What?

JIM
These are things that might be a little scary to a guy.
You could listen to him when he talks.
You could move a little closer to him.
I don't think you should unbutton any buttons.

BONNIE
Okay.
Say you are walking down the street
and you see a cute guy walking a dog.
Do you
pet the dog and smile at the dog
pet the dog and smile at the guy
touch the guy on the arm and wink at the dog?

ALICIA
Pet the dog and smile at the guy.

PHIL
What has this got to do with it?

JIM
He doesn't even have a dog.

RED DICKS
What's his favorite color?

ALICIA
I don't know.

RED DICKS
It's worth knowing. You can tell a lot from that.

ALICIA
Like what?

RED DICKS
Well, a guy who likes grey
is going to be your indecisive kind of guy.
Yellow, he's kind of passive,
maybe gay, you know,
I'm not saying necessarily,
just could be.
Your pink man is a philanderer
and a flirt.
But red:
a guy who likes red is going to be easily aroused
he likes sex every way you can imagine
he's going to be a tiger in the sack.

JIM
This is maybe not what we're talking about here
a tiger in the sack
this is a girl you're talking to.

ALICIA
I'd like a tiger in the sack.

RED DICKS
Really?
Have you ever taken the purity test?

ALICIA
I don't think so.

RED DICKS
Have you ever:
held hands with someone?

ALICIA
Sure.

RED DICKS
photocopied parts of your body, such as your face,
hands or feet

ALICIA
Uh, no.

[At some point in here, the chicken will come
"back to life;"
one of the grownups can put the chicken in the car
and close the door.]

RED DICKS
been on a date?

ALICIA
Of course.

RED DICKS
been on a date past one a.m.?

[as the test goes on,
she responds more slowly or hesitantly
or with difficulty or embarrassment
at the increasing intimacy of the questions]

ALICIA
Of course.

RED DICKS
worn a strapless gown?

ALICIA
Yes.

RED DICKS
slow danced?

ALICIA
Yes.

RED DICKS
necked?

ALICIA
Yes.

RED DICKS
French kissed?

ALICIA
Yes.

RED DICKS
hot tubbed in mixed company?

ALICIA
Yes.

RED DICKS
in the nude?

[silence]

ALICIA
Yes.

RED DICKS
had someone put suntan lotion, cocoa butter, or baby oil on you?

ALICIA
Yes.

RED DICKS
played doctor?

[more hesitantly now]

ALICIA
Yes.

RED DICKS
played Twister?

ALICIA
Yes.

RED DICKS
played Naked Twister?

ALICIA
Yes.

RED DICKS
been picked up?

been picked up?

ALICIA
Yes.

RED DICKS
picked someone up?

ALICIA
Yes.

RED DICKS
had a one night stand?

ALICIA
Yes.

RED DICKS
I think she's ready.

POLLY
If you don't mind my saying,
I think you could use a little help with your makeup.
I think if you want to go for this dewy look
you're going to need some powdery, shimmery
products
instead of these creamy moisturizing ones.
You're going to want to give your T-zone some
extra blotting power
with a sweep of loose powder.
Go for the glitter on the eyes.

Loose sparkle eye powders, blush powders.
Forget the frosts on the lips,
go for clear gloss. Clear gloss.
Or else you could use

"Honey Rose"
or
"Tulip"
or "Tea Rose"
or "Oyster Pink"

RED DICKS
Or, "Almost Kissed"

BONNIE
Or "Baby Kiss"

SHIRLEY
Or "Sweet Nothing"

POLLY
"Desert Rose"

BONNIE
"Positively Pink"

POLLY
"Blush Rose"

BONNIE
"Dusty Rose"

SHIRLEY
"Cinema Pink"

RED DICKS
"Pink Champagne"
Or "Balla Balla"

BONNIE
"English Rose"

RED DICKS
"La vie en Rose"

SHIRLEY
"Peony Peach"

POLLY
"Belle de Jour"

PHIL
"Baby Lips"

[silence;
the others look at Phil]

POLLY
Well, you have a lot of choices.

ALICIA [overdosed]
I,
you know,
sometimes
I can't stop thinking about
cutting myself
on my arms and legs, you know,
with razors,
not killing myself

or anything
but just
cutting myself
and then I guess I'd wear
long-sleeved shirts
or something
because I know that
hurting myself
isn't really
solving anything
but I can't seem to stop
thinking about it.

[she turns and runs out at full speed;

Polly gets into the back seat of the Lincoln Town Car
and shuts the door.

Shirley takes up the brushes next to the drums
and does a quiet, contemplative solo with them.

JIM takes off his shirt,
lights the outdoor barbecue grill with lighter fluid,
then puts a trail of lighter fluid along the ground
and suspends himself horizontally above the flames
on two saw horses
and roasts himself like a hog on a spit.

or else he has picked up the lighter fluid
and managed to get it on his hands,
and lit his hands on fire;
he turns front with both hands burning,
looking awkwardly, but calmly, from side to side,

looking for something to put out the fire.
Finally, he goes over to the kids' swimming pool,
and extinguishes his hands.

PHIL, meanwhile, has been standing in the kids'
pool,
fiddling with a radio, which explodes,
giving him an enormous electrical shock,
and then something else also explodes with a huge
ball of fire and smoke
as JIM climbs down from his rotisserie and puts
his shirt back on.]

SHIRLEY
A lot of people think
that they're entitled to happiness.
I never thought that.
I always wished for happiness
but I never thought I had a right to it.
I thought happiness was something I had to make
for myself,
not something like manna that fell from on high.
I have some friends who get indignant
at the least obstacle to their happiness
as though it were an outrage.
I always thought you had to win your happiness,
under conditions some of which were burdensome
others favorable.

BONNIE
When I first met Walter
he would talk and talk about the most boring things

on and on
not quite "how to get up in the morning," but almost.
He would burst into tears on my shoulder.
He was—well, obviously, he was afraid of his father.
The house he grew up in
it was just draped in black.
He never remembered any nursery rhymes from
his childhood
or songs he learned.
And then, when I had to put him in Manhattan
State Hospital
underneath the Triborough Bridge,
and I called his mother and begged her to help
his father got on the phone and said
"stop it, you're upsetting Walter's mother,"
and he hung up on me.
And they never came to visit him.
The last time I saw him
when I was leaving after a visit
I told him I loved him, and he cried.
He was so fat from the drugs they were giving him.
He walked like a fat man.
And his hair was turning gray.
And they had him at work there
making those ugly, clumsy ashtrays.
And he had been such a beautiful boy.

[The garage band plays

A COUNTRY LOVE SONG

while all those on stage sing along

and Polly opens the window of the Town Car

and sings vocals from the front seat under a
spotlight.

As the song comes to an end, Edward enters, sits
on the edge of his bed,
takes off his rollerblades.]

RED DICKS
A guy like you
you're growing up.

EDWARD
I guess I am.

RED DICKS
Do you have a girlfriend?

EDWARD
No.
How come you ask?

RED DICKS
Guys your age, usually they do.

EDWARD
I like girls okay.
But for me, I don't know,
my idea of a good time is listening to the radio
playing a little air guitar
roller blading
if I had my choice finding out a little more about
women

or doing something else
I think I'd rather
learn the secret of cartooning
how to identify different kinds of airplanes
the fundamentals of Greco Roman wrestling
how to build a business
the secrets of Jiu Jitsu
how to train a dog.

And frankly, if you want to know what I think
I'm getting a little sick of seeing sex dragged
through the dirt,
glorified
misrepresented in every way, shape, and form
I read through postings I find on the Internet
these so-called personal experiences that are so
outrageous and far out that only a fool would
believe what he is reading.
Or on the television set
all these bikini clad women parading across the
screen
holding Brand X Beer or breakfast cereal.
What kind of message does this send out?
Everyone else feels fat and ugly by comparison
everyone is insecure and angry
so all the men go out and rape someone
And is sex all that big a deal in the first place?
I'm not so sure.
I myself vowed a long time ago
to wait for someone very special,
to share that part of myself

with the one woman I fell in love with
and spent the rest of my life with.
And now, after almost 14 years of waiting,
masturbating to hold myself together sexually,
what do I find?
That adults are trying to get me involved in
pre-marital sex.
Don't you people realize
that sex is a distraction from the real world,
that what the politicians want is for you to think
about sex all the time
and if that's all you think about
everyone will soon be reduced to poverty
without any health care or social security or pensions
because you haven't even been paying attention?
Yes.
Yes.
It happens that I did break my vow
and I did have sex with someone
I went with this girl for two months,
both of us getting very serious about the relationship
and expressing our wishes to remain virgins until
our wedding
and then it started with a touch here,
a stroke there,
and then one night,
we talked for almost three hours
about whether or not we should make love.
and so we did
and pretty soon I was moving my penis towards

her vagina,
and in a half a second,
I had an orgasm.
All the buildup
all the excitement of finally having sex—
it all rushed out as fast as it could,
and I spent the next hour feeling horrible
about ruining her first time with such a poor
performance.
and all my years of hard work down the tube.
And it wasn't even that wonderful
what I did feel was nothing more than masturbating
without my hands.
The oral sex we'd been having for months
had been far more satisfying.
Suddenly I understood
how so many guys out there
wanted to have sex with as many women as possible.
Maybe they all felt as cheated as I did
Now I knew sex for what it was.
And now I have no interest in sex.
None.
Forget it.

[He lies down and falls instantly asleep,
like a narcoleptic.

Silence.

A very quiet conversation follows
with Phil and Jim sitting on opposite sides of the bed,
talking over Edward.]

JIM
You forget how it is to be a kid.
Sometimes I look back at the family photograph album,
and it comes back with such a rush.
You remember these moments exactly the way they were
as though it was yesterday.
Do you ever do that?

PHIL
Well....
Sure.

JIM
You don't?

PHIL
Sure.
Sure.

JIM
But not as though you like to.

PHIL
Unh-hunh.
Did your father ever take pictures of you nude?

JIM
What?

PHIL
Did you father take pictures of you nude?

JIM
Well, no.
I mean, I guess when I was a baby
you know,
in the bathtub,
yeah, sure.
Did your father take pictures of you nude?

PHIL
Yes.

JIM
Where?

PHIL
In the bedroom mostly.

JIM
What was he doing in the bedroom?

PHIL
Well, taking pictures and
having sex with me.

JIM
When you were a boy?

PHIL
Yes.

JIM
He did?

PHIL
Yes.

JIM
How did he do that?
Was he nice to you?

PHIL
He was gentle.

JIM
Were you thinking it was wrong?

PHIL
That what was wrong?

JIM
That your father was having sex with you.

PHIL
Well, he wasn't having sex with me at that time.
He was just massaging me.

JIM
Oh. I thought you said...

PHIL
That was later.

JIM
But when he massaged you,
did you think that that was wrong?

PHIL
No.

JIM
You never did?

PHIL
When he massaged me with his mouth,
I thought that was wrong.
But, you know,
I thought I'd get used to it, and I did;
and eventually it made me feel warm.

JIM
Oh.
Did you like it?

PHIL
Sometimes.

JIM
Why did he do that?
Did you ask him why he did that?

PHIL
He told me that it was a way to release the tension
and the
knots in your muscles
when you got worked up from sports and anxiety,
and it was
just a way to relax.

[Phil begins to shiver uncontrollably,
hugging himself to keep from shivering.]

JIM
Did you ever massage him?

PHIL
Yes.

JIM
Did he give you directions?

PHIL
He just said no.

JIM
No, meaning
what?

PHIL
Meaning if I skipped over his penis, he said no.

JIM
So, what did you do?

PHIL
I started to touch his penis and
massage it in the way he did me.
And then, one time
he took my hair in his hands
and wanted me to massage his penis with my
mouth.

JIM
How old were you?

PHIL
I was seven.

JIM
Were you afraid of your father?

PHIL
Yes. When he

gave me swimming lessons,
he would
grab my
hair and
dunk me under the water and hold me down for 20
or 30 seconds,
and then he
would lift me up; and
I would cry out,
and then he'd
dunk me under again.

JIM
Was this, like, playful?

PHIL
No.
He wanted me to
struggle,
and he wanted me to
fight.
And I was afraid he would
kill me
accidentally.

[Polly, emerging from the Lincoln Town Car,
goes to Edward's bed, wakes him up gently.]

POLLY
I'm sorry things didn't work out with your girlfriend.

EDWARD
It's okay.

POLLY
These things do happen, you know.
So many times, for most people,
the first time is so bad,
and they think they never want to make love again
or that it was wrong
and yet
love
love is the most wonderful thing we have as human
beings
this closeness to others
caring
compassion
and these feelings of empathy and caring for
another
this is the whole basis for society
for civilization.

And if you were ever to get together again
with the girl you cared for
there are things you can do
that will give her happiness
or simply fun
there's nothing wrong with that
pleasure: that you give her as a gift
selflessly
because you care for her

For instance, you know, talking
you can't do enough talking with a woman
or reading her a book in bed

women like this
or when you're making love
not to carry on a whole discussion
but just to say how much you love her.

EDWARD
Yeah?

POLLY
And taking off a woman's clothes
you need to treat her with the care
well
with the care of the person you love most in the
world
and very slowly
and in a dim light
because a lot of women are self-conscious about
their bodies
and as each new part of her body is revealed
kiss her there softly

EDWARD
Unh-hunh.

POLLY
And touching
touching needs to be gentle
a lot of guys will just grab a woman's breast, you
know,
and that hurts
a really gentle caress
just gently brushing over a nipple

or even just holding her breast
this is a real trigger

EDWARD
It is?

POLLY
And
a woman likes to be touched all over her body
before she makes love because
when she is really excited
her whole body feels like a penis.

EDWARD
It does?

POLLY
Of course, if you're making love with an experienced woman
she will know some things to make you feel more at ease
and some other things you will like
tickling you with her eyelashes
on your cheek and neck and stomach
rubbing her nipples over your chest and stomach
and thighs
taking you into a bath with her
soaping you all over
up and down
reading an erotic story to you in the bath
and afterwards
taking you to bed and giving you a massage

and then guiding you inside her
so that before you know it
having done nothing yourself
she is holding you gently, tightly inside
kissing your neck, your cheek
holding you
her arms around you
you've forgotten entirely where you are
all you feel is
complete love
safe and warm
forever

[silence;
Edward looks around;
no one speaks;
he gets up slowly, uncertainly from the bed,
and leaves, slowly, not running,
looking back and around from time to time in
confusion,
and then he is gone.]

POLLY
Probably I should kill myself.
I mean, I've lost my bearings altogether.
I suppose I could identify a picture of a spoon
or a sailing ship
if I were given a test
I could identify a duck, a mushroom, a horse,
a cherry
but I would only think I was fooling

the examiners
thinking I had my wits together just because
I could tell a bucket from a coffee mill
and repeating sentences:
The dog fears the cat because it has sharp claws
repeating:
The dog is afraid of the cat but only because of its
claws
and that would be wrong
that would count against me
they wouldn't even know what should count
against me
and who did this to my fucking hair?
Did you do this?

RED DICKS
No.

POLLY
Look how it is
you did this when I wasn't paying attention?

RED DICKS
I didn't touch your hair.

POLLY
How am I supposed to manage
when I have nothing to wear.
I don't have any top to put on
unless I take some skirt and pull it up around my
neck
and then what is it?

Something cream with something brown?
Do you know someone who would put that on?
I go to Saks and say to the saleslady
do you have thongs?
She pushes her eyeglasses up her nose and says
for underwear?
Right, I say, for underwear.
No, she says, we don't have thongs,
we have bikinis.
Well, let me see your bikinis
and she says,
these are 100% cotton

[she is pacing frantically back and forth]

Cotton! I say.
Ugh!
Who would wear a cotton bikini?
What has happened to civilization for god's sake
it's all downhill from here on out.
They come in a package of three, she says.
I don't want a package of one, I yell at her.
And pretty soon, they're calling over the store detective
telling me to pipe down
Pipe down, I say,
I'm a fucking shopper!
The reason you have a job is because I am here
demanding things!
And so the next thing I know
I'm being manhandled,

I find myself back out on Fifth Avenue
and I'm supposed to count myself lucky that I'm
not in jail—
that's what happened to me
the last time I tried to shop at Saks!
And now I have this crap to wear!
And nothing to eat but this goddam bagel!

[she throws the bagel across the stage]

Would someone just get me something to eat
a cup of coffee and a cigarette

[yelling]

I'm a frantic person!
Someone!
I'm just a little bit out of control!

I need a friend here.
Could you help me with this?

What the fuck ever happened to style?
Oh, sure, you say,
why don't they just lock her up
sure, lock her up.
A nice mental hospital in the country.
And then the same crazy people would just come
around:
[in a different voice:] did you see Philip Blum.
Philip Blum? Who the fuck is Philip Blum?
[in a different voice:] Did you see him?
No, I did not.

[in a different voice:] Last night or this morning?
Where would I see Philip Blum?
[in a different voice:] Walking around the ward.
I did not. What was he doing, walking around?
[in a different voice:] Just walking through the ward. Did you see him?
Oh, I don't know. Maybe I did.
[in a different voice:] Was he carrying anything?

[One or two of the others
is just pacing back and forth
as a reaction to all the frantic stuff that's going on.]

What would he be carrying?
[in a different voice:] A syringe perhaps.
Yes, he was carrying a syringe.
[in a different voice:] For what purpose?
You're asking me. To give injections I suppose.
[in a different voice:] Did he give an injection to you?
Yes. Yes, he did!
[in a different voice:] And did you fall asleep?
Yes. But not for long.
[weeping now]
Not for long.
I begged him: put me to sleep forever.
I'm worn out
and I don't know what I might do next.
I don't think of myself as a bad person
am average person, sure,
not a saint

I'm the first to know it
but not an evil person
who fucks her own children!

[Edward enters,
having returned, obviously,
because he is interested.]

EDWARD
Sometimes
things move so fast
it makes me dizzy.

POLLY
I know.
What do you wish I would do?

EDWARD
I don't know.

POLLY
Maybe you should come with me.

EDWARD
Where?

POLLY
Come with me.

Don't worry.
I'll take good care of you.

[she takes his hand
and leads him over to the Lincoln Town Car,
opens the back door.]

Let's get in back.

[He gets in,
she follows,
and closes the door behind her.

Bonnie turns on the radio
and we hear

BIG MUSIC.

Bonnie pulls her skirt half way down her butt
and does a dance to the music
that is half-wantonly flirtatious towards the men
and half-hostile and half three or four other things;

Phil and Red Dicks, meanwhile, engage in a
"roughhouse" dance,
throwing each other to the floor,
and jumping on each other's stomachs and butts,
one pulling the other upright and then throwing
him down to the ground again,
jumping on him,
grabbing his head or hair and hurling him to
the ground,
kicking his legs out from under him,
both of them screaming with horror and delight
as the violent dance goes on and on,
neither really hurting the other;

Shirley just walks around during all this
with her shirt pulled up to her neck;

and Jim tops everyone with a wild, licentious
striptease,
twirling his shirt round and round before tossing it
across the stage,
shimmying with a sock between his legs,
lots of wild stuff
stripping all the way down to a fig leaf.

Then the music comes to an end,
and Jim is the only one who had been dancing till
the end;
he is naked and feels instantly embarrassed;
in silence, with no one else moving or speaking,
he retrieves the items of clothing he had thrown
wildly in the air,
trying to cover himself with the clothes as he picks
them up,
finally coming to his cowboy boots,
getting one of them on after a struggle,
getting the other one half on,
when Red Dicks comes at him for a pas de deux,
and Jim partners with Red,
one boot halfway on,
holding Red up in the air,
then dipping Red's head toward the floor,
finally releasing Red and resuming picking up
his clothes.

A cellular phone rings.
It rings over and over.

Everyone looks at the cellular phone

that lies in the middle of Edward's bed.
No one moves.

Finally, Shirley picks up the phone—
and hands it to Bonnie.
She hands it to Phil
who hands it to Jim.
Jim stands with it uncertainly.
Red Dicks snatches it out of his hand and answers
it.

RED DICKS
Hello....
Richard!
Yes.
Yes.
No.
He's not...uh...here.
No, she's not here.
They're not here.

[everyone looks at the car as he says this]

You're coming home.
Good!
Good!
I'm sure they'll be....
Yes.
I'll tell them.
See you soon.
Bye.

[silence]

JIM
You know
I think what a man wants most when he comes home
is just a little time to himself
like a dog circling on the rug before he lies down
just a little space to get acclimated
read his mail, check out the game on TV

PHIL
I don't know.
A man comes home
the first thing he feels is tension.
He's thinking, right:
I remember where I am
Home, this is where the female always makes the rules.
Where the rules are subject to change at any time without prior notification.
Where no male can possibly know all the rules.
Where, if the female suspects the male knows all the rules,
she must immediately change the rules.
Where the female is never wrong.
Where, if the female is wrong,
it is due to misunderstanding
which was a direct result
of something the male did or said wrong.
Where the female may change her mind at any time.
Where the male must never change his mind
without the express written consent of the female.

Where the female has every right to be angry or
upset at any time.
Where the male must remain calm at all times
unless the female wants him to be angry and/or
upset.
Where the male is expected to mind-read at all
times.
Where if the female has PMS all the rules are null
and void.
Where the female is ready when she is ready.
Where the male must be ready at all times.
Where the male who doesn't abide by the rules
can't take the heat, lacks backbone
and is a wimp.

JIM
Oh, I think you've just got some differences here
between men and women, and I say,
vive la différence.

PHIL
I think I see him coming.

BONNIE
What?

PHIL
Richard.
I think that must be him.
You recognize that car?

[All look off to one side.]

JIM
No.

JIM
No.

PHIL
I think that must be him.

JIM
Right.

[Phil takes off in the opposite direction.
After a moment, Jim follows him,
then Bonnie, then Shirley, then Jim and Red Dicks.
The stage is empty.

The radio miraculously lights up and comes on

and we hear, at maximum, blasting volume:

Screamin' Jay Hawkins sings "I Put a Spell on You"

and after a few moments
Edward and Polly get out of car
and slow dance naked to the music.

Richard enters.
He is in his fifties.
He stands, lit by a spot,
and watches them dance.

After a long, long while
Polly sees Richard,
turns
and runs out.

We've entered a state of suspended animation,
as though we have gone into slow motion.]

RICHARD
What are you doing?

EDWARD
I...
I should get dressed.

[He moves towards his bed,
to get a sheet.]

RICHARD
I leave
my wife with you
and ask you, like a man, to take care of her,
and all you can think to do is to
is to get naked with her?

EDWARD
Did anyone know you were ever coming back?

RICHARD
This is your explanation?
Is this how it is for you to be my son?

EDWARD
Your son?
Is that how you think of me?
You never had anything for me but orders.
Do you remember
one weekend,
driving to the country

I was six years old
you got so angry at me
for something I had done I don't remember what
you pulled the car off onto an exit road
and got out and pulled me out of the car by my hair
and took me around to the front of the car
in front of the headlights
and I tried to pull away
and you knocked me to the ground
in front of the car, in the headlights
and I was crying
do you remember anything of this?

RICHARD
No.
This is not what I remember.

EDWARD
and one afternoon in the country
you left me playing with a friend
and you went off for tea with Mrs. Perry
but you didn't come back until after dark
and I was waiting for you beside the road
I saw you driving toward the house
and I waved to you
and you drove right past
because you still had Mrs. Perry in the car with you
and you kept on driving
and then you came back an hour later
I was still waiting for you by the road

RICHARD
I'm sorry.
If you say it was true, I believe you.
I'm sorry.

EDWARD
You were always exploding
always angry
cursing at the other drivers
calling them sons of bitches
so that I was always afraid of you

RICHARD
I'm sorry.

EDWARD
Always afraid you would turn on me
I thought you might kill me
push me out of the car
or crush me.

RICHARD
Oh, no. No.
I couldn't have done that.

EDWARD
How did I know?
You were in such a rage
or else silent, thinking,
holding your jaw, covering your mouth with your
hand
so sad and discouraged
we all made you feel your life had been worthless.

RICHARD
No. No.

I'm just a person, too, you know.
I always felt your hatred of me.
I thought, well, okay,
leave him alone,
don't force yourself on him
maybe one day he'll come around
see something in you that he likes
when I explained things to you
it made you squirm
I talked too much
it always turned into a lecture
I couldn't help myself
and I would see your attention drift off
I could see you wanted to get away
I didn't know how to get you back
the best I could do was try to be cheerful
wrap up what I was saying
let you go
and then, playing catch
I could tell,
you'd rather be playing with a friend
tossing a ball back and forth with me
it was nothing but your filial duty
you remember we went on a fishing trip together
one time to Canada.

EDWARD
Yes, one time.

RICHARD
Yes.

EDWARD
It was fun. I had a good time.

RICHARD
So did I.

I never knew what else to do.

EDWARD
So I've become a cold person, like you.
Usually I don't even know what I feel.

RICHARD
I loved you.

EDWARD
No, you didn't.
I loved you.

RICHARD
I don't think so.

[Edward runs out.

Richard sits on Edward's bed,
his head in his hands.

After a few moments,
Jim enters uncertainly.]

JIM
Is there something
maybe

I can do?

RICHARD
I can't say
that I've been a perfect person.
I abandoned the mother of my son
and I abandoned my son himself
to pursue another woman.

Other women really.

When I was a boy my son's own age,
I slept once with the mother of a boyhood friend
of mine
who lived just down the road,
a woman in her forties
Well, I slept with her more than once.
I slept with her the whole summer long,
going over early every morning
after her son had gone off to his summer job,
a divorced woman
and I was just a boy.
I remember her still,
I think of her still almost every day

[Polly enters.]

RICHARD
Polly.

POLLY
Yes.

JIM
Excuse me.
I'll just be....

[he leaves]

RICHARD
Was I gone so long?

POLLY
Yes.

RICHARD
You've always been my one true love.

POLLY
Oh.

RICHARD
You didn't know that?

POLLY
No.

RICHARD
When I first saw you
I thought
there couldn't be
a more pure vision
of absolute beauty.

POLLY
When we first met
you were happy to be with me all the time.

RICHARD
It's my fault?

POLLY
No.
It's just the way you were.

I remember
when we first arrived in St. Remy
the tall ceilings in our hotel room
with blue sky painted there,
and birds;
we made love,
and lay next to one another,
the summer breeze coming in through the open
windows
cooling our bodies,
I felt so dizzy from jet lag
and making love
and the summer breeze coming from the garden,
I thought: I've gone to heaven.

RICHARD
I remember that.

POLLY
And I thought at the time
I could never leave you.

RICHARD
I felt
such sympathy for you.
I thought: I could care for you forever.

I thought: I see deep inside you
your most secret self
and I will always care for you.
I will always wish you well.
I will always hope for your happiness.
To keep things away from you
that bring tears to your eyes
that cause you grief
that make you feel small or hurt
unfairly treated
those things in your past
your mother's goodness—but still, as good a person
as she was
as much as she loved you,
you always felt her distance
her coolness toward you
I thought: you will never feel that again.
Situations in your life
ordinary things, not knowing where the money
would come from
for your rent
I thought: you will never feel that fear again
that sense that things were so hard
and you didn't know where the answer might
come from
that sense of vulnerability
I'll hold you in my arms all night
my stomach pressed against your back
my face nestled in your hair
holding you the whole night, every night,

no harm will ever come to you
not ever.

POLLY
But then, do you remember when our bedroom
ceiling was falling
and you said,
"Polly, that ceiling has been up there for a hundred
and forty years
it's not going to fall now."

And I said, "Yes, but it's falling now."

And you didn't believe me until it fell
and you said you would believe me from then on.

RICHARD
Yes.

POLLY
Do you remember when I woke up one night
more than four and a half years ago
and I was sitting in the armchair in our bedroom
awake and sobbing
because it had been a year of you not getting
divorced...
six months after the time when you promised me
it would be over
and it was far, far from being over
and you gave me excuses like
"it doesn't mean anything...our marriage is over..."
and "Divorce will happen, like the sun rises and
sets,

the divorce will happen"
nothing made sense to me
I felt horrible to have people ask me
"so, are you and Richard going to get married?"
a question that should have made me happy or coy
or blushy
or giggly or secretive
and it made me sick to my stomach and humiliated
and I was faced with the choice to either tell people
that you were married
still with no divorce in sight
or I could lie—
both options made me sick and resentful
I knew you had seen that this was painful to me
you had seen it
and dismissed it as trivial, wrongminded, petty,
insignificant
I showed you over and over that it was painful...
truly painful
I sat in the chair sobbing, loudly
you woke up and saw me
you looked at me
and said with such contempt in your voice
"Boy, you've really worked yourself up over this
haven't you?"
and you rolled over
to go back to sleep

RICHARD
Yes, I remember that.

POLLY
and I thought
My God, I'm a complete idiot
I'm the little blond bimbo
the great fuck with the hot little dresses and the fun
and it's all so sexy and fun
and we'll travel to the south of France and all
around the world
and we'll show everyone how well we shop
and how in love we are and how romantic it all is
but don't you dare fuck with my family
and what's really important...
don't you dare ask me to rush getting a divorce
from the mother of my children
because this is serious and real
and someone real might get hurt
You showed me over and over again how
insignificant my pain was
You told me flat out that you would not get a
divorce one day faster because I wanted it
than you would without my insistence...
that it had to be on your schedule and not mine
And I had to decide then...
am I willing to be this person?
This bimbo, this loved thing, this doted upon object,
on the outside of "real" "important" "significant"
stuff—
like potentially upsetting wives and children—
am I willing to be that in exchange for having
Richard.

And I said "yes"
And I was wrong
And I came up for air a few more times over the
years
I called you from Louisville and I told you
"I cannot do this for another year,
I can't do this for a few more months, I can't, I can't.
I can't."
I made that call after sitting in the bathtub
for the fifth night in a row
crying for hours and slamming my head against
the tiled wall.
Spurred on by the sad fact of meeting new people
who saw we were in love and asked me the dreaded
questions
"will you and Richard get married?"
I made the call to let you know that I had a definite
limit.
A time beyond which I could not continue.
I called to tell you that the ceiling was falling
and I guess you thought
"that ceiling has been up there for a hundred and
forty years
it's not going to fall now"
The ceiling fell
I fell
As I had predicted I would
As I told you I would
As I tried not to as hard as I could
That's what happened to me

RICHARD
So it doesn't matter now
that I am finally really about to be divorced
because I have said this for years
over and over again
and it never happened and the damage has been
done
it's too late

POLLY
Right.

RICHARD
Because a person needs to be first in another
person's heart
and know it
and know it absolutely
or it is just too corrosive.
It's just poisonous, finally
poisonous

POLLY
Yes.

RICHARD
You know,
you never wanted so much to make love with me
You were interested sometimes
and sometimes, I think, took real pleasure in our
making love
but you never found me irresistible
the way I found you

you didn't want me more and more and more
the way I wanted you
you could wait to make love with me
or not make love for days and days and not care
about it at all
and I often thought
of course, it could be I'm not so appealing
I'm not so hot or so exciting to make love to
but maybe even more than that
it's simply that I'm not the right kind of guy for you
at all
not even the category of person who thrills you.

Or maybe you're just not carried away by love of
me
the way I am by you.

Which came first, do you think,
the rejection I always felt from you
or the disrespect you felt from me?

Every night you rejected me
and every time you returned from taking a trip out
of town
you rejected me
so that I came to dread your coming back
because your coming back
meant not that you would return
but that you would say you couldn't return
and I would feel your rejection again in the biggest
way
you would come back and savage me

[silence]

But really after what you've just said now
there's nothing more for me to say
except again and again how sorry I am
for hurting you, the best and only true love of my life
the whole point of living
was to find you and love you
and take care of that love
pay attention to it
and make sure I never lost it
and so I haven't done the one thing in life I should
have done
and without you
the whole point of life is over
and I feel my life has ended
and I see that I'm the one who is responsible for that
so I feel a grief beyond anything I've ever felt
for myself and for the pain I've caused you
I'll never ever forget the picture of you in the bath
in Louisville
crying and hitting your head on the tiles
never
and to know I did that

I wish you could see through the pain I've caused
you
so that you might still be able to understand
something of me
and see that I have loved you completely and still do
and somehow find your way back to me

and, if that turns out not to be possible
at least for you to know
in spite of the terrible mistakes I made
how much you were truly loved
what a precious person I always felt you are

POLLY
I can't see that.

RICHARD
You thought I thought of you
as a bimbo outside of anything
"real" or "important" or "significant" to me?

Everything I've done and felt and known and lived
for these past five years
was about you
was filled with your spirit
and your tastes and your hatreds and your loves
and your humor and your idiosyncrasies
and your whims
your sudden turns and your steadiness
your confidence in me
the depth of your feelings
and the ferocity of them
everything I did was about you
and now without you my life is over.

You thought I thought of you as the great fuck
in the hot little dresses
You never were a great fuck
You were the worst fuck I ever had

I loved to make love with you
because I loved you
and I loved who you were
and I cared for you
and I always wanted to be close to you
as close as I could be
You were inhibited and frightened and closed off
to adventure
repulsed and I don't know what else
and I always thought it was because you had been
sexually abused
as a child
by a grownup
or by the other kids in the woods
that you always used to joke about
and say how tough you were and you didn't care
what they did
but I've never known a woman
so averse to just opening up and having a good
time sexually
and experimenting and trying things
and seeing where it might take you

No
only because I loved you so much
did I live with what I always thought was
a frustrating and unsatisfying sex life
for you as well as me, I'm sure,
that I only thought maybe, maybe one day
if you ever came to love me and trust me enough
you might overcome whatever trauma of the past

had made you this way
and if you never did
I loved you so much
that a great fuck was way way down the list of
important things
to me about you
the biggest thing was always that I loved you
completely and forever

I loved your brains and your sensibility
we were soulmates
we felt and thought the same things in the same
ways
all the little subtle things in life felt the same to us
the same things were funny and stupid and
heartbreaking
the same things were pretty
the same things were good to eat
we liked the same light in the sky in Provence
we liked the same roads
we liked the sounds of the cicadas
we liked the same room in the hotel
we felt the same about Nostradamus's house
and about the people who ran it
and about the little stone pool back away from the
house
we liked the same things when you decorated the
living room
we liked the same scenes in the same plays
ten thousand million little things held us together
like no one I've ever known

I wanted to be inside you
inside your love
inside your feelings
inside your thoughts and how you felt the world
I wanted to feel things as you felt them
I wanted to be in your heart
and so often I felt I was
I felt we were together in that way
and in that way
you were the greatest fuck I ever had
but not the great fuck in the hot little dress
the great fuck because of who you were in your
heart
and how I loved you more than life itself

I remember
when we went to see the Greek play
The Danaids
in the abandoned marble quarry
and I thought:
we are connected to this human life
and to one another
for all eternity.

[They sit looking at one another
while we hear the Handel Sarabande from Suite
No. 11 for Harpsichord.]

Then Richard shoots Polly.

She is shot in the head, and astonished.

He shoots her again.

She is open-mouthed with surprise and anguish
and slips slowly to the floor.

He shoots her again.

She jerks involuntarily and lies still.

He puts the pistol into his mouth
and blows his brains out.
Brain and blood splatter behind him.]

RADIO TALK SHOW VOICE
Usually, in life,
we're so busy doing things,
we don't stop to look at each other anymore.

2ND VOICE
That's so true.

TALK SHOW VOICE
But you won't be here forever.

2ND VOICE
No.
Right.

TALK SHOW VOICE
You won't even be the same person tomorrow.
Things go by so fast,
and then they're gone.
Your children grow up
and get married
and you never took the time to look at them.

2ND VOICE
Like that couple in upstate New York.

TALK SHOW VOICE
Who's that?

[While the radio talk continues,
Phil and Jim come in and pick up Richard and
carry him out;
Shirley and Bonnie carry out Polly.

Red Dicks picks up the odd Coke can,
bit of clothing as the radio show continues.]

2ND VOICE
You heard that:
this man who shot his wife;
she was sleeping with their son,
near Utica.
TALK SHOW VOICE
Oh. Oh. Right.
Well, not their son.
His son. Her stepson.

2ND VOICE
That's the one.
He shot her
and then he shot himself.
And then it turned out they weren't married after
all.

TALK SHOW VOICE
Right.

2ND VOICE
He died. But she lived.

TALK SHOW VOICE
I understood he lived, too.

2ND VOICE
He lived? I didn't know that.

TALK SHOW VOICE
Yeah, he lived.
I guess, you know, he sort of lobotomized himself
but he was still able to pump gas
so they gave him a job there
and I guess he does okay.
They say that he seems happy.

2ND VOICE
I didn't know that.
But I did know that she
even though he shot her a couple of times—
once in the head—
she lived;
and she recovered,
well not completely, I guess—
she had a little trouble with her memory,
but otherwise she was okay.

TALK SHOW VOICE
And she moved into a trailer
with the stepson

2ND VOICE
Right.
In the trailer park off the old Route 32.
And they lived there together
raising pit bulls.
I heard they have thirteen pit bulls
living with them there in the trailer.
And the husband's in the trailer next to theirs.
I guess you could say
they lived happily ever after.

TALK SHOW VOICE
Right.
Well.
That's a love story.

2ND VOICE
Yeah. That really is.

[silence]

TALK SHOW VOICE
Okay!
Well,
here's some more music
a familiar old song.
This is Hank Snow singing "I Don't Hurt Anymore."

2ND VOICE
I like this song.

TALK SHOW VOICE
I've got to say,

I love this song.

[The garage band picks up the Hank Snow piece
and drowns out the radio

as Red Dicks straightens up,
throwing things into the kiddie pool.

END

True Love was composed, in collaboration with
Tom Damrauer, for Laurie Williams as Polly. It
was written with the dramaturgical assistance of
Greg Gunter. The piece was inspired by Euripides's
Hippolytus, and the works by Seneca and Racine
based on the same story, and incorporates texts
from those writers as well as from Leo Buscaglia,
Kathryn Harrison, the letters of Simone de
Beauvoir, Andy Warhol, Valerie Solanas, Wilhelm
Reich, the transcript of the trial of the Menendez
brothers, Gerald G. Jampolsky, M.D., Jean Stein's
biography of Edie Sedgwick, and texts posted on
the Internet, among others.

SUMMERTIME

A hundred slender white birch tree trunks.

A scattering of casual, summer-house furniture all covered in white muslin.

Grass grows on a desk,
and there are stars in the sky.

A woman's white summer dress hanging from a tree branch.

Later on, there might be 300 wine glasses half-filled with rose wine.

There is not so much a set for a play, as an installation piece
in which a performance occurs.

Violin music, quietly in the distance.

Tessa wears something in the colors of Spring.
She may have a flower in her hair.
She sits at the desk.

James enters.
He, too, is wearing something the color of Easter eggs,
and he carries a bright yellow umbrella.

JAMES
Excuse me?

TESSA
Yes?

JAMES
I didn't mean to barge in...

[he closes the umbrella]

I was told I might find a translator here.

TESSA
Oh, well, I...
I do some translation sometimes.

JAMES
You are?

TESSA
Tessa.

JAMES
Tessa.

Right.
Good.

I have a few things
I need to have put into Italian.
You see,
I work for someone
a photographer
who took photographs
and then asked certain people to look at the photographs
and say things or write things
that he would then put with the photographs.

TESSA
Captions.

JAMES
Yes. Right.
Well, no, not exactly.
More like thoughts or I don't know, feelings.

That is to say, he asked Roberto Calasso to write something
or, as it turned out, he thought he asked Roberto Calasso
whereas in actuality he asked a journalist named Francesco Ghedini
to speak to Calasso and ask Calasso to write something
do you know Calasso?

TESSA
I know *of* Calasso, sure.

JAMES
Right,
and Francesco said he had spoken to Calasso
and that Calasso had written these things
the things I have here.

TESSA
I see.

JAMES
but actually Calasso never did write them
I guess Francesco made them up
or even someone else made them up and told
Francesco
that they had been written by Calasso

TESSA
This is really complicated.

JAMES
What is?

TESSA
This whole story.

JAMES
Right.
Well: life itself.

TESSA
Right.

JAMES
So, when the proofs were sent to Calasso for his
final approval
because the book is going to press -
Calasso said he had never heard of these things
and if we printed them he would sue.
And so we had to stop the presses
and I came here to talk to Calasso.

TESSSA
Calasso is here? What, for the summer?

JAMES
I guess.

TESSA
What's he doing here?

JAMES
I don't know, I guess he's on vacation.

Anyway,
when he heard what had happened with Francesco
he didn't want to get Francesco into trouble

TESSA
Francesco.

JAMES
I don't know why
I suppose because he understood Francesco, you
know, is just trying to make a living
and Calasso felt sympathy for Francesco, I guess,
because Calasso's a nice man

and so he suggested maybe someone else could
sign the words
and he suggested Benigni

TESSA
Roberto Benigni.

JAMES
Right.
Because Benigni is well known as a lover in a way
a person who loves life and women
And Calasso knows Benigni and he said he would
call him -
because he's here too, vacationing...

TESSA
He is?

JAMES
Do you know Benigni?

TESSA
I know *of* Benigni.

JAMES
Right....
and the pictures are...uh...
did I say what the pictures were?

TESSA
Nudes.

JAMES
No.
Did I say that?

TESSA
I guessed.

JAMES
Well, yes.
Or, no.
Not entirely.
Some are nudes, but some are not.
I mean, many are not.
And there are men, too. And old people.
And children, I mean: as friends.
You know.

[silence]

Love.

[silence]

Sex for sure. But: also love.

TESSA
Oh, well, love.
No wonder it's so complicated.

JAMES
Right.

TESSA
These days especially.

JAMES
Right.

TESSA
With what we all know now

what we've come to know.

JAMES
Exactly.

[silence]

JAMES
Anyway the texts are in English
because we have them in type for the American
edition

TESSA
and Benigni doesn't speak English

JAMES
Right. Well, not so well.

TESSA
So you need them translated back into Italian.

JAMES
Right.

[silence]

TESSA
No problem.

JAMES
What?

TESSA
No problem.
I can do that.

JAMES
Oh. Oh, great, thank you.

TESSA
Do you have them?

JAMES
Sure.
They're right here.

TESSA
So.
Why did you want Calasso to speak about love?

JAMES
Because he's, well,
he's Italian....

TESSA
Right.

JAMES
You know,
from Europe,
from an ancient civilization in a way,
the old world.

TESSA
Greece and Rome.

JAMES
Right.
And still in touch with the deeper ways of life
and love

the things that are deep in human nature and eternal

TESSA
close to the dreamtime of civilization

JAMES
Right.

TESSA
The time of mythology.

JAMES
Right.
Deeper than Freud, even.

TESSA
Right.
Deeper than Freud.

[silence]

JAMES
Or, you know, I suppose we could have gotten a woman to write about it.

TESSA
Right.
Though probably that wouldn't have helped.

JAMES
No.

[silence]

Do you think I could wait here while you do it?

TESSA
This could take a while.

JAMES
Right. Of course,
and you'd rather have some privacy I guess.
I only thought,
if you had any questions.

TESSA
Sure, sure. You can stay.
You can sit there.

[silence]

JAMES
Do you mind if I just lie down?
I'm sort of jet-lagged.

TESSA
No. Fine. Please do.

JAMES
Thanks.

[he lies down;
she looks at the text for a while, quietly.]

TESSA
This line -
"deer heart" -
what is that?

JAMES [sleepily]
Um...

I don't know.
I guess it's just something that...uh...you know
someone thought of.

TESSA
Unh-hunh.
I mean, it's supposed to be an animal, a deer,
a fawn, a wild animal,
but at the same time it should suggest sweetness:
d-e-a-r.
In English, you have this play on words.

JAMES
Yes. Right. I suppose you do.
That's one of the challenges of translation I guess.

TESSA
Well. Yes, it is.

[Music comes up.

Francois walks vertically down the sky,
or steps out of a wardrobe
or up out of a steamer trunk
or through the wall
or out of the trees.

He carries a rose umbrella;
and he too wears flowered or brightly colored clothes
and has a flower in his buttonhole]

FRANCOIS
Are you free for dinner?

TESSA
No.
I'm busy.
As you can see.

FRANCOIS
Everyone has to eat.

TESSA
I'm not dressed.

FRANCOIS
I have something for you.

JAMES [waking up]
Uh, excuse me.

[he hands her a crimson satin slip]

TESSA
Oh, Francois.
This is a slip.

FRANCOIS
Everyone's wearing slips these days.

TESSA
As a dress?

JAMES
Pardon me.

FRANCOIS
Yes.

TESSA
To go out?

FRANCOIS
Sure.

TESSA
Not in Martha's Vineyard, I don't think.

FRANCOIS
Of course in Martha's Vineyard.
It all started here.

TESSA
I like it.

[she steps out of her dress
and into the slip;
she wears, otherwise,
black boots, and socks that are falling down around
her ankles;
or else, she takes off the dress and doesn't put the
slip on,
wearing nothing else but stockings and red high
heels]

JAMES
What is this?
I beg your pardon,
but you seem to have interrupted something here.

FRANCOIS
Do you believe in love at first sight?

TESSA
No.

JAMES
What's going on?

FRANCOIS
It's the truth.

TESSA
So?

FRANCOIS
So what?

TESSA
So why do you tell me this?

FRANCOIS
Because perhaps this is how it is for us.

TESSA
How can this be after all these years we've known
one another?

FRANCOIS
Because sometimes you don't see the other person
at first.
And then suddenly you do.
You sense something in one another.
You might not even know what it is.
In fact, probably you never know,
the connection is so deep,
beneath the place where language even starts.

And then, if you let the moment pass, it is
past forever.
And what you never know is:
was this a great love or not?
Was this your one great love
that you've just missed.
Because each of us is given only one great love
in life.
That's what all the poets have known.
We've forgotten it in our times.
I think we get too caught up in our daily lives.
But people used to know:
you are born,
you have one great love,
you die.
There's nothing else to life.
That's why, in Romeo and Juliet,
after they find their love,
they die.
Because that's the truth of it:
birth, love, and death,
that's all there is.
Your great love may come at the beginning of
your life,
or in the middle,
or near the end.
Or not at all.
But there is only one
and if you miss it,
you've missed it forever.

JAMES
This is exactly what I meant to say to you.
This is what I myself was thinking when I first
met you.

TESSA
Is this what you always say to women?

FRANCOIS
No.

JAMES
I was going to say the very same thing to you
but I was afraid you would think I was too forward.

FRANCOIS
Do you dance?

TESSA
Of course I dance.

JAMES
Excuse me.
Wait a moment.
Uh...I beg your pardon.
Goddammit.

[Music comes up.
They dance -
not just for a moment
but this dance is a long performance event of
its own.

James paces back and forth,

wanting to interrupt, feeling too uncertain and shy, until finally he does.]

JAMES
Well, look, finally,
I don't mean to interrupt, but...

TESSA
I'm sorry.
James, this is my friend Francois.

JAMES
Yes, so I gather.
It seems that I happen to doze off for a minute and now you're dancing with someone else.

TESSA
What?

JAMES
You're dancing with someone else.

[she hurriedly puts on the slip -if she didn't have it on]

TESSA
Someone else?

[the following is all on top of one another]

JAMES
Well, yes.
Excuse me,
Tessa and I...
I thought we...

well, I might have been mistaken,
but I thought we were...
taken up with one another.

FRANCOIS [withdrawing]
Oh, I beg your pardon.
I didn't realize.

TESSA
What?
Taken up with one another.
What he means is...

FRANCOIS
I didn't realize....
I didn't mean to intrude.

TESSA
You're not intruding.
This is a...
we have a business relationship.
I mean we are...
I am working for him
in the sense that...uh....

FRANCOIS
That's quite all right. I'll just be....

JAMES
Business relationship, yes.
I suppose so, but I thought there was something
more than that.
I thought...

FRANCOIS
Possibly we'll have the pleasure again....

[he exits;

at the same moment, Mimi enters,
coming out of the woodwork or the woods
also with a brightly colored umbrella
and brightly colored clothes.

She doesn't speak for a while;
she just stands there, drinking an iced tea, and
watching.]

TESSA
What have you done?

JAMES
Done?
I hope I haven't done anything.
I certainly didn't mean....

TESSA
This was my friend!
I was dancing!

JAMES
Yes, I see.
And I didn't mean to....

TESSA
What are you,
some kind of stalker?

JAMES
No. No.
All this happened totally by chance
by pure chance.
Stalker!

TESSA
We might have been....
I mean, you can't tell what you might have
interrupted....

JAMES
I know.
I'm sorry.
Well, in fact, of course,
I don't mean to presume,
but I also thought that perhaps you felt....
that is to say,
we met,
and frankly I felt something right away,
and I even thought perhaps you might have felt
something, too.

TESSA
Felt something?
For you?

JAMES
Yes, for me.
I thought I sensed something special possibly.

Are you telling me you didn't feel some connection?

TESSA
No. No, I didn't.

JAMES
I was just a stranger with whom you were doing business
and, knowing nothing about me, you let me sleep here with you
and you felt no connection?

TESSA
Sleep with me?

JAMES
From the first moment I saw you
I thought
here is a wonderful person
and I thought you felt something of the same
but now you seem, well,
as though you might be denying your impulse.

TESSA
Impulse? I don't have an impulse!

JAMES
What do you call it?

TESSA
I call it nothing.
Are you crazy?
You thought
we were in love?

JAMES
Not that I thought we were in love,
but that perhaps there was some feeling of
a connection.
You have such beautiful eyes.

TESSA
Eyes? Eyes?
I have nothing to do with my eyes.
They have nothing to do with me.
Get out! Get out! Just get out!

JAMES
I'm sorry. I apologize.
I'm leaving.
I wouldn't think of staying another minute.

TESSA
Then go!

MIMI
Excuse me.

[Tessa wheels around to see Mimi]

TESSA
God, Mimi, am I glad to see another woman.
I am so sick of men
and all their talk of love and sex

JAMES
I don't think I mentioned sex.

MIMI
Love, I hate love

TESSA
do you know has it ever been anything but a cover
for some kind of manipulative bullshit
some kind of exploitation

JAMES
I don't think I was trying to....

TESSA
has anything ever done more damage to me
than love?

MIMI
These men what is sex to them
but some way to avoid any sort of reality altogether

TESSA
call it love
and it's nothing but a hideout.

MIMI
I know just how you feel.
I feel the same way exactly.

TESSA
A woman wants another person with whom she
can relate

JAMES
And so does a man.

TESSA
one who sympathizes

MIMI
who can know how she feels

JAMES
Just like a man.

TESSA
and know who she is in some deep sense

MIMI
accept her for exactly who she is

JAMES
As a man hopes as well.

TESSA
not try to keep just to the surface of things

MIMI
avoid the real involvement with the deeper things
that are inevitably more complex

TESSA
and sometimes not entirely easy to deal with

MIMI
but this is the real human exchange
the exchange with the inner being
that feels really good and consoling

TESSA
and, as far as that goes, really hot

MIMI
and sexy

TESSA
Exactly.

JAMES
Excuse me, but is there maybe something
are you two having some sort of....?

TESSA
Certainly not.

JAMES
Because I thought I sensed...

TESSA
You sensed something again?

JAMES
If not on your part for her
then possibly on her part for you.

MIMI
Certainly not.

JAMES
I think so.

MIMI
Absolutely not.

TESSA
I am a person without any involvements whatsoever!
And that is exactly how I intend to keep it!

JAMES
And all the while
doesn't it mean anything to you
that I think I love you?

TESSA
Love me?

MIMI
You think you love her?

JAMES
It happened so suddenly -
who's to know?
it was all the most fortuitous event
but, in fact, this could be our real chance in life,
Tessa.

TESSA
I hope not.
[to Mimi]
He could be some kind of narcoleptic.

JAMES
You don't know anything about me.
We've only just met.
Maybe I seem like a jerk to you

TESSA
Well....

JAMES
but that could be just because it's an awkward time
I'm not at my best

something like that
I mean everybody has these potentials within them
to look like a jerk
or even to be a jerk
but they might be more
like 90% of the time or even 98% of the time
really fine people
or good people
or funny
or even,
you know,
hot.
I might be like that
and then that would be good for us
because I tell you
I'm crazy about you.

TESSA
You walk in on me with some random project.
You don't even know me.

JAMES
You don't think I do?
People are smarter than we think.
We think
it takes a long time to get to know someone
and in a way it does
but we know so much from the first second
it's not just the words another person speaks
we right away take in
their, you know, body language

the way they hold themselves
cock their heads
how their hair falls and how they push it away from
their eyes
whether impatiently or gently
whether they are irritable or thoughtful people
gentle or violent
caressing or insensitive
how they smell
whether they look directly in your eyes
or they can't look up from the ground
or meet your gaze directly
or their eyes dart from side to side
because they are anxious in a way
they will never change
I saw you
and I knew:
I've looked for you all my life.
I love you.

[Francois enters,
sees Mimi, starts to sneak back out.]

MIMI
Francois!

FRANCOIS
Oh,
Mimi.
Imagine that. It's been...

MIMI
A long time.

FRANCOIS
Yes. Precisely.
How extraordinary.

TESSA
You know each other?

MIMI   FRANCOIS
We were...   We had a...

FRANCOIS
We lived together...

MIMI
Briefly.

We spent the weekend together in San Remy.

FRANCOIS
A wonderful time...

JAMES
Excuse me, but we were having a conversation here.

MIMI
Until what?
You walked out the door...

FRANCOIS
We were outdoors at the time.

MIMI
Right. In a little outdoor cafe.

TESSA [to Mimi]
You never told me this?

FRANCOIS
So, technically speaking...

JAMES
Perhaps you would excuse us....

FRANCOIS [to James]
I'm sorry....

MIMI
You walked out of the cafe
and got into some woman's car.

FRANCOIS
Not some woman.
That woman was a friend.
I mean,
I had known her....
which is to say
I had been friends with her at one time
and then there she was in San Remy
she asked for my help.

MIMI
Your help?

TESSA
Who was this?

JAMES
Do we care about your love affairs?

FRANCOIS [to James]
I beg your pardon.

[to Mimi]

It seems she was there with a fellow
who wouldn't let her out of his sight
and she needed to phone her husband
so I said I would drive her to a telephone I knew
by the side of the road
where she could make a call
with the motor running as it were
and I could bring her back.

MIMI
But?

FRANCOIS
Well, but it turned out, of course,
the phone was out of order
and then she was frightened to return
so she convinced me to drive her to another town
down towards Les Baux
and

[shrugs]

by that time it had become so late
and I thought you would have been angry
so that, for me to return....

MIMI
So instead you disappeared.

[He shrugs.]

Men! Men!

You appear and then you disappear!

[She turns away from him,
not knowing which way to go.

Four people come out of nowhere
simultaneously,
in mid-sentence:

Natalie,
Maria,
Frank,
and Edmund.

They are all dressed in summer clothes,
beachwear perhaps,
or linen things in greens and whites.
They all wear sunglasses.

This is a multiracial and differently abled cast.]

MARIA
...which is not what I meant to do at all.

FRANK
So you say
so you always say when you do these things

EDMUND
That happens to me all the time
finding I've done something I never meant to do

FRANK
and yet how could you not mean it
when it happens over and over again

NATALIE
Me.
I do what I mean to do
and when it's done
I've done it.
What do I care?

MARIA
Francois!

NATALIE
Mimi!

[Francois spins around one way,
Mimi spins around the other.]

FRANCOIS
Maria!

MIMI
Natalie!

NATALIE
What are you doing here?

MIMI
Yes, well...
I might ask the same of you.
And yet, how wonderful to see you.

[to Tessa]

This is my friend Natalie.
This is Tessa.

MARIA
Ah, Tessa!

TESSA
Mother!

MARIA
I didn't realize you knew Francois!

TESSA
Well, *know* him.
I don't know that I *know* him.

FRANK
It would seem that's just as well.
And yet,
we step out of the house for what seems a few
minutes
and already you're having a house party.

MARIA
It's alright, Frank,
she's a grown woman,
this is her home, too,
she should do as she likes.

FRANK
And yet, entertaining men.

NATALIE
Can you just say
how wonderful to see you
and that's that?

MIMI
What's what?

NATALIE
I thought,
well,
I thought
getting to know you
you changed my life.
Really.
Everything I thought.
Who I was.
Who I thought I was.
What I meant to do with my life.
How I meant to live.
How it was to see the world with new eyes
and feel all my feelings completely transformed.
And yet it seems
I meant nothing to you!
Nothing!
I thought you would be my whole life!

[She bursts into tears,
turns around
and disappears.]

MIMI
Natalie!
Natalie!

[Everyone is looking quizzically at Mimi.]

It was just a casual thing, you know.

Not that I'm not really fond of her.
Women,
sometimes they like a dalliance with another woman
or the warmth of friendship
whatever
but I am definitely heterosexual.
I just happen to be someone who likes men.
I like men!
That's just who I am.
Of course maybe I've had some relationships with
women

JAMES
Exactly what I thought.

MIMI
But I've had a lot of relationships with men,
I shouldn't say a lot
but, on balance....

JAMES
Who are these people?

[Note: Throughout the piece, all the characters are
meant to inhabit the setting with a physical life
independent of the dialogue and actions-
that is, they are meant to lounge and do their nails
and write books
and despair and try on various outfits and practice
solo dances
and perform tai chi and carry on lives as others
occupy center stage.]

TESSA
This is my family.

MIMI
And friends.

TESSA
And friends.

JAMES
I thought we were going to be alone.

TESSA
Where did you get that idea?

EDMUND
No one is alone.
We all come into the world with a family.
We all have a past.

MARIA
And a present, too, it would seem!

FRANCOIS
None of us starts a new day carte blanche, do you think?

JAMES
Yes. Yes, I do.
Why does a bride wear a white wedding dress?
Because she starts anew.
But what chance is there for us?

TESSA
What chance was there ever?

JAMES
This is a minefield!

FRANCOIS
A battlefield.

MIMI
A rubblefield.

JAMES
How is anyone supposed to know where to put a
foot?

FRANK
You're a friend of my daughter?

JAMES
Your daughter?

FRANK
Yes, Tessa is my daughter.

JAMES
Well, friend I don't know.
I'd certainly like to be.

FRANK
Indeed.

MARIA
And, in fact, Francois,
what exactly are you doing here?

FRANCOIS
It's not entirely clear to me

what I'm doing here.
As it started out
what I thought was
it was a perfectly straightforward life plan
as clear as the plot of a novel
I was setting out in life
to find a woman I could love
and who loved me
and then one thing led to another
I found myself with a friend
the next thing I knew I was at a chateau in the country
where there were many people
there was a party
I couldn't find the woman I had come with
you know

[he shrugs]

I became disoriented.
But as I think about it
I think
is this not how life is?
You think you are doing one thing
it turns out you have been doing something else entirely
life has no plot
you only think it does
while all the time something without a plot is happening to you
over and over until you reach the end of your life

and you think you've had a beginning and a middle
and an end
but all you've had is a start and a stop
and a lot of disorientation in between
trying to get a grip
hoping for true love
maybe you have a chance and you lose it
you don't know where it went
you're not sure if you had it
or who it was with
maybe the time you least thought it was meaningful
at all
that was your one chance
you walked right past it
while you were pursuing another woman
and then you kick the bucket....

[Maria slaps Francois.]

FRANCOIS
What?

MARIA
How can you flirt with her like this?

FRANCOIS
Flirt with her?
Flirt with whom?

MARIA
I was always the one who loved you.

FRANK
Excuse me.

I'm feeling a little....

MARIA
I called you all the time.
You never called.

FRANK
I don't think this is meant for me....

FRANCOIS
Maria, please,
this is hardly the right occasion....

MARIA
What?
You can't bear to hear the truth?

EDMUND [kindly]
Frank,
would you do me a favor?
Would you get me a little milk for my tea?

FRANK [disoriented]
Milk. Yes. Of course.

[he leaves]

JAMES [stupefied, looking at Maria]
So, this is your mother?

TESSA
Yes! Yes! So you see!
This is what I grew up with!
What chance did I have with a family like this?
And you want to fall in love with me?

How can anyone expect me to form any kind of
relationship
with another human being?

[Tessa goes to the couch
where she lies down,
face buried in a pillow,
like a Balthus girl,
disconsolate.

James follows her to the couch, uncertain what to
do to help.
During the following conversation,
James moves toward her, then away,
toward her again, then away.

Finally, James finds a blanket
and gently puts it over Tessa;
she accepts the blanket without acknowledging
him.]

MARIA
So
you ignore me,
you neglect me,
you're always running around with these sluts

MIMI
I beg your pardon?

MARIA
Actresses, then, actresses!

MIMI
Sculptors!

MARIA
Artists. Whatever.
I love you, Francois,
I was always the only one who ever loved you.
You will end up alone and lonely
because you can't know what it is to be loved.
You think I am clinging and demanding

FRANCOIS
And neurotic, frankly.
Let's be honest.

MARIA [to Francois]
You think you'd like to get rid of me
but I could take care of you forever, Francois!
Sometimes, Francois, I think you are a good person
if only sometimes you wouldn't try so hard
if you would just relax
let life come to you
take it as it is
don't always be on the prowl
because, in the end,
all we have is one another
you're not a boy any longer
you won't live forever
and what you will have had will be your friends
these days like today
where nothing special happens to you
but you have been with me

[she is weeping now]

I don't want to go through life
always bickering, always unhappy
feeling cheated
I could be content just to have a glass of wine
to dance
to hear you sing
I don't care what kind of voice you have
I love you
I can be with you as long as we have on earth
it's not so bad
just to love and be loved

FRANCOIS
On again off again!
On again off again!
You are a lunatic!

MARIA
I'm a person who says what I feel
when I feel it.
With me you always know where you stand.
You can count on it.
That is a kind of certainty and security
that is almost impossible to come by in this world.
We could have another chance, Francois!

FRANCOIS
Would you stop this holding on to me?
Can't I take a breath?
Can't I go out to dinner?

You are a married woman!
This is disgraceful!
Can't I do my job without you calling
tracking me down,
you'd think you were my wife
asking me, can you see me now,
can I come with you,
where are you now?
Who are you with?
Are you having an affair?
You're more than neurotic

[Barbara, the cook,
enters wiping her hands on a dish towel,
stands there listening to Francois.]

you're psychotic
with your crying and your pleading
and what else
your taking pills to go to sleep
pills to wake up.
I have to live my life,
you would suffocate me,
you would pull me down and bury me alive!
I wish you were dead!
Dead!

[silence;

all this time,
James is getting a cup of tea for Tessa, which,
again,

she accepts from him
but without acknowledging him]

BARBARA
So this is how people speak to one another these
days?
Men.
Who wants you?
With a man, every act of love is an act of rape.

A man will swim through a river of snot,
wade nostril-deep through a mile of vomit,
if he thinks there'll be a friendly pussy waiting for
him
on the other side.
He'll screw a woman he despises,
any snaggle-toothed hag,
and furthermore, pay for the opportunity.
A man will fuck mud if he has to.
And why is that?
Because every man, deep down,
knows he is a worthless piece of shit
hoping some woman will make him feel good
about himself.

Eaten up with guilt, shame, fears and insecurities
obsessed with screwing,
to call a man an animal is to flatter him;
a man is a walking dildo,

a completely isolated unit,
trapped inside himself,

incapable of love, friendship, affection or tenderness
his responses entirely visceral, never cerebral
his intelligence a mere tool of his drives and needs;
a half-dead, unresponsive lump of flesh,
trapped in a twilight zone halfway between humans
and apes.

Why did god create man?
Because a vibrator can't mow the lawn.

I went to the County Fair.
They had one of those "Believe it or not?" Shows.
They had a man born with a penis *and* a brain.

Why were men given brains larger than dogs?
So they wouldn't hump women's legs at cocktail
parties.

My feelings about men
are like a Jew just released from Dachau.
I watch the handsome young Nazi soldier
fall writhing to the ground with a bullet in his
stomach
and I look briefly and walk on.
I don't even need to shrug.

Men pretend to be normal
but what they're doing sitting there
with benign smiles on their faces
is they're manufacturing sperm.
They do it all the time.
They never stop.
They are suffering from testosterone poisoning.

You know what they say:
What do you call a man with half a brain?
Gifted.

Why do men name their penises?
Because they want to be on a first-name basis
with the person who makes all their decisions.

What do you call the useless bit of fatty tissue
at the end of a penis?
A man.

Will all these people be staying to lunch?

FRANCOIS
I wouldn't eat a lunch you made if it were the last
piece of uncooked shit on the planet.
What is it with you women
you think men can't live without you.

Have you noticed
how uncomfortable it is for most women
to put their elbows on the table while they eat?
Because the table is too high for them.
But for most men,
it is uncomfortable not to put their elbows on
the table
because they are taller.
But it's not proper to put one's elbows on the table.

And why is that?
Because etiquette is a system that defines as
appropriate

what is natural for a woman,
and defines as inappropriate what is natural for
a man.

[In the middle of this,
a slimy young Italian guy enters
to deliver a pizza.
He stands there holding the pizza box.]

So, of course,
similarly,
perhaps one should not be so surprised that
pornography,
which appeals to men
is condemned,
while soap operas and romance novels,
the female equivalent of pornography
is acceptable.
And so, of course, men have become ashamed that
they are men.
And so women control men as they wish, at their
whim,
they get men to do whatever women want them
to do.
The women get the men to do the dirty work, the
violence,
the bad stuff
whatever women want but don't want to do with
their own hands
so they can have whatever they like
and blame the men for it.

BOB [holding the pizza box as he speaks]
And yet, I think, nonetheless,
forgiveness is possible.

FRANCOIS
You do.

BOB
Well, sure.
Really under any circumstances.

Uh, primarily, uh, uh, the, uh, the...
primarily the question is
does man have the power to forgive himself.
And he does.
That's essentially it.
I mean if you forgive yourself,
and you absolve yourself of all, uh,
of all wrongdoing in an incident,
then you're forgiven.
Who cares what other people think, because uh...

EDMUND
Was this a process you had to go through over a
period of time?
Did you have to think about it?

BOB
Well, no.
Not until I was reading the Aquarian gospel did I,
did I strike upon,
you know I had almost had ends meet because I
had certain

uh you know
to-be-or-not-to-be reflections about of course
what I did.
And uh,

EDMUND
I'm sorry, what was that?

BOB
Triple murder.
Sister, husband. Sister, husband,
and a nephew, my nephew.
And uh, you know, uh, manic depressive.

EDMUND
Do you mind my asking what instruments did
you use?
What were the instruments?

BOB
It was a knife.
It was a knife.

EDMUND
A knife?

BOB
Yes.

EDMUND
So then, the three of them were all...

BOB
Ssssss...

(points to slitting his throat)

like that.

EDMUND
So, uh,
do you think that as time goes by,
this episode will just become part of your past,
or has it already...

BOB
It has already become part of my past.

EDMUND
Has already become part of your past.
No sleepless nights? No...

BOB
Aw, no. In the first three or four years there was a couple of nights where I would stay up thinking about how I did it, you know. And what they said... they told me later there were so many stab wounds in my sister and I said no, that's not true at all, you know. So I think I had a little blackout during the murders, but uh...

[he sits,
making himself at home]

Well, uh, they said there was something like thirty stab wounds in my sister, and I remember distinctly I just cut her throat once. That was all, you know, and I don't know where the thirty stab wounds came from. So that might have been some kind of blackout thing. You know, I was trying to re- re- re- uh, re- uh, uh, resurrect the uh, the crime -my initial steps, etc. You know, and uh, and uh, I took, as a matter of fact, it came right out of the, I was starting the New Testament at the time, matter of fact I'm about the only person you'll ever meet that went to, to do a triple murder with a Bible in his, in his pocket, and, and, listening to a radio. I had delusions of grandeur with the radio. Uh, I had a red shirt on that was symbolic of, of some lines in Revelation, in the, in the New Testament. Uh I had a red motor...as a matter of fact, I think it was chapter 6 something, verses 3, 4, or 5, or something where uh it was a man, it was a man. On a red horse. And, and, a man on a red horse came out, and uh, and uh uh, and he was given a knife, and unto him was given the power to kill and destroy. And I actually thought I was this person. And I thought that my red horse was this red Harley Davidson I had. And I wore...it was just, you know, it was kind of a symbolic type of thing. And and and uh, you know, uh after the murders I thought the nephew was, was the, was a new devil or something, you know. This, this is pretty bizarre now that I think back on it. I thought he was a new devil and uh, uh. I mean basically I love my sister, there's no question about that. But at times my sister hadn't come through uh for me. You know and I was in another, one of these manic attacks. And uh, and uh, uh, uh, you know, uh, I was just uh, I was just you know, I mean I was fed up with all this you know one day they treat me good and then they tell all these other people that I was a maniac and watch out for me and etc. and like that. And uh, uh, so I went to them that night to tell them I was all in trouble again, you know, and could they put me up for the night, you know, and they told me to take a hike and uh so uh, believing that I had the power to kill, uh you know, that was that for them. You know. I mean when family turns you out, that's a real blow. You know. But uh, back to the original subject of forgiveness. If I forgive myself I'm forgiven. You know that's essentially the answer. I'm the captain of my own ship. I run my own ship. Nobody can crawl in my ship unless they get permission. I just (he nods) "over there." You know. "I'm forgiven." You know. Ha-ha. You know. (Laughs.) It's as simple as that. You know. You're your own priest, you're your own leader, you're your own captain. You know. You run your own show, a lot of people know that.

Who ordered a pizza?

TESSA
I did, but that was hours ago.

BOB
Well, here it is.

TESSA
I'm sorry, it's too late.

[Frank returns, holding a glass of water.]

BOB
Too late?
I don't think so.
Who's going to pay for the pizza?

FRANK
Here you are Edmund.

EDMUND
What is this?

FRANK
You asked for a glass of water.

EDMUND
No, Frank.
[he laughs]
Not a glass of water.
A little milk for my tea.

FRANK [confused]
I'm sorry.
I don't know what I was thinking.

EDMUND
Never mind.

FRANK
No, no,
I'll be right back.

[Frank leaves.]

BOB
Who's going to pay for the fucking pizza?

EDMUND
I'll pay for it.
Give it to me.

BOB
Plain cheese.

EDMUND
Right.
Here.
Keep the change.

BOB
Thanks. I appreciate it.
Which way did I come in?

EDMUND
That way.

BOB
Are you sure?

EDMUND
I'm sure.

BOB
Don't fuck with me.

EDMUND
I would never fuck with you.

BOB
Right.
Thanks again.

[Bob leaves.]

BARBARA
I'll take the pizza.

[Barbara exits with the pizza.]

MIMI [to Francois]
You know,
I myself knew a woman,
I won't say who,
who was in love with a man who was married,
and this married man went away on vacation with
his wife.

FRANCOIS
Mimi, this is
this is probably not a perfect moment.

MIMI
And the woman I knew, who was left at home,
spent every day thinking
not just what *she* was doing at every moment
but what this *man* was doing at every moment, too,

MARIA
Who was this?

[Francois paces back and forth, moping his brow
as Mimi assaults him with this story of their past]

MIMI
knowing, as she got up in the morning
that her lover was waking up with his wife

MARIA
Who was this, Francois?

FRANCOIS
I wouldn't know.
This is some sort of I don't know what.

MIMI
and behaving as he always did in the morning
lying in bed,
turning over to embrace his wife
perhaps making love

MARIA
Are you saying that you were married?
That you have a wife?

FRANCOIS [to the others]
There's not a shred of truth to this.
Essentially.

MIMI
and lying there under the covers afterwards
as his wife went to make a cup of tea for him
bringing it back to bed

MARIA
All this time you've been married
and I never knew?

FRANCOIS
No, not married.
Of course, in the past....
in a different time,
at another time,
as you yourself are married at the present time.

MIMI
the conversation then, the planning for the day,
the breakfast in the cafe

MARIA [totally thrown, sinking to the ground, talking to herself]
How could this be
and I didn't know?

EDMUND
There's only so much pain a human being can endure
before they cave right in.

MIMI
his reading things out loud from the newspaper
every moment, for two weeks,

FRANCOIS
How can you say this?

MIMI
this woman thought all the time, every moment,
of what her lover was doing
waiting for the moment that he would return
and call her

FRANCOIS
What could I have done?
Given the circumstances!

MARIA
I can't believe I never knew this!

MIMI
and come by and take her out to dinner
and spend the night with her

MARIA
How do human beings keep themselves from
knowing things all the time?

MIMI
she knew the hour and the minute that he would
return

MARIA
This is inconceivable.

MIMI
and when at last he did return
and the woman waited by the phone for him to call
he did not call that evening

MARIA
We do this with everything.

MIMI
he might have been delayed by the weekend traffic
and he did not call late that night
or early in the morning

FRANCOIS
Well, I couldn't call.

MARIA
We make ourselves unconscious
and then we wonder why we are so tormented.

MIMI
not from home or from the road saying he had
been delayed
he did not call all that next day or night
he did not call until the following day
in the afternoon

FRANCOIS
I couldn't very well get to a phone.

MARIA
Couldn't get to a phone?

MIMI
from his office

FRANCOIS
Mimi....

MIMI
to suggest dinner the following week.
So what did this woman do?

FRANCOIS
What?

MIMI
She waited for her lover.

She waited until the time he said for dinner.
She waited for him,
and she is still waiting.

[She sinks to the ground
next to Tessa
so that now, Tessa, Maria, and Mimi are all on the
ground.]

EDMUND
Human beings are as tough as cockroaches, really.
They can take so much more than they can imagine.
But, at a point, you can crush them.

JAMES
You know,
I can understand how perhaps he couldn't call.
I mean, I myself have been in a similar situation.
Sometimes it's not easy to call.

[silence]

TESSA [speaking quietly, sadly to James]
So
it turns out
you mean you meant nothing of what you said to
me.

JAMES
What?

TESSA
You lied to me.

JAMES
I never lied to you.
What are you saying?

TESSA [still quietly]
I think you did.
You came to me with someone else still in your heart.
You said you loved me.
But, in fact, you weren't free to say such a thing at all.
Part of you still belonged to someone else.
Part of you was stuck to someone else.

JAMES
What who are you talking about?

TESSA
This other woman you didn't call.

JAMES
It was not.
I was just saying -this was long ago.
I was not stuck to someone.
I mean,
of course, as you say yourself, we never shed our pasts entirely.
But I wasn't *stuck* to anyone.

TESSA [close to tears]
I'd like to be able to trust someone, you know.
You see the sort of life I've had
I could turn out to be a totally fucked up person myself

[now she is crying]

and what I need more than anything is someone I
could trust
and I thought
even though you were a jerk
I could trust you.

JAMES
I'm a jerk?

TESSA
I mean, I'm sorry,
I mean even though you came on to me,
well, face it, James,
the way you came on to me
it wasn't exactly so suave
but I thought you were sincere
and honest
and innocent

[she is sobbing]

and for a moment I thought:
oh, I could trust you
I could trust you
and now it turns out
you're just like every other man!

[she curls up in a fetal position
underneath the desk]

JAMES
I'm not!

I'm not!
I'm not like a man at all!

[He throws himself to the ground in a heap,
bouncing and rolling several times
before he settles down in a funk.]

FRANCOIS [trying to whisper, or speak privately]
Maria, I think, perhaps, frankly,
we just need to make love
it's been so long
we need to be close to one another again to have
some hope.

MARIA
Are you serious?
This is disgusting.
I wouldn't touch you.
I wouldn't touch you.
Not now.
I could vomit.

FRANCOIS [still trying to keep this conversation
from the others]
We've just gotten off track.
If you come to bed with me it'll go away.
It always does.

MARIA
You're pathetic.
You've never really made love to me.
To *me*.
You don't even know who I am.

You don't even notice.

FRANCOIS
You're really crazy if that's what you think.

MARIA
Oh, I'm crazy?
You think you're in love with someone
who is repulsed by the very smell of you
and I'm the one who's crazy?
Everyone kept telling me what a great guy you were.
So I looked past the fact that you bored me to tears.
I suffered through your endless inane monologues
about rocks.
I tried to see you for what you think you are,
strutting around the house as if you were a man:
you're a fucking dwarf!
I could kick you across the room.

MIMI
What a beast.

FRANCOIS
What do you mean, I'm a beast?

MIMI
Yes!

TESSA
Would you people get out?
Would you just get out?
Don't you know some people are trying to lead
their lives

trying to lead lives that are not all FUCKED UP?

Don't you people know
how you treat people
this is who you are!
A person is not what job he does
or how the neurons work inside his skull
or how he looks in the suit he wears
but how he is with other people
and this then is the world he makes
for others to live in
whether this world is happy or savage!

[silence]

FRANCOIS
It's true. It's true.
I am a beast.
Oh, god.
I'm sorry.
What can I do?
I can't say that I can't do anything about it
because I have to try
that's my responsibility
but I can't seem to do anything about it.
God, what a loathsome person I've become.

MARIA
Francois I never want to see you again.

FRANCOIS
What's wrong with me?
What do you mean?

MARIA
Just what I say.

FRANCOIS
Never?
You never want to see me again?

[to James]

You know when people say never,
I never believe they really mean it.

MARIA
Okay, then, okay:
For five years!
I don't want to see you for exactly *five* years,
not a moment before!

[she vanishes]

FRANCOIS
Oh right! Great!

You never know where you stand with women, do
you?
Whatever you do is wrong.
One day they call you a satyr,
the next day an impotent idiot.
You can never tell what they want.
In a word, then, the poisoning has begun.
The man has been used, that's all.
One of a number of equally acceptable items
taken down from the shelf, used, put back,
never valued for himself, no,

but only for what can be gotten out of him.
And then women will complain about physical
satisfaction!
Or gossip to her friends about her lover.
A man, on the other hand, would consider it a
betrayal of her trust,
her privacy.
It never occurs to a woman to think he
might have miscalculated about her
Might have second thoughts about *her* -
in giving her what she needs to feel secure,
having given away himself
so that he no longer *possesses* himself
so that he no longer knows who he is
or if he even exists any longer!

[he turns on the radio at full, hostile volume,
rips off his shirt in a rage and throws it across the
stage
and does a quick, hostile, sexually suggestive dance
step
and then he takes off his belt and hurls it across the
stage
and does another hostile dance step;

this is strip music he is working to
and soon he is taking off his shoes and hurling
them across the stage
then unzipping his trousers
and he is totally into a striptease
-still with anger and defiant sexuality -

and he does the full Dionysian thing,
completely into it and wild.
This goes on for a long time -a full performance.

Eventually the music stops,
and he is left alone there,
suddenly embarrassed.
He stops, looks around;
everyone is just looking at him,
and he is humiliated.
Sheepishly, he starts to gather up his clothes
and awkwardly put them on.]

FRANK
Here you are, Edmund.

EDMUND
What is this?

FRANK
Your tea.

EDMUND
My tea?
Frank, do you never listen to me?

FRANK
What?

EDMUND
I asked you for milk for my tea.

FRANK
Milk?

EDMUND
Do you never pay attention to me?

FRANK
I'm sorry.
I'll get it for you right away.

EDMUND
Never mind.

FRANK
No, no, I'll be right back.

EDMUND
Never mind, Frank, it doesn't matter anymore.

FRANK
I said I'll get it!

EDMUND
Fuck it!
I don't want it!

FRANK
I said I'd get it goddammit!
And I will goddam get it!
Am I not always getting things for you?
Get this, get that,
you stand here like the Prince of Wales
while I fetch things for you night and day
and one time I happen to get the wrong thing
and you say I never listen to you?

EDMUND
Because in fact you don't!

I think I have no respect for you
or common courtesy
certainly no real sympathy
or empathy
or love as one might expect
even from simply another human being passing in
the night.
Think how it is:
you are sleeping with another person.

FRANK
That's not true.

EDMUND
You are sleeping with Maria.

FRANK
Oh, Maria. Well....

EDMUND
Well, what?

FRANK
Well, she's my wife.

EDMUND
You mean, yes, you are sleeping with Maria.

FRANK
Sleeping with her yes.
But she's my wife, my wife.

EDMUND
So?

FRANK
It's not as though we were lovers.

EDMUND
You say you're not.
But you sleep with her.
You love her.
You love to be with her.
She makes you laugh.
She thrills you.

FRANK
Yes, yes, yes.
So?

EDMUND
Well, there are many kinds of lovers in the world,
many kinds of relationships,
marriages even, you might say.
You are married to her.

FRANK
Only in the sense of being married
not in the sense of being married as you use the
term.

EDMUND
You sleep in the same bed.

FRANK
So what?
You can sleep with us, too, if you like.

EDMUND
I beg your pardon?

FRANK
Well, we *are* friends.

EDMUND
Who?
You and I?

FRANK
Well, yes,
also you and I.
I mean you and I *are* friends, aren't we?
I hope.

EDMUND
You hope?
You hope?
What do you mean you hope?

FRANK
Forget it! Just forget it!
I'll be right back, goddammit!

[Frank leaves.]

EDMUND
Forget it!

And what do you suppose happened when I went
over for dinner
the other night?
I arrive, and he says, what is it you're doing here?

I've come to dinner, I say.
Did I invite you to dinner, he says. No I don't think so.
Why don't you have dinner with me, I say.
I can't. You know, he says, this is too much. I can't....

Just dinner, I say. Nothing more.

You say so, he says, and then you just want to stay on after dinner....

When you talk this way, I say to him, I begin to feel like I'm expecting a death sentence.

Then we argue, he says, you cajole me, you don't leave
and you don't leave, I begin to feel cornered.

I shout at him: I'm just talking about dinner!

Next thing you know, he says,
you think there's no reason you shouldn't spend the night....

If we just sleep together, I say to him, just sleep in the same bed, nothing more

And then, he yells at me for no reason at all, when you fall asleep
I look at you and I see how ugly you are when you're relaxed.

What, I say, what?

That's when you're at your ugliest, he says, when

you're asleep
so that I can't stand it.

When I'm asleep I'm ugly, I say, that's what you're saying?

Or really any time after twelve o' clock, he says: old and ugly

Every night? I say. Are you saying every night?

Yes, he says, yes. Almost every night. Ugly and repulsive. Like another person altogether. So that I hardly recognize you except I say to myself: right, yes, there you are again the way you really are. Last night I woke up with palpitations and a pain in my head and I thought: right, there you are again, attacking me in the middle of the night when I'm defenseless.

I'm attacking you? I say!

Like the time you tried to hypnotize me while I was asleep, he says, setting my nerves on edge so I had to hit you in the face that time to get you to stop, you remember that and you said you were being eaten alive by worms.

I did not. You didn't hear a word I said.

EDMUND AND MIMI TOGETHER
I hang on every fucking stupid word you ever say!

EDMUND
Every stupid word I say!

You are stupid.
Stupider than ever.

MIMI
And black and venomous. Poisonous really,
more poisonous now than ever before.

FRANCOIS
Ever before when?

EDMUND
Before you used to give me that filth at the dinner
table
-on purpose, on purpose -so that it made me shiver?

MIMI
Before that?

FRANCOIS
Before you would seek some intimacy with me,
force yourself on me,

FRANCOIS AND EDMUND
demanding I make love to you....

MIMI
Excuse me, would this be after you had turned
your back on me?

FRANCOIS AND EDMUND
[not necessarily exactly together, but both of them
saying the line on top of one another]
Excuse me, if I remember correctly you always
turned your back on me, always.

FRANCOIS
I was supposed to pursue you,
put my arms around you so I was always in the
position of the suitor,

EDMUND AND MIMI
you were always cool, no, cold,

FRANCOIS
I was supposed to be the beggar the suppliant
and then,

EDMUND AND MIMI
[not necessarily exactly together, but both of them
saying the line on top of one another]
if I *had* to turn over because my arm had gone to
sleep
and my shoulder feels broken
and I have a pain in my head,

EDMUND AND MIMI AND FRANCOIS
and I turned over because I couldn't bear the pain
of holding you in my arms,
then did you

FRANCOIS
ever,

JAMES
ever,

MIMI
ever once,

FRANCOIS
did you ever a single fucking time turn over and
hold me
the way I held you?

FRANCOIS AND EDMUND AND MIMI AND
JAMES -EVERYONE
[not necessarily exactly together, but all of them
saying the line on top of one another]
No.

EDMUND
Did you ever pursue me the way I pursued you?

FRANCOIS AND EDMUND AND MIMI AND
JAMES -EVERYONE
[not necessarily exactly together, but all of them
saying the line on top of one another]
No.

FRANCOIS AND EDMUND AND MIMI AND
JAMES -EVERYONE
[not necessarily exactly together, but all of them
saying the line on top of one another]
You just got finished saying I come over to dinner
and try to stay the night.

Is this not pursuing you?

Oh, sure! Now! Now! Now it's too late!

Why is it too late?

EDMUND

Because I woke up this afternoon in the middle of the afternoon with women's voices in the apartment below and I thought I had come to live finally in a home invaded by sluts! And I began to cry! I'm a man, and I began to cry! I can't take this bullshit forever! What kind of person do you think I am? Do you know why the earth has governments and dictators and none of the other planets do? Because this is the only planet where all the inhabitants do not say what they think, where people lie all the time, lie and lie and lie all the time, and I am sick of it. No, you cannot stay for dinner. No! Just fucking leave me alone!

Love! Love!
Do you think love is possible these days?

EVERYONE [variously]
No. No. Love is not possible these days. No. No. No.

[Music.
A big hostile dance
with everyone throwing everyone else to the ground over and over again,
venting their aggression
by running into the walls and trees,
throwing themselves to the ground all together
in repeated synchronous movements,
until, finally, still seething with rage or disgust,
or given over to hopelessness and despair,

they are exhausted,
sprawled on the ground or on the couch or in a
chair,
and the music ends.]

Act Two

FRANK [gently]
Here's your milk.

EDMUND
Thank you, Frank.

FRANK
I'm sorry.

EDMUND
Thank you.
I apologize.

FRANK
One looks for things
and finds something else.

There's no simple story of boy meets girl
any more
these days.

And other stories, too,
are gone entirely.

And those people
who once loved in some other way
they're gone forever, too,
their lives, their loves

their sensibilities
we will never see anything that remotely resembles
them again.
How people used to love
the ways for which we now have complete contempt.

We think because the past is no longer who we are
that the age that came before us is stupid
and that how we are today
or what it is we wish to be
is the true way and the good way -
even if, in fact, we are tormented every hour of
our lives -
and, in any case, our true way is passing too
to yield to yet another true way
and who's to say the past
did not have pleasures as deep as those the future
holds
or deeper
or perhaps simply different?

The aging gay man who had to keep his life a secret
and found ruses and manners to hide himself
and find another who would share his inner world
we don't know how it is to live like this today
that sense of nuance and subtlety
the decor of a home
that would suggest but not declare
the inner life of its host
that finely developed ability
to discriminate the gentlest hint

all this is gone
and it would be wrong to mourn its loss
and the suffering that so often went with it
and yet I still have friends who are lost
because it is lost
their lives
the lives they thought they would live all their lives
vanished suddenly
with nowhere to go
just as all of us
will one day be gone

our lives unrecoverable
the civilizations of the past
so distant from us
as to be more alien than foreign countries
human beings we recognize
are in some way related to us
and yet so different we cannot know
their inner lives
the only lives that matter
their private lives
the lives they thought they lived
are lost forever

and even as we live today from day to day
each day is lost as we live it
never to return
we shed our lives as we live them
we die each day
our lives becoming first stories

and then barely remembered dreams
the fleeting stuff of mortality
so that even as we live
we disappear
and all that we have treasured most
disappears along with us.

[James sits down next to Tessa,
trying to entice her into conversation.]

JAMES
You know,
maybe everybody does have a past.

[silence]

And, you know,
it's like they say,
when you go to bed with someone,
you bring six people to bed with you,
each other,
and the other person's parents
and your own parents.

[silence]

Well, or maybe even more people than that
because....

[silence]

TESSA
Are you trying to start a conversation with me?

JAMES
Yes.

TESSA
You should probably say something else.

JAMES
Right.
I was only just saying
it's like, you know,
you were saying you have this family
and this past you can't escape
and I was only saying....

TESSA
Right.
And I was saying,
maybe you want to talk about something else.

JAMES
But what I was saying was that other people
are not just your past
they are also your future.

TESSA
You mean, you're planning on having an affair with
someone I know?

JAMES
No, no, no.
I mean, what we are is humanity,
I mean, part of humanity,
we just have to accept that,

we can't separate ourselves from that
from one another
so all of us all the time...
you know...

TESSA
What?

JAMES
Are part of humanity.

[silence]

You can't escape that.

[silence]

I'm a person too, you know.
You feel you grew up with certain
difficulties in your upbringing
but so did I!
So did everyone I suppose
and this is our chance
to love one another
because of our backgrounds
to console one another
to feel close *because* of the pain we've felt
to feel intimate
and to know even better how to take care of
each other
because we know how important that is
and how it feels
and just where another person needs support.

Being fucked up, you know,
might be a *basis* for love.

TESSA
You're an American.

JAMES
Yes?

TESSA
I don't think I could like an American
or love an American
or really even have fun with an American.

JAMES
Aren't you an American?

TESSA
I'm half Italian.

JAMES
So you can't love someone who is all American?

TESSA
I don't think so.

JAMES
That's crazy.

TESSA
Why?

JAMES
Because Americans are just -Americans.

TESSA
So?

JAMES
Well, they're just Americans.

TESSA
So?

JAMES
So, what is that?

TESSA
Well, I don't know.

JAMES
So, you see?

TESSA
No, I don't see anything.

JAMES
You see, you could come to love me.
I'm crazy about you, Tessa,
you know, if somebody's crazy about you,
you can't resist it finally
because it feels so good to have someone be just
crazy for you
and just love everything about you and everything
you do
and just be delighted in you
and laugh at your jokes and feel for you
and love to do things with you
and look out for you

and all that sort of thing
I think I'm going to become irresistible to you.

TESSA [smiling]
You do?

JAMES
I'm really pretty sure of it.

Think, how,
you know,
I found my way to you,
which, in a way,
you have to believe is the most important thing
in life
so you have to believe I know how to do the most
important things
to have enough a sense of adventure to throw
myself into the world
to see what happens
and to come up successful,
this couldn't be such a bad partner for someone.

TESSA
But what if you're not, I don't know, funny
or fun or something.

JAMES
I might not tell jokes
but I might just be ridiculous
which, in time, once you got to know me
could be constantly amusing to you.

Plus I think you're in a situation where anything
could happen.

TESSA
I guess that's true.

JAMES
What else do you want of life?

TESSA
What do you mean?

JAMES
To live a life where anything could happen.
And then, of all the anythings,
you can choose what you like.

TESSA
I guess.

JAMES
Well, then.

TESSA
There's just a whole lot to fight your way through
these days
how men are,
for that matter: how women have become
all the stuff
you know what I mean
you watch television
I'm doing a twelve-step program
I'm trying to work it through
but simple love

even if you're an OK guy
I don't think you can get there from here anymore.

I was just wondering a little while ago
how it would be if we were sleeping together
and I imagined we had to sleep on a giant mattress
on the floor
and you were chilly
and the cat was giving birth to eight kittens in
the room
and it made you cranky.

So I went out to buy you some
red thermal underwear
and I came back with the wrong thing but by then
you weren't cold anymore but you needed a travel
toiletry bag.
So I went back to the store for groceries
and the store was an Arabian camel tent
with pyramids of canned foods and regular check
out grocery scanners
and I bought ten dozen yellow and red roses
and a bunch of six foot high gladiolas
and a silver mesh Gucci toiletry bag for ten
thousand dollars

And when I got home
you were asleep
wearing the red thermal underwear that was too
small for you
and a pair of red gloves

with each finger labelled with random words on
colored tapes

and you were wearing my black RayBan sunglasses
that you had already stretched out and ruined with
your giant head.

I crawled on top of you and started kissing you
and you opened your eyes and yelled,
"How the fuck am I supposed to pay for a ten-
thousand-dollar
toiletry bag?!"
And you climbed up on the scaffolding at the foot
of the bed
and started throwing the yellow and red roses at
me -thorns first
and there were thorns stuck all over my arms and
legs and chest
and the roses were hanging off me
and I was rolling around the mattress trying to get
them off
and you told me you knew a guy named Todd
who had thrown batteries at his girlfriend and
killed her
when she had done something like that
and then you smashed a tape recorder under
your boot
and took out the batteries and threw them at my
head
and you climbed higher and higher up the scaffolding
saying that the higher you went the more the
batteries would hurt

and that even a penny could break my skull
from way up there.

[silence]

That's what I see when I fantasize about our being
together.

[She looks at him for a moment
and then turns away from him.

In rage and despair, he grabs a chair,
takes it to an upstage corner, and sits facing into
the woods.

Maria appears]

FRANCOIS
Maria!
How time flies!

MARIA
No wonder your family won't speak to you
and every woman you've ever been with has gone
crazy
or killed herself.
Did you ever think about that?
It's not them, it's you!
You're like a baby with a switch blade.
So fucking needy
and when you get everything just the way you
want it
you attack whoever gives in to you
for being weak and pathetic and worthless.

FRANCOIS
Okay. Okay.
This is how it is.
We're through.
Forget everything I ever said to make up.
The truth is: Frank is a better person than I am anyway.
I've never been a good person
or even an acceptable person
I'm actually a person of almost despicable character.
You should go back to Frank
what more could you want?
He's a wonderful person
loving and kind and considerate and generous.
What could you have been thinking
not just to be grateful for that?

MARIA
Probably you're just saying that,
but I think it's true.

FRANCOIS
It is true.
In fact, all you've ever done is string me along
out of some sense of discontent
you never could define!
You never loved me if you think about it.
Your heart has always been with Frank.

MARIA [to Frank]
What he says is true, Frank.
I do love you.

I'm sorry for all I've done to hurt you.
I don't know why I ran away from you.
I think I never felt you wanted me
but I want you, Frank,
let's never leave one another's side again.

FRANK
It's too late, Maria.

MARIA
Too late?

FRANK
I'm sorry.
I would never do anything to hurt you
because I do love you.
But now, you see, without you,
I've turned more and more to Edmund
for solace and companionship and,
finally,
love.
And now I couldn't betray him
after all he's done for me
his being there for me
his loyalty
he's completely won me over
and I think I never could find my way back to you.

EDMUND
Don't say that, Frank.
The truth is, you've never left her.
You've never been with me.

I've always felt you left half yourself behind.
And you could never let go completely
and be with me
the way I need someone to be
for my sake.
Go back to her.
She's your family.
You'll never be happy without her.

FRANK
Love these days:
it is such a strange and difficult terrain
so often we don't know where we are
or whether we're in the right place at all
we can't find a place that feels like home
our hearts are lost.
And I have to admit,
the place that feels like home to me
is with you, Maria.

MARIA
Oh, Frank,
I'm so happy
to feel we can start out again in life together
and have a whole second life.
One doesn't just throw away a marriage on a whim
for some fleeting romance or sudden passion
all those years
the chance of having an entire lifetime together
that's the truest treasure of all.

Shall we all have a drink -

or shall we have some tea?
Is this tea, Tessa?

TESSA
I don't think it's hot.

[Maria spills it down the front of Francois's trousers.]

FRANCOIS
Oh! Oh!
Yes, it is hot.

MARIA
Oh, Francois, I'm so sorry.

FRANCOIS
No, you're not!

MARIA
Here, give me your trousers,
you don't want to have a stain.

[she unbuckles his belt, starts to take off his trousers;
Tessa slowly stands up,
horrified by this further display of her family's behavior]

TESSA
Mother!

FRANCOIS
Excuse me. Please.
I don't think I'll be taking off my trousers.

TESSA
Mother!

MARIA
I'm only thinking what's practical!

FRANK
Let's all take off our trousers, then,
so you don't feel embarrassed.

FRANCOIS
Frank, you are the perfect host, but...

TESSA
Are you going to do this?

[he takes off his trousers
as Maria helps to remove Francois's;

meanwhile,
Gunter and Natalie enter;
they stand, their clothes disheveled,
obviously having been in bed together,
looking at what's going on]

FRANCOIS
I don't think this is necessary,
a little tea can't hurt.

MIMI [to Natalie]
Natalie, where have you been?
And who is this?

NATALIE
This is Gunter.

MARIA
Hello, Gunter.

FRANK
Hello, Gunter.

GUNTER
How do you do?

MIMI
Is this your idea of getting even with me?

NATALIE
I don't know what you mean.

MIMI
Oh, yes, you do.

GUNTER
I'm not taking off my trousers.

MIMI
Oh,
taking off your trousers.
Right. Good idea.
I have an idea.
All the men take off their trousers
and I will make a sculpture of all of you.
I've always thought:
what would it be
to do a whole set of modern torsos?

GUNTER
Is this what people do here?

Everyone takes off his trousers?

JAMES
I'm not taking off my trousers I can tell you that.

EDMUND
I'm taking off my trousers.

NATALIE
Here.
I'll help you with your trousers, Gunter.

[Natalie goes for Gunter's pants.]

GUNTER
No, no.
I don't remove my trousers.

NATALIE
Come, Gunter.
What's the difference?
You could be wearing a swimming suit.
Lift your foot, Gunter.

GUNTER [seeing all the other men taking off their trousers]
Well, I don't know if this is right.

MARIA
Come along, James.
Is it James?

JAMES
Yes.

MARIA
Don't be shy.
We're among friends here.
Let me help you get your pants off.

JAMES
I don't think so.
I'm not a stripper.

MARIA
Of course you're not.
Taking off your trousers doesn't make you a stripper
or all men would be strippers.

TESSA
How can I have a relationship with a man
when my mother takes off everyone's pants
who comes into the house.

[Maria starts to take off his trousers]

MIMI
Now, if you will all lie down,
come,
lie down here in a row
on your backs, not your fronts,
not too close together....

[Tessa has ended up sitting in a corner,
like a Schiele doll,
her knees pulled up under her chin,
her dress pulled up to her waist,
and she is naked under her dress

and looking forlorn,
like a broken doll,
her head tilted over to one side.]

NATALIE
Come, Francois.

FRANCOIS [as he cooperates, led by Natalie]
You never think
I may have feelings, too.
Just because it seems to you I am indifferent
or cold
or interested only in conquests,
but I am a vulnerable person too in my way
I want just as much as you
to have a deep and meaningful relationship
but it may be that in my own way
I don't know any better than you in your way
just how to go about achieving it.

MIMI
that's good
I'll show you what I'm going to do
I'm going to make
plaster casts of your torsos
five male torsos I will call them.

Here, Francois,
I'll take you first.

[she starts to mix water and plaster of Paris
in a bucket;

Natalie gets Francois settled,
his head in her lap;

in fact,
though all the men have their pants off,
Mimi will never get beyond the cast of Francois;

suddenly, now, there is a tableau:
the men all lying down, propped up on their
elbows,
the women arrayed around them
as though at a picnic;
we are at a salon
where there will be a philosophical conversation]

MARIA
I love art
and artists
people who make things in general
creative people
there are people who make things
and the other sort
and my feeling is
I love a person who makes something.

[Sentimental Italian music comes up
under the dialogue,
a violin or mandolin]

Because art
art is where we discover
in the freedom of our imaginations
what it is to be a human being

FRANCOIS
Or else, we discover it in love.
Because human beings are social animals
not isolated imaginations
and so we discover truly who we are
in our relationships
that's where we can see the full complexity
and wonder of a person
where we see the mystery of what it is to be a
human being.

FRANK
Of course, you're talking here
not just about sensual love
what the Greeks called *erotike*
but also about love as friendship,
what they called *philia*.

Because the Greeks thought
love is not just a sentiment
but is actually the physical principle of the universe
itself
the very stuff that binds the universe together.
And without it the whole world just falls apart.

GUNTER
This is fine for you to say
but it's not so clear you can know what it is to love
and so what it is to be a human being
unless you live the life of a bourgeois person in a
bourgeois country
because

under Stalin
the Russians only made love an average of 1.2 times
a month
the same is true in Bulgaria as I happen to know
and then not very happily
and mostly in the doggie position
this is a statistic
this is a fact.
And some people, in prisons,
they forget entirely how to reach out to another
human being
to touch another person in any way
that isn't cruel.

How do you think it is for the street hookers
who live in the alleys of Istanbul and Havana?

TESSA
You look around the world,
and you think:
should there be love in a world like this?
Of should there only be politics?

JAMES
This is true.
I think this is true.

FRANK
Still, we carry on.

TESSA
We shouldn't.

MARIA
No matter what,
you can't stop living.

GUNTER
And yet, it can seem strange
to live in a world where, just to get a lipstick,
you have to choose between

Red
or Hot Red
or Classic Red
or Real Red
or Radiant Red
or Russian Red
Reggae Red
Love that Red
Uptown Red
Drop Dead Red
Red Red Red
Crimson Splendour
Guerlain no 102 Rouge Boléro KissKiss Hydro-soft
Guerlain no 103 Rouge Satin Tango KissKiss
Hydro-soft
Guerlain no 104 Rouge Passsion KissKiss Hydro-
soft
Cherry
Crushed Cherry
Cherry Blossom
Very Very Cherry
Cherries Jubilee

Hard Candy Tramp....

[silence;
bewilderment and awe at Gunter's knowledge of
lipstick]

FRANCOIS
The world can be so confusing,
what are the rules, what is allowed, what is not
allowed
and we live in constant anguish.

You have to reinvent your relationship every day
discover all over every day what it might be
what a woman wants
what you yourself might want.

MARIA
And then, sometimes
you might live apart from your wife or lover
and so you have love affairs
or you even agree to have love affairs
even while, at the same time, in your own way,
you remain faithful to one another in your love for
one another
whatever you might be doing physically
and yet, no matter how you sort it out,
even at the moment you are going to bed with
another person
it makes you feel even more alone and betrayed

FRANCOIS
And then

when you say, for example, do you love me?
then she replies I don't know you
because in fact she never will, she never will.

JAMES
Why not?

FRANCOIS
Because I rediscover who I am every day,
it's a moving target, you can't hit it.
How can you have love at all these days?
These days,
it's not easy for a man and a woman to fall in love.

MARIA
It never was.

GUNTER
One needs courage.

EDMUND
Human beings.

MARIA
It turns out life is nothing but loose ends.
It's not that, just because one has many love affairs
or love affairs with people one shouldn't
that that makes you a person incapable of love
or a person who has no feelings
I myself
I pray for a better world
a world where there will be no such thing
as unrequited love and pain and suffering

and women can return the love of any man
where people live in peace
where the whole world will be like Tuscany
the evening sunset on the vines
and olive trees
a golden glow
roses growing up the sides of farm houses
a glass of wine in the lingering twilight
grandchildren playing down by the arbor
reading by the pool
the circus performers from the village
coming out to the house for lunch
entertaining the children with their clowning
and juggling
the family in the kitchen
making dinner together
the children picking fresh vegetables
the neighboring farmer holding forth
reciting Dante by heart
stanza after stanza
and bursting into song
arias from Verdi
the mother sitting at the hearth
giving her breast to her baby
fresh herbs
the fennel and the basil
the roasted garlic and the fish stew
we'll have our own wine
from the vines nearby the house
our own olive oil

from the trees on the nearby hillside
we will laugh and cry and tell stories
we will have love affairs
and no one will be hurt
aunts and uncles will gather every Sunday
to take care of the children
while we have a nap in the upstairs bedroom
oh Tuscany Tuscany
how I long for you and love you.

FRANCOIS
In the olden days
you were married for life, that was it
and then you have your love affairs.
But nowadays these love affairs cause nothing but
pain or death,
and it seems you shouldn't have them.

EDMUND
Or you might say,
this wonderful married love
this is not for me.
What I long for is a moment
and nothing more
an intense moment
a moment even of pain
or especially of pain
never mind the falling in love
the consummation
the lifelong pleasure
let us cut right to the end of it

the searing pain
that lets us know
we did once long and love
we are alive
and this awful pain proves it
over and over again.

FRANK
This is not my idea of love.

GUNTER
Or it may be
rather than feeling the pain ourselves
we like to inflict it on others
to enable them to feel what we ourselves cannot
and this can be a form of generosity
giving the sensation of life to another
life at its most intense and intimate

MARIA
Oh, Gunter, really....

[Natalie now launches into an aria
whose sole purpose is to get Mimi's attention
and seduce her.]

NATALIE
Sometimes you might like to say to someone
hey! go ahead
do your worst
stick it in me,
up my ass,
piss on me,

double up your belt,
make it sting
make me lie still
make me whimper
make me beg

Because I like to feel some leather
up between my legs from time to time
with a little silk
a knee up in my crotch
nails down my sides
bone against my clit
a little bit of rubbing
The old double dildo
and you've got to like an animal from time to time.

Or you might say to your partner
make it hurt
spank me, pinch me
give me an enema
bite me, burn me,
but watch out for the joints, the nerves,
watch out for the blood vessels, you know
I'm taking this for granted,
this will be safe
think about the front of the thigh,
the shoulder, the upper arm,
use a little soap and water,
alcohol, Betadine,

keep it perpendicular to the skin
make a gentle cut

wait a minute before the blood begins to flow
and then another cut or prick
like lightning going through the body

and when it's done
rub it with wine
stain it
leave a mark there
because these marks are here for life
these are commitments being made
we're never going back

MIMI
never.

NATALIE
And what do you need in life finally but
some bandaids
smelling salts
sterile cotton

MIMI
bandage scissors

NATALIE
bolt cutters

MIMI
aspirin

NATALIE
spare keys

MIMI

a marlinspike

NATALIE
ice pack

MIMI
hydrogen peroxide

NATALIE
rectal thermometer

MIMI
KY jelly

NATALIE
tweezers.

MIMI
And then you can feel free to say to your mate
you could tie me down
so I can't jump when you cut me
you know
Do it slow
then work me over
this is what I like
and tell me bedtime stories

NATALIE
You could powder me.
You could oil me.
You could dress me up.
You could take me out.

[Mimi, having gotten caught up in Natalie's fantasy,

has been worked up into a sweat.
She takes a deep breath now.]

MIMI
There.
I'm done.

I call these plaster casts of torsos
my erection series
because
no matter what a man does
when he feels the heavy warmth of plaster on his
torso
he can't keep himself from getting an erection
don't ask me why.

[Silence.
Mimi and Natalie are fixated on one another.
All the others look at Francois.

Maria bursts into song,
an aria from an Italian opera,
leading to a chorus

so that everyone joins her in singing the opera,
even Tessa;

while they sing,
Mimi takes Natalie by the hand
and guides her into the woods
or to the steamer trunk,
opens the trunk, and gets into it with Natalie and
closes the lid;

and also, while they sing,

beautiful things ascend from beneath the ground
to heaven

or rose petals rain down

or ten thousand brightly colored beach umbrellas
descend from the skies;

at the end, there is silence,
and the sound of the surf]

GUNTER
Dear God,
did you hear these women singing together?

MARIA
Thank you, Gunter.

GUNTER
But, no,
could you hear yourself?
I am speaking of you and your daughter.

TESSA
I was only singing.
I wasn't listening.

GUNTER
The two of you
mother and daughter
your voices flowing in and out of one another
like quicksilver
like a mountain brook

like satin sheets

MARIA
Oh, Gunter, really.

GUNTER
Like the spring breeze in the branches
like the silk camisole
beneath the summer dress

MARIA
Gunter, please.

GUNTER
Like the summer light
falling on the pillow
in the late afternoon
and the ocean waves are quiet
as the tide goes out once more

FRANK
Gunter.

GUNTER
My mother sang to me every night
when she put me to bed
and sometimes my grandmother would join her
the two of them singing to me
their duets and solos
from the operas we had attended all together
and I have often thought
one never knows
what one seeks in life

why this man loves a woman with fair hair
or this woman needs a man who seems substantial
while that woman needs a man who is tender
or even weak
a man may love a woman
or a man may love a man
but why will he love this woman or that man
these things that make us long for another human
being
or need another
that make us unable to sleep
or make us tremble
make us perspire with a passion we don't understand
it is so specific and so sickening and so potent
it frightens us
we run from it
we choose instead some more peaceful seeming
love
some love we can bear from day to day
even though eventually it may come to bore us
and we forget what it is that makes our knees buckle
until, by accident,
we come across it again in the most unexpected
place
as I have just done this moment
with you, Maria, and with you, Tessa
hearing the two of you sing
I recognize: I love you
I love the two of you together, singing
and I need you

I want you
I need to marry you
please, Maria, please
[he is on his knees and weeping now]
I beg you
I can't help myself
I can only plead that I can't help myself
or else I would
I only thank god in this moment
that the passion I can't resist is this one
instead of, as it could have been -
who knows? we seem to have no control of these
things -
a passion to whip someone or shoot them
I beg you, Maria
I beg you, Tessa

MARIA
Gunter.

GUNTER
come with me
sing to me
I'll take care of you as you've never been cared for
before.

FRANK
Gunter.

GUNTER
What do you say, Tessa?
I pray to God
I'll give you anything you want.

EDMUND
This is too bizarre.

GUNTER
The Mormons love two women all the time
or three or four

EDMUND
Because of the way they sing?

GUNTER
Perhaps!
I don't know.
And why not?

JAMES
This is insane!

GUNTER
I don't say it's not insane.
I apologize for it.
But I can't control the way I feel.

MARIA
You should!

GUNTER
I can't.
I won't.
I love you, Maria.

MARIA
You are a creep, Gunter!
No one likes this sort of weird

kinky kind of thing.
I am a normal person, Gunter,
with normal sorts of normal feelings.

GUNTER
What I feel feels normal to me.

FRANK
I've never heard of such a thing.

GUNTER
This happens all the time
someone becomes transported by another person
this is what is called love.

MARIA
This is sick.

JAMES
Sick.

MARIA
Sick.

FRANCOIS
Do you think you can just come in and take another man's love
right from under his nose
and this is an acceptable thing to do.

GUNTER
I tell you, I can't be blamed.

FRANCOIS
Who would you ever blame then

if not you yourself?
Would you blame a man
who likes to be tickled with pheasant feathers?

GUNTER
No. No, I wouldn't.

FRANCOIS
That was a bad example.
Would you blame....

GUNTER
You can't blame anyone for love.
You can weep for them
but you can't blame them.

I could be so happy with the two of you
so filled with joy
it would overflow and fill your whole world
so that finally
you would be happy, too,
I know it
just as my mother and my grandmother were
taking care of me when I was a little boy
chastising me when I had done wrong
spanking me if I needed it
and sometimes I must admit
I did need it.
And we could be just this happy together
if you would just give me a chance.
I beg you, Maria.
I beg you.

[he has Maria's foot, which he is trying to kiss;
and she is trying to get away from him;

Francois comes and gently pries Gunter loose,
and takes him to one side,
putting an arm around his shoulder]

FRANCOIS
Here, here, Gunter, come with me.

GUNTER [weeping]
I love her.
I'm afraid I can't get over it.

FRANCOIS
Many people have had to get over it, Gunter.
She is a wonderful woman,
with a big heart,
but she can't love everyone.

[Francois helps Gunter to a place to sit down,
where Gunter sits in absolute desolation
and then gradually rolls under the desk in a fetal
position.]

MARIA
I wish I could love you, Gunter,
I would if I could,
but it is the nature of women
they are able to love only one man

or two

or so

but there comes a limit
or not
but with me this is how it is.

[Bertha, an elderly woman, enters.]

BERTHA
I'm terribly sorry
we've been having a party next door
and suddenly I looked around and my little boy
was gone.
I suppose he just ran out.
Have you seen my son?

MARIA
Oh. No.
I'm sorry.
Let's look for him.

EDMUND
Could he have come in through the kitchen?

FRANK
Or he might have come in through the terrace.

MARIA
Oh, how unsettling.
I remember I lost Tessa when she was a tiny little
thing
and we didn't find her for hours
do you remember Frank
and she was down by the ocean playing in the surf
and just as I spotted her

she tipped upside down in the water like a little cork
and of course she couldn't swim
and so she couldn't get herself right side up
I got to her just in time
and I thought
thank God
if we'd found her a moment later
it would have been too late.

[an awkward silence at this story she shouldn't
have told Bertha at this moment]

FRANK
I'm sure he's fine.
Children these days are tough little creatures.

MARIA
We should branch out
so we cover all directions.

JAMES
How old is your little boy?

BERTHA
He will be forty-three on his next birthday.

[Silence.
Everyone -on the verge of scattering in different
directions -stops.
They all look at the same time toward Gunter,
under the desk.]

Gunter!
Whatever are you doing there?

I was worried sick!
Where have you been?

GUNTER
I don't know.
I was taken outdoors by -someone -
I don't see her here.

[Hilda, an even more elderly woman enters.
She shouts everything she says.]

HILDA
Have you found him, Bertha?

BERTHA
It seems he has been here all the time.

HILDA
What have you been doing, Gunter?

GUNTER
I'm sorry.

MARIA
And this must be your grandmother?

HILDA
I beg your pardon?

MARIA
Would you be Gunter's grandmother
he was talking so much about.

HILDA
Not at all.

I am his mother's lover.
We have been together fifty-seven years this
September
and never had an unhappy day.

MARIA
Oh,
well,
I'm so glad to hear it.

FRANK
Relationships can be so complicated these days.

HILDA
Relationships have always been complicated.
Why is it people these days think they have invented
complications?
Bertha and I had a hell of a time getting together
it was never easy
all the people who thought they had a corner
on the one true way of living on earth
and they ought to bury anyone else who had hold
of a different stick

BERTHA
Hilda....

HILDA
but we did it
because what the hell is the point of life
if it's not to live it?

FRANK
Yes, well, no doubt.

HILDA
What?

FRANK [shouting]
I say, no doubt.

HILDA
What the hell,
do you think I'm hard of hearing?
It's a timid age we live in.

BERTHA
Hilda....

HILDA
The landscape of love has always been a rocky one,
filled with swamps and pitfalls
brambles and sticky bushes
and slipperly slopes and precipices
what the hell has ever been the point
except to slash your way through the underbrush
to score?

BERTHA
Of course, without hurting anyone.

HILDA
Of course. I'm not a Visigoth.
Although sometimes, let's face it,
shit happens.
You give it your best effort.
I try to be very, very careful -
but you can't hold back
just because there's no such thing as life insurance.

Sometimes we don't find anyone.
Sometimes we hurt someone.
Sometimes it doesn't last.

BERTHA
Hilda....

HILDA
Sometimes a love has the lifespan of a butterfly.
So does life itself.
We make the best of it.
Because time is running out.
Time is running out!
This is the only shot you've got!

BERTHA
Hilda....

HILDA
You've got to set a course and damn the torpedoes.
And what do they mean you can pursue happiness
but you can never find it.
Why do they tell you such a thing,
just to keep you from doing it?
Bertha and me: we've found happiness.
We are happy people.
I recommend it!

BERTHA
Hilda: sometimes she gets a little carried away

HILDA
On a rant....

BERTHA
But she's really a very nice person.

MARIA
Will you stay for tea?

HILDA
No, thank you, it's naptime for Bertha and me.
And for you, too, Gunter.

GUNTER
I was having a little nap.

HILDA
You're going to be much more comfortable in your
own bed.
Come along, Gunter.

BERTHA
Thank you so much for looking after Gunter.

MARIA
Not at all.

BERTHA
Come, Gunter.

GUNTER
Goodbye.

[Bertha exits, followed by Gunter.]

HILDA
Nice chatting.
You'll have to come and visit us sometime

if you like to get naked in a hot tub.
Bertha likes things a little kinky
but I'm always telling her:
not with the guests, Bertha,
not with the guests!
People don't like things out of the ordinary.
Well, they're young.
Once you get to be my age,
you like to make sure you haven't missed anything.
Do come and visit us.
You're lovely people.
And don't forget,
for us it's open house every day.

[She leaves.

Barbara enters, carrying the pizza box.]

BARBARA
Have you decided about lunch?
The pizza's getting cold.

MARIA
Oh, Barbara, we forgot all about it.
Come, people, what would we like?

TESSA
Whatever.

JAMES
Do you have any peanut butter?

FRANK
Salmon would be nice.

EDMUND
Just some raspberries for me.

[Bob enters.]

MARIA
Raspberries?

EDMUND
Some pale yellow raspberries.

BOB
This is the same place.

MARIA
Oh, it's the pizza man.

BOB
Did you phone for another pizza?

EVERYONE
I didn't phone.
Did you phone?
No.
No, I didn't phone.

EDMUND
We didn't phone.

MARIA
I'm terribly sorry if there has been some confusion....

BOB
You know, pizza is not returnable.

MARIA
I don't think anyone here is going to pay for a pizza
we didn't order.

BOB
I am not taking this pizza back to the pizza parlor.
Who is going to pay for the pizza?

TESSA
What is this, some form of extortion?

EDMUND
I'll pay for the pizza.
Here.

BOB
Last time, if I'm not mistaken
you gave me a good tip as well.

EDMUND
Here's a tip.

BOB
What's happened?
You've lost your job since we last saw one another?

EDMUND
OK. Here.

TESSA
This is enough.
I, for one, have to get back to work.
Maybe no one else has to work,
but I have to work.

And work is good.
This is another way to spend your life.

MARIA
Work?
What are you working on, Tessa?

TESSA
I am doing a translation for James.

MARIA
A translation.

JAMES
About love.
And women.

MARIA
Love, of course. Love.
Well, we know.

TESSA
What do you know?

FRANK
What is it you have?
It's not as though none of us has ever worked.

MARIA
Or loved.

FRANCOIS
Or loved.
All of us have worked.
It may be we can work with you.

FRANCOIS
Let me see.

TESSA
Please don't get mixed up in this
and make everything all topsy turvy.

MARIA
Well, I don't think anyone would make it topsy
turvy.

FRANCOIS
What is this?

JAMES
It's for a book.
It has some photographs and some text.

FRANCOIS [looking at the pages on the desk]
Right. Right. Right.
I think we can help with this.
I think, you know,
what you have is good
but it doesn't go quite far enough.

JAMES
Far enough?

FRANCOIS
I think love is more intense, clearly, than what you
have here....

JAMES
I don't think you ought to get....

FRANCOIS
You know, tragedies
and people fighting
slamming car doors,
driving off and leaving a woman by the side of the
road at night.
At least,
this is what I hear.
Probably I could help you.
Let me have a pen.

MARIA
Here.

TESSA
Pardon my saying so
but I don't think any of you knows anything about
love
and now you think you're going to write the book!?

FRANCOIS
We're not going to write anything
or even change what has been written.
But, well....
for instance, this, with this photograph:
"a slender, lovely, graceful girl,
just budding into supple line" -
who would say such a thing?
it would be pretentious
of course I'm not a writer,
still, nonetheless....

MARIA
Who could speak of love
if not you?

FRANCOIS
That's kind of you to say.
Not that I know so much
but perhaps I can help a little bit.

[handing the paper to Maria]

Now this is just a suggestion, but,
you might try, for example -
here....

[as she reads it and passes it to Frank
who passes it to Edmund who passes it to James
while
Francois continues]

JAMES
Everyone seems to be an expert....

FRANCOIS
And then, too....

[he begins to edit another bit of paper]

you might say....just as an example....

TESSA
What is this?

FRANCOIS
What is what?

TESSA
"in copulating
one discovers
That."

What is "That?"

FRANCOIS
That's what Roberto wrote.

TESSA
Or Francesco.

FRANCOIS
Or Francesco.

TESSA
I know that.
But what is "That."

JAMES [sitting, head in hands]
God.

FRANCOIS
That's what I have translated from his Italian.

TESSA
I thought it was already in English
and you were translating into Italian.

FRANCOIS
Oh.

TESSA
So now you are translating from English into

English. Okay.
But the "That" that you have in that.
[pointing to the piece of paper]
What is "That"?

FRANCOIS
That's what he says.
It's his idea, it's his sentiment.
What do you mean, what is that?
I'm not going to change it.

TESSA
Look here at the phrase:
"In copulating
one discovers
That."
What is the "That" that one discovers.

FRANCOIS
Oh, "That."
Well,
I don't know.

TESSA
You don't know?
You are translating this
whatever you are doing to it
and you don't know what it means?

FRANCOIS
It's a mystery.
It's an unknown.

It is the great, wonderful unknowable deep knowledge
one discovers that is different for everyone.
Possibly.
I don't know.

I'm just trying to bring a little depth and sophistication and complexity to the text
because, let's face it, our young friend James here is, after all,
an American
and it may be that he doesn't know a great deal about love.

TESSA
Who doesn't know anything about love?

FRANCOIS
I don't say he doesn't know anything about it,
possibly just not so much
in its details and subtleties.

TESSA
Are you crazy?
You know nothing about love, nothing!
I've never known a man
who had so much tenderness as James
so much caring
a man so solicitous
who had so much regard for another person
and so much respect
and loyalty

and steadfastness
and dependability and sweetness.
Someone you could count on
when you're feeling vulnerable
to take care of you
even when you yourself are maybe not so friendly
in a bad mood
to have the strength and goodness
not to be put off by that
but to stay right with you
until you could accept his caring
and his kindness
and his carefulness
and his thoughtfulness
and his gentleness
and his honor

[silence;
everyone is stunned by her outpouring of affection
for James;
no one is more stunned than James;
then she realizes what she has done
and turns away]

MARIA
That's lovely, Tessa,
and yet, to be fair,
it's not as though Francois knows nothing about
love.
In fact, he knows a great deal about love, about
passion

and excitement
about what it is to thrill to life
and to be thrilling to a woman
to make a woman laugh
to make her quiver and cry with happiness
to make her weep with sorrow that her life will
ever end
to hold a moment in her heart as though it were
forever
and you would never let it go
and you long for it and pine for it to return
you carry it with you in your heart your entire life
you cherish it
you never forget it
because it was the moment that made your entire
life worth living.

[silence;
everyone is stunned by this confession of love for
Francois]

FRANK
Indeed,
I think I know something about love myself,
about patience and forbearance and generosity
about wishing for happiness for another person,
Maria:
whatever might bring that to her
wishing that for her
even if it means
not having such happiness oneself

but taking real joy in the happy life of another.

[silence;

Francois takes Maria's hand]

FRANCOIS
Maria.

MARIA
Francois.

[A love song of the 50s or a heartbreaking aria by Caruso
on a record with scratches and crackles.

Francois and Maria leave together.

Frank starts to follow them out, stops, looks after them.]

JAMES
Will you go away with me?

TESSA
Live with you, do you mean?

JAMES
Yes.

TESSA
How could anyone do that
when you see how hard and painful it is?

JAMES
Not for everyone it seems to me.

TESSA
For everyone. Yes. For everyone.

[Edmund is watching Frank from the other side.]

JAMES
And yet, at the same time,
maybe love is something that will grow,
these things
you never can tell
not every love begins like in the movies
where a person is swept off her feet
sometimes it grows and deepens over the years
you grow together
until in old age
you are so close
so intimate
you are like the home you live in
indivisible
and so deeply happy in the place you live
you can't even understand it.
Maybe this is not your only choice
but this could still be one of your options, Tessa.

How about just going out to dinner with me?
There's no food in the house, right?

[silence]

There's food in the house, but you don't feel like cooking.
Am I right?

TESSA
Right.

JAMES
You throw on a little something,
we go to Tre Scalini,
what's to lose?

TESSA
Well....

[Frank continues to look in the direction in which
Maria left.]

JAMES
How many times have you eaten at Tre Scalini?

TESSA
My parents took me there when I was a kid.

JAMES
Now you go back as a grownup.
Tessa, time is passing,
you've been to Tre Scalini only once in your life
already you're a grownup
you could get to be sixty years old
still sitting home
waiting for the right person to call,
hoping to go to Tre Scalini one more time before
you die.
Let me take you out.
Let's go somewhere.
Maybe go on from dinner to a party

maybe stay up all night
go for a walk on the beach in the early morning
maybe not
this is how it is to be alive
it's no big deal.

[Edmund turns and leaves.]

TESSA
I don't know.
Nowadays it seems to me
you have to be so brave
even to accept a dinner invitation -
and to fall in love
that seems like a calamity,
even life or death,
and at the least a swamp.

[Frank turns around -sees Edmund has gone]

And, anyway,
I'm not dressed.

JAMES
I have something for you.

[he hands her a red satin slip]

TESSA
This is a slip.

JAMES
Everyone's wearing slips these days.

TESSA
As a dress?

JAMES
Yes.

TESSA
To go out?

JAMES
Sure.

TESSA
Not in Martha's Vineyard, I don't think.

JAMES
Of course in Martha's Vineyard.
It all started here.

[she steps into the slip;

[Frank, looking lost,
sits on the couch.]

TESSA
I like it.

JAMES
I thought it would be good on you.

JAMES
Do you believe in love at first sight?

[a long pause]

TESSA
Yes.

[James and Tessa kiss -a long, long kiss.]

JAMES
Do you dance?

TESSA
Of course I dance.

[They dance.

Frank puts his head slowly into his hands.

The lights fade to twilight and darkness.]

WINTERTIME

Beautiful heartbreaking music:

Dawn Upshaw singing "lorsque vous n'aurez
rien a faire" from Massenet's Cherubin.

It is snowing.

Icicles hang from a summer dress on a tree branch.

A forest of white birch.

A white summer house set in the white winter
woods.

The desk is covered with snow,
the piano is covered with snow,
the fireplace mantel is covered with snow.

And, since the house is closed for the winter season,

all the furniture is covered in white muslin.

The snow is beautiful, peaceful,
not a cold winter storm
but rather a snowfall of beauty and solitude,
just after Christmas.

Jonathan and Ariel enter through the woods
and through the non-existent "wall" of the house
carrying their cross-country skis.

Neither of them wears a winter coat.

Jonathan puts down a suitcase in the snow.

ARIEL
Oh,
I love it here
the beauty and the quiet

and being here with you

I've never known anything like it

JONATHAN
Never?

ARIEL
No. Never.
I'd like just to sink into it with you.

JONATHAN
Into the snow?

ARIEL
Into the snow

and into you
into the world
falling through space
and feeling safe and warm and held close
there's nothing better.

I think this is why there is music
and painting
because there was love first
and music is how it feels:
weightless in outer space
with nothing but feeling you want to cry
this is probably why people invented dancing
and talking
not so they could say: look out, there's a bear
OK take this stick and we'll kill that tiger
but so they could talk to each other
and feel how it is to be with the person they love
feeling they really exist with the planets and the stars
and so they already have eternal life in the present
moment
even if they know they are going to die,
they feel already that they are living forever.

I think of the earth flying through the universe.

I love you.

JONATHAN
Do you dance?

ARIEL
I am dancing.

[they dance -
not just for a moment, but, rather:
they dance;
and it is its own scene,
a long, romantic dance
with the beautiful music.

Maria, in a negligee, enters with a glass of champagne in her hand.]

MARIA
Oh, Jonathan.

[the music stops]

JONATHAN
Mother!

[she immediately exits]

JONATHAN
That was my mother.

ARIEL
Your mother.

JONATHAN
Yes....

JONATHAN AND ARIEL TOGETHER
I thought....

JONATHAN
Yes, I thought so, too.

ARIEL
That we were going to be alone.

JONATHAN
Yes.

[Francois enters to look
holding a champagne glass in his hand, wearing
his bathrobe.]

FRANCOIS [with a bit of a French accent]
Ah,
Jonathan,
how wonderful to see you!

JONATHAN
Francois.

FRANCOIS
And this is?

JONATHAN
Oh,
this is my friend Ariel.

FRANCOIS
Hello. I am delighted to meet you.
I am Francois.
And the two of you: you are friends, you say?

[Maria has returned, wearing a robe]

MARIA [with a bit of an Italian accent]
Francois and I, we are friends, too.

JONATHAN
You know, mother, I think everyone knows what....

FRANCOIS
What everyone knows and what everyone says
are sometimes two entirely different things.

MARIA
And should be....

FRANCOIS
And should be....

JONATHAN
This is America, Francois; we are a plain-speaking
people.

FRANCOIS
So you say and yet it seems to me people lie to me
all the time,
lie and lie, I never know what to believe in America.

MARIA
If what you are doing is speaking to me in some
roundabout way....

FRANCOIS
Speaking to you!
Of course not,
of course not.
Of course to be sure
you might lie about some things at some times
a person cannot be criticized for this
certainly I would not be one to judge

even though
I myself am a truthful person
but when I talk about lying I am not always talking
about you,
necessarily.

MARIA
I thought we could be alone here, if that's what you
mean.

JONATHAN
So did we.

FRANCOIS
So did I, that's all I'm saying.

JONATHAN
Perhaps we should leave.

FRANCOIS
No, no, no, perhaps we should leave.

MARIA
Not at all, this is our house, too.

FRANCOIS
Well, your house.

MARIA
I think of it as our house.

FRANCOIS (to Maria)
I think of it as your house.

JONATHAN
I think of it as my house.

MARIA (to Jonathan)
I think of it as your house, too.

JONATHAN
Forget it, Ariel and I will leave.

MARIA
I won't hear of it.

JONATHAN
I don't think we can all stay....

[Frank enters carrying a suitcase,
and snow shoes.]

FRANK
Maria!

MARIA
Frank!

FRANK
Francois!

FRANCOIS
Hello, Frank.

JONATHAN
Ariel, this is my father.

FRANK
Jonathan!

ARIEL
Hi.

FRANK
How do you do?

MARIA
Frank, I didn't think you would be here.

FRANK
No. No. You wouldn't. I mean you didn't
and I don't know why you would.

MARIA
No, I didn't.

FRANK
I came just to get away
to be alone
to have some time by myself

FRANCOIS
after the Christmas holidays with all the parties

FRANK
to have a little quiet time as it were.

MARIA
Of course. It's just that you said you wanted to hear
some music.

FRANK
Music?

MARIA
Mozart. Or Puccini. I don't know. At Carnegie
Hall?

FRANK
Oh, yes.

MARIA
So, of course, I thought....

FRANK
Of course. And yet, I thought:

ARIEL
a chance to be alone.

FRANK
Exactly.

[Edmund enters,
carrying a suitcase
and ice skates,
having come, as arranged, to be with Frank.]

EDMUND
Oh, Frank, you're already here,
I wondered....

Oh, Maria.

MARIA
Hello, Edmund.

EDMUND
Francois.

JONATHAN
Edmund.

EDMUND
Jonathan.

FRANCOIS
Edmund.

[silence]

EDMUND
Lovely. We know who we are.
And who is this?

JONATHAN
This is Ariel.

EDMUND
Hello, Ariel.

ARIEL
Hello.

FRANK
So!

FRANCOIS
Well

MARIA
we are all here.

FRANK
We didn't know you would be here.

MARIA
No.

FRANCOIS
No.

EDMUND
No.

JONATHAN
We didn't.

ARIEL
No.

FRANK
I see you've brought your ice skates, Edmund.

EDMUND
And you have snow shoes?

FRANK
Yes, well, you know I don't skate.

MARIA
What's the fun of snow shoes,
it just seems like hard trekking to me!

FRANCOIS
Well, what's the fun of snow?

EDMUND
What's the fun of winter?

FRANK
What's the fun of the whole fucking four seasons
except for the occasional, rare peaceful summer
afternoon when you can sit on the porch completely

alone and have a gin and tonic by yourself?

[silence]

ARIEL
The truth is:
I love all the seasons.

FRANCOIS
Do you?

EDMUND
How lovely.

MARIA
I think, when a person is in love
she does love all the seasons.

FRANCOIS
And what did you think you might do?
I see you've brought your skis.

ARIEL
What do I want to do?

FRANCOIS
Yes.

ARIEL
You mean now?

FRANCOIS
Yes. Or on New Year's Eve.

ARIEL
On New Year's Eve, or in the New Year I guess

or at least before I die
I want to go to all the strange, distant places in the world
to China and Afghanistan and Uzbekistan
geographically, I mean, actually in the real world
and also in Jonathan's heart and in our hearts together
to explore the whole world before I die
so that I'm not up in the ether somewhere
looking back at the earth
and saying
oh, that was my only life on earth
and I hardly got to know it at all
and I want it to be just with Jonathan
and no one else
so that I'm not lost
and adrift in the world
disoriented, disconnected,
not knowing where I belong.

FRANK
That's very charming.

MARIA
Perfect.

FRANCOIS
Absolutely right.

FRANK
I'm happy for you.
Happy for Jonathan, and for you.

EDMUND
Who could hope for anything more?

FRANCOIS
For two people to be in love
and to have such a longing for such faithfulness
to one another
this is what we all hope for
and this young woman, Jonathan,
you are such a lucky young man
to have found already a woman with such an
openness to love
and to life and to the world
to speak so directly from the heart
not afraid if someone thinks, oh
she is a bit naive or a little sentimental
no,
to be brave
not to care if she seems foolish
to put her heart out into the world
she is a very special person
so attuned to every little breath of life
so perceptive and delicate
such a sensitive vessel
an exquisite person really
if such a thing may be said about another human
being these days.

[silence]

MARIA
Are you in love with this young woman, Francois?

FRANCOIS
I beg your pardon?

MARIA
You speak of her with such how would you say.
Have you known this young woman before?

FRANCOIS
Before when?

MARIA
Before today.

FRANCOIS
No, no, no, of course not.
I meet her at this moment
but anyone can tell
she is a very special soul.

MARIA
You can tell that on first encounter?

FRANCOIS
Well, yes.
I feel I have known her all my life.

MARIA
You do!

JONATHAN
Ariel, have you known Francois before today?

ARIEL
Are you kidding?

MARIA
He greets you with such how would you say,
such enthusiasm
such warmth
such knowingness.
And he is, after all,
as they say:
well-known.

FRANCOIS
What does this mean: well-known?

MARIA
I'm making no judgment
this is who you are
and if you are the sort of despicable person
who can't keep himself from women
therefore,
I am making no judgment
this is who you are.

FRANCOIS
You are so I don't know,
practically a paranoid schizophrenic with your
suspiciousness.
One greets young love.
So full of hope.
So full of, I don't know,
one doesn't say innocence any more these days,
and yet....a certain
lack of experience, I suppose one could say,
not that, of course,

a lack of experience
deprives one of wisdom
or even maturity
I mean, love: it knows no age really. Or anything
else.
Love of any kind is a wonderful thing.

EDMUND
One is always happy to see another person in love.

FRANK
Love is the very balm of existence.

EDMUND
The world can't do without it.

MARIA
And yet, in fact, it seems you know her.

FRANCOIS
What would it matter if we did know one another?

JONATHAN   MARIA
What would it matter?

FRANCOIS
People know one another
People have known one another in the past
People have never never known anyone in the past
this is how people are
and this is good
for people to have had experience of life
to bring to another person not ignorance
but knowledge

the experience they have had of the world
we are not all virgins!
We don't even want to be virgins!

JONATHAN
Is this true
what he says?

ARIEL
That we are not all virgins?

JONATHAN
That he has known you?

ARIEL
Are you crazy?

FRANCOIS
I am only saying
it would not be bad if we had known one another
in the past.

JONATHAN
Oh. I understand.
It seems you're not denying it.

FRANCOIS
I would not dignify it with a denial.
Of course I am denying it.
But I do not make denials
I am not going to base my life on denials!
This is like mother like son with the paranoid
schizophrenia.

ARIEL
It's the same for me, too.

JONATHAN
What is?

ARIEL
What he said:
exactly what he said.
I'm not going to spend my life
defending myself against wild talk.
I'm just introduced to these people for the first time
and the first thing you do is accuse me
of having had a love affair with one of them?
Is this how it's going to be for us?

JONATHAN
But this is not normal.
Normally I would never ask you such a question.
But this is my mother's lover!

ARIEL
What does that have to do with me?

JONATHAN
It has to do with both of us!

[she turns and runs out]

JONATHAN
Ariel!

[he turns to the others]

We were going to be engaged!

MARIA
Engaged!

JONATHAN
That's why I brought her here,
to be alone,
so that I could propose to her on New Year's Eve.

MARIA
How wonderful!

JONATHAN
And now look what's happened!

BERTHA
People! People! Quickly!
Help! Hilda she is drowning!

[Bertha, an elderly woman,
comes running through the woods to the house.]

FRANK
What?

BERTHA (still running into the house)
We were ice fishing
and we had our lunch with us
by the side of the what, you know,
the hole you fish through
and she reached for a sandwich
and fell through the hole
and I couldn't reach her
and she has disappeared
disappeared under the ice.

FRANK
My God. We'll come right now.
Let's get a rope.

EDMUND
Or a pole, a ski pole.

[everyone is rushing around
gathering up their athletic equipment,
everyone talking at once]

FRANCOIS
Or a ski, a ski is even longer than a ski pole.
I have a ski.

MARIA
Blankets. Blankets.
We'll take some blankets from the bed.

JONATHAN [to the others as they rush around]
If you take a snow shoe
you can break your way through the ice
because she might have floated away from the hole
and you'll need to open up more water.

HILDA
Bertha! What the hell do you mean
running away and leaving me there!

[Hilda, another elderly woman,
soaking wet, dripping water,
enters fast, shivering.]

BERTHA
Hilda!

HILDA
I'm freezing my butt off
you leave me to drown.
What the hell is going on
you had a tea party you had to get to?

BERTHA
Oh, Hilda, I'm so happy.
I'm so happy.

JONATHAN
Are you the drowning person?

BERTHA [weeping]
I thought you had drowned.
I thought you were gone forever.
I thought I would never find you.
Oh, god, I am so happy.

HILDA
What the hell happened?
Did you push me in?
Did you think you'd have a little joke?

BERTHA
Of course I didn't push you in.

HILDA
Did you think you'd be better off without me?
Doesn't anyone have a blanket?
I'm freezing my butt off and you're standing there!

BERTHA
Excuse her.

Hilda, she is a frank talker.

HILDA
What the hell, I just fell through the ice,
you expect some chitchat?

BERTHA
I came to get help.

JONATHAN
Who is this?
Is this a neighbor?

HILDA
A neighbor, yes!
And wouldn't you think there would be a little
neighborly offer
of some coffee or hot chocolate.

MARIA
Oh, of course. I'm sorry.

[Maria rushes out.
Others help Hilda into a chair,
pile blankets and overcoats over her.]

HILDA
I don't mean to complain.
Ordinarily I'm not such a bitch
but I just fell in the water and damn near drowned.

FRANCOIS
Here, let's wrap you in a blanket.

FRANK
And put this coat on as well.
You can't be too warm after such a chill.

EDMUND
Have my sweater.
Let's put this around your feet.

HILDA
There you are, Bertha.
You've been wishing I were dead,
you almost had your wish.

BERTHA (weeping)
Hilda, how can you say such a thing!

FRANK
We should get you into a hot bath really.

HILDA
She thinks if she had me out of the way
she could take up with Ursula.

BERTHA
I don't.

EDMUND
Would you like a hot bath?

HILDA
You do.
You think I don't notice?
I hear you talking to her on the phone
the way you giggle

the way you are excited when she calls.
Are you ever excited when I call home?
No.

EDMUND [to Frank]
I could run the bath.

HILDA
Do you ever giggle when I say things?
No.
What do I do that pleases you?

BERTHA
Every day you are alive pleases me.

HILDA
What is that?
Yes, for sure, I think you like me,
I think I am a good companion for you,
you like to sit with me by the fire after dinner
we can talk
we can say, oh, I read this book,
I saw this television show,
oh?
and how was that?
But as for thrills,
I don't think you feel them from me.
You don't think my jokes are funny.
You don't think what I have to say is worth thinking
about.
Your first instinct, everything I say,
is to disagree,

not to think,
the way you do with Ursula,
oh, this is an interesting insight
I'd never thought about that,
don't you think that's amazing, Hilda?
No. No, I don't.
I think she's a dumbkopf.
No one else would give her the time of day.

[Maria returns with coffee.]

MARIA
Here.

HILDA
Thank you.

[Silence.]

BERTHA
I love you, Hilda.
I thought I myself would die if I had lost you.
I can't live without you.

FRANK
You know, one doesn't want to seize on any little thing
some doubt one has of another's love
or faithfulness
and blow it up.
Otherwise there's no end to it.
There's something every day you can make a case out of
if you choose.

JONATHAN
Unless it's clear someone is being unfaithful to you
and then you don't want to wander around oblivious
to the fact that you are being betrayed behind
your back.

FRANK
Still, as a grownup
one has to let the little things pass
even if sometimes some little rumor might possibly
be true
one has to let it pass for the sake of a larger love.

JONATHAN
If sometimes some rumor might be true?

FRANK
I'm not saying whether it is or it isn't.
I'm only saying
as man to man
you keep your eye on the goal line
you don't let yourself get caught up
in the details along the way.

JONATHAN
Unless, in fact, you can easily hear in the other
person's voice
that she hates you.
As I could hear when Ariel spoke to me.
And then things are clear enough.

FRANK
I didn't hear that.

JONATHAN
Did you hear the way she spoke to me?

FRANK
No.

JONATHAN
The contempt in her voice.

FRANK
No.

JONATHAN
The scorn.

FRANCOIS
I didn't notice it.

FRANK
No.

FRANCOIS
This jealousy and suspicion,
it's like a rising tide,
it could swamp all boats.

JONATHAN
Did you hear her say:
"I'm not going to spend my life
defending myself against wild talk."

FRANCOIS
Perhaps it was a little wild.

JONATHAN
The sneering.
The derision in her voice.

FRANK
I didn't notice it.

JONATHAN
I did.

FRANCOIS
Still, seizing on these things -
sometimes women speak this way
even if in this case she didn't
sometimes they do
possibly sometimes we deserve it I don't know
but one lets it pass
water off a dog's back
if one wants to change the mood
and move on toward making love.

JONATHAN
I don't think, anyway,
that anyone is going to change the mood in this house
where all of you are in such a tangle with one another
that no one ever knows if they are standing on solid ground
and you come here
and create such an atmosphere
how could anyone ever propose marriage in this house?

Thank you, you people have ruined everything.

FRANCOIS
I don't think we have ruined everything.
I think you yourself might have ruined your own
engagement
I don't know.

JONATHAN
Is that a fact?
Is that what you think?

[he picks up the little delicate desk chair and slams
it down
and picks the chair up and slams it down again
and picks it up and grabs it in his arms
as though he would rip it in half;

and Jonathan struggles and struggles to pull the
chair apart with his hands
and falls to the ground, wrestling with the chair,
and, kneeling on the ground, slams the chair over
and over on the ground,
breaking its legs, breaking its back, smashing it
to bits,
reducing it to wreckage.

And then he slowly gets up,
looks around at the others -who are all standing
back, away from him -
and turns and leaves.

Silence.]

MARIA
We can fix it.

FRANK (looking at the chair)
I don't think so.

MARIA
We can have an engagement party for them
just the family
to show we are sorry and we care
and then they will feel relaxed and happy together
and everything will be perfectly all right
and then we can all just slip away and leave them
alone here.

Unless, Francois, you would rather stay.

FRANCOIS
Stay?

MARIA
With Ariel.

FRANCOIS
Maria, why do you go on with this jealousy and
suspicion
you see what it does
you see what it did.

MARIA
She is a beautiful girl
who would blame you?

FRANCOIS
No one would blame me,
and yet it seems you do.

MARIA
Of course I do!
Everyone knows who you are as a person.
Who can trust you?

FRANCOIS
Or it might be said:
who can trust you?

MARIA
Haven't I been faithful to you?

FRANCOIS
How can it be faithful to me
if you are married to Frank?

FRANK
Let's face it, Maria, you're not a faithful person.
You have many fine qualities
but you have never been a faithful person.

EDMUND
I didn't know Maria's faithfulness was such a
concern to you.

FRANK
Of course it is!
She's my wife.
We had an understanding, Maria and I,
we might have the occasional flirtation

EDMUND
Flirtation, you say. Flirtation!

FRANK
because we are adults
and we know these things happen
but we wanted to be faithful to one another
fundamentally
to have a lasting marriage
and so we might have our flings

EDMUND
Flings!

FRANK
but never, never where we live
or with anyone the other one knows
but always out of town.
And I know Francois.

MARIA
You've known Francois for years.

FRANK
That's what I mean.

MARIA
So why do you make an issue of it now?
You have Edmund for your special friend.

FRANK
You had Francois first.

MARIA
And now you have Edmund.

FRANK
And now I have Edmund -
What of that?

EDMUND
What of that?

MARIA
What are we arguing about?
Are we in a tizzy about chronology?
Now today in the present moment
you are not faithful to me!

EDMUND
Or to me either.
Even now after all these years
Maria remains first in your heart.
You know, Frank,
I can take your marriage,
your involvement with your children,
I understand
and I think it is a good thing and a fine thing
and shows what a good heart you have
but always, when it comes down to it,
if she is in trouble, or she needs something,
Maria is first in your heart
and
I need to be first in someone's life.

[he leaves,
not in anger, but in pain]

FRANK [to Maria]
And so do I, to be candid.

[he leaves -in a different direction -
also not in anger, but in pain]

MARIA
And so do I.

FRANCOIS
Well,
so do I.

HILDA
Who doesn't?

BERTHA
Come, Hilda,
we will get you into a hot tub.

HILDA
Don't think you can get into a hottub with me now,
Bertha.
[getting up to leave]
You think I'm easy.

BERTHA
I don't think you're easy, Hilda.

HILDA
Oh, yes, yes you do, you think I'm easy,
but a person doesn't forget
if you leave them in the icy water to drown.

[she leaves, Bertha following]

BERTHA
I didn't leave you, Hilda.
I would never leave you.
I went for help
because
let's face it
when you're soaking wet
as you well know
nobody can lift you by themselves.

[A love song:

Hahn: L'Heure Exquise from In Love With Love

We listen for a few moments, and then:

Francois sits down with a stack of paper,
writes something on a piece of paper,
lights the paper on fire with his cigarette lighter,
and watches it burn before he drops it to the floor.

He writes something on another piece of paper,
and lights it on fire.

Maria watches him for a while before she speaks.]

MARIA
What are you doing?

FRANCOIS
I am writing down my memories of you
and lighting them on fire
one by one
and when the last one is burned up
you will be gone from my heart.

MARIA
This is lunatic.
You can't do this.

FRANCOIS
Oh yes, I can.
I can't get rid of all my memories of you all at once
but I can do it one at a time
and, at the same time, it gives you fair warning.
You can see the countdown to the end.

Or, you have an option
you can go away with me
and I'll stop burning up my memories.

MARIA
I can't go away, this is my house.

FRANCOIS
And so?

MARIA
It's my house, I live here.
I can't leave.

FRANCOIS
And I can't go on.

MARIA
Why not?

FRANCOIS
Because how it is:
when you feel you might be losing me

as you have felt over these Christmas holidays
then you run to me
and we make love
over and over and over again
until we are exhausted
and you feel sure that you have me again
and so that makes you feel confident
that you can drop me and go back to Frank
because he is your husband and
by then, you are afraid he doesn't love you anymore
because he is jealous
or he is angry
or he feels lost or left out
and so you go back to him
and I guess you make love to him over and over
and over
until he feels reassured
and I am, by this time, crazy because you have
dumped me
and so you run back to me
and you make love with me over and over and over
again
until you have me again
and then you dump me again.
So it turns out,
the way to keep you
is to make you feel anxious and uncertain
and if I show my love for you
I lose you.
So I have to behave backwards:

if I love you I have to reject you,
and if I don't love you I should seem to love you,
so that I have to live an opposite life
and I can never show you the love I really feel
for you
because if I do, I will lose you,
and this is what people call crazy
and if you do it and do it over and over and over
you become crazy.
Because our whole love for one another
is not just a thousand times coming together
but also a thousand rejections.
Not to mention you
because you are already crazy
and anxious
running back and forth
never doing what you might want to do
but only going where anxiety drives you
back and forth back and forth
like a ping pong ball.
Frank feels OK: ping
Francois feels OK: pong
Frank feels OK: ping.
So this can't go on
or we will all end up in the hospital with padded
walls.
So I am being decisive.

MARIA
No.

FRANCOIS
Yes.

MARIA
No.
Francois, you know you are the only one I love.

FRANCOIS
You say this and you say this
and yet
how can you say this?

MARIA
Because you know it's true.
I belong to you.
My heart belongs to you.

FRANCOIS
And yet you go home to Frank
and you sleep with Frank.

MARIA
Only on Friday nights.

[silence]

FRANCOIS
Only on Friday nights?
What do you mean?
You didn't tell me this.
You sleep with him on Friday nights?

Why on Friday nights?

MARIA
I wouldn't know.
That's all.
That's how it always has been.
This is our bargain.

FRANCOIS
You trade a home for sex?

MARIA
Certainly not.
I have a home.
Frank lives there.
And that's what Frank wishes
and because I love him in a way, you know,
as one loves a husband
that's how it is.

[Frank has returned
to have the last word with Maria.]

FRANCOIS
So then
that's what I am saying:
you love him.

MARIA
Not the way I love you
because when I see you I quiver.

FRANK
I beg your pardon.

FRANCOIS
I beg your pardon?

MARIA
I quiver
because even if you are a bad person
you are an eager person
you are an enthusiastic person
so
I love you.

FRANCOIS
You sleep with him every Friday night?

MARIA
You shouldn't get so attached to that.
It's nothing.

FRANCOIS
How can I get it out of my mind?
Why do you tell me this?
Now it's worse than I imagined.
So.
That's it,
you are going to have to choose.

FRANK
I beg your pardon.

MARIA
Try to be a mature person, Francois.
How can I choose?

FRANCOIS
How can you not?

MARIA
Frank.
He is a good person.
And I wouldn't want to give him pain
(any more than I need to).
We have children together.
We are still our own family
and you can never leave your family.
If you love me
you can understand that.
And want me to be happy.
And it's such a little thing
it means nothing to us
but to Frank, you know,
it's important.

FRANCOIS
Ah, to Frank, it is important!

FRANK
I beg your pardon.

FRANCOIS
No. No.
Excuse me.
I am leaving.
I am leaving.
I am going for a walk in the ice and snow.
Because nothing is important to me!

[he leaves]

MARIA
The point is
of course we did have an out of town understanding
until you accused me of being a slut with that
puppeteer
in New Hampshire.

FRANK
I'm sure I never said quite that.

MARIA
Oh, yes, you did.

FRANK
I think what I said was you had become known
as a person who would sleep with anyone.

MARIA
I was younger then.

FRANK
Yes?

MARIA
I had an appetite for life, Frank!

FRANK
Not for the whole of life, it seems.

MARIA
Yes. The whole of life.

FRANK
The whole of life includes other things
such as the paradox of faithfulness and freedom.

MARIA
The what?

FRANK
The difficulty of being both faithful
and still discovering freely and completely
what it is to be a human being.

MARIA
I couldn't do both at the same time.
It was too much.

FRANK
You were doing neither one.

MARIA
What are you saying?
I thought I was doing too much freedom.

FRANK
You were an addict, Maria,
not a free person.
It's no different than if all you liked in life was
reading novels
or eating lettuce
and you let everything else fall by the wayside
and you think you're alive
because you embrace your novels or your lettuce
but you're not
you're not completely alive.

MARIA
I thought I was.

I thought I should be.
I thought this was my only chance to be alive.

Sometimes a woman likes sex, Frank,
and not always something gentle and considerate
sometimes a little wild or it could be ridiculous
like a ride on the handlebars of a bicycle
and therefore she will do something wrong to have this
and not be very proud of having done it
but not be needing a lecture afterwards
from a person pretending to be a sort of moral authority
or even actually being a sort of moral authority
but even if he is
being a little boring and depressing because of it
a little like a heavy thing
as much as she hates to say it
because she may feel this person is a really good person
deep down
deeply good and kind and considerate
and deserving real love in return because of that
not just some stifling person who ought to be snuffed
but in his own way
even if it is not her way
in his own way even lovable
but possibly lovable by someone else.

And also I love you, Frank.

FRANK
No.

MARIA
Yes.

FRANK
I don't mean to just dwell all the time
on some narrow aspect of our relationship
because it's true you've been steadfast with me
a good partner in life
solid and considerate

MARIA
Thank you, Frank.

FRANK
Or, maybe not entirely considerate,
in a way taking advantage of me
thinking of me as the provider
never thinking what performing that role cost me
or what else I might have wished to do with my life
but, most of all,
I never felt you loved me
really loved me.

MARIA
I don't even understand what you mean.
I never promised to love you
in some romantic way.

FRANK
What other way is there?

MARIA
I don't even understand
what it is you have in mind
to love in the way you mean.

[Edmund has entered,
to speak with Frank.]

FRANK
The love I mean is to love someone else completely
to be unable to stop yourself
to be so excited by them and carried away
so in love with how they are
or what they do
you just can't help loving them
cherishing them
enjoying them.

[silence]

And you see,
even now,
you don't rush in to say, oh, but I did, I do.

[silence]

And, finally,
I've come to feel that living with you
I'm living alone
isolated
in a cold world,
all by myself.

MARIA
I'm sorry.
So do I really.

FRANK
Still,
I feel such a bond with you
it seems that every day when I get up in the morning
I can't decide whether I most want to hurt you
or give you something.

MARIA [gently]
I know.

FRANK
I can't go on like this

MARIA
Neither can I.

[she leaves, in sorrow]

EDMUND
You say you can't go on,
but you always do go on.

Because how it is:
when you feel you might be losing me
as you have felt over these Christmas holidays
then you run to me
and we make love
over and over and over again
until we are exhausted
and you feel sure that you have me again

and so that makes you feel confident
that you can drop me and go back to Maria
because she is your wife and
by then, you are afraid she doesn't love you anymore
because she is jealous
or she is angry
or she feels lost or left out
and so you go back to her
and I guess you make love to her over and over and
over
until she feels reassured
and I am, by this time, crazy because you have
dumped me
and so you run back to me
and you make love with me over and over and over
again
until you have me again
and then you dump me again.
So it turns out,
the way to keep you
is to make you feel anxious and uncertain
and if I show my love for you
I lose you.
So I have to behave backwards:
if I love you I have to reject you,
and if I don't love you I should seem to love you,
so that I have to live an opposite life
and I can never show you the love I really feel
for you
because if I do, I will lose you,
and this is what people call crazy

and if you do it and do it over and over and over
you become crazy.
Because our whole love for one another
is not just a thousand times coming together
but also a thousand rejections.
Not to mention you
because you are already crazy
and anxious
running back and forth
never doing what you might want to do
but only going where anxiety drives you
back and forth back and forth
like a ping pong ball.
Edmund feels OK: ping
Maria feels OK: pong
Edmund feels OK: ping.
So this can't go on
or we will all end up in the hospital with padded
walls.
So I am being decisive.

FRANK
No.

EDMUND
Yes.

FRANK
No.
Edmund, you know you are the only one I love
why do you be idiotic about Maria
when you know she doesn't matter to us.

EDMUND
How can you say this?

FRANK
Because you know it's true.

EDMUND
I think you are lying to me, Frank.
You are always lying to me
because you wish something would be true
but it isn't.
You are a weak spineless person, Frank,
feckless, feeble and ineffective.

But I love you like a cicada.

FRANK
A cicada?

EDMUND
Yes.

FRANK
Like a grasshopper you mean?

EDMUND
Do you know what a cicada is?

FRANK
I thought I did.

EDMUND
There was a time long ago, in prehistoric times
when cicadas were human beings
back before the Muses were born.

And then when the Muses were born
and song came into being
some of these human creatures were so taken by
the pleasure of it
that they sang and sang and sang.
And they forgot to eat or drink
they just sang and sang
and so,
before they knew it,
they died.

And from those human creatures a new species
came into being
the cicadas
and they were given this special gift from the
Muses:
that from the time they are born
they need no nourishment
they just sing continuously
caught forever in the pleasure of the moment
without eating or drinking
until they die.

This is the story of love.
If you stay there forever in that place
you die of it.

That's why people
can't stay in love.

But that's how I've loved you.
And how I love you now.
And how I always will.

I thought you were a person who would give
yourself entirely to me
you said you were the sort of person who
if you were betrayed in love
you would throw rocks
through the window of the person who betrayed
you
and I called up all my old lovers when we got
together
and said I was no longer available
but you
you
you insisted your family was your family
and your friends were your friends
and there was no reason to drop family and friends
because it had nothing to do with love affairs
and friendships don't have to end when you stop
sleeping with someone
and when I told you I felt jealous
however irrational that was
you said you couldn't be controlled by my
irrationality
and you would continue to see your friends
what if I didn't
that was my choice
so when I said then I would see my old lovers
you said, why would you do that, you said you
didn't want to
I said I will do it if you do
you said that was infantile

I was doing it just to get back at you
whereas you were doing it because you wanted to
do it
and I said then I want to do it, too, I always wanted
to do it
and you said you never wanted to do it
I said I got the idea from you, I think it is a good
idea
I will do it, too
and you said, if you do, I will leave you without
thinking twice about it
you will leave me, I said
you will leave me?
yes, you said,
because you are an adolescent
and I only want a relationship with an adult, you
said,
so I said, fine, fine, forget it
see whoever you want
have your marriage if that's what you want!!!

[Frank and Edmund look at one another for a
moment.
Music comes up:
music from a performance they were to go to
or that they went to in the past -
Una Furtiva Lagrima from Donizetti's L'Elisir
d'Amore.

The two of them listen for a few moments,
looking at one another,

and then Edmund goes offstage for a moment
and returns with a door on wheels.
He wheels it out,
looks at Frank,
and slams the door (which is miked to resonate).

Frank looks at the door,
looks at Edmund,
looks at the door,
walks over and slams the door.

Edmund slams the door.

Frank turns and leaves.

Edmund slams the door.

Frank returns and slams the door and leaves.

Maria enters and slams the door.

A performance piece of opera and door slamming.

All the other family members (but not Hilda or
Bertha)
come out and slam the door in turn
over and over
watching one another do it

and, by the end of the music,
they are finally all on stage together,
gathered around the door.]

FRANCOIS
You see, Jonathan,

this feeling of jealousy
or the feeling of having been betrayed
or thinking you are not loved
or not loved enough
that you are not first in another's heart

you can't indulge it
because, if you do,
the next thing you know
you are blowing up the world
so at a point
you stop yourself
you say,
good
I am loved
of course I am loved
I am not a cockroach
I am a loveable person
and for sure somebody loves me
and so, here is this lovely young person
who loves you

JONATHAN
Who is that?

FRANCOIS
Ariel.

JONATHAN
She doesn't love me.
She hates me.
She speaks to me with such hatred in her voice.
Do you know what she is doing now?

FRANCOIS
No, I don't.

JONATHAN
She is getting her stuff together.
Because she is leaving.
And as far as I'm concerned
she can't leave too soon.
And who are you to lecture me, anyway,
or even speak to me?

MARIA
How can she be leaving?

JONATHAN
Because she doesn't love me.
And probably because she is sick of you.

FRANK
I don't think she can be sick of your mother,
Jonathan.
What has your mother done wrong?

JONATHAN
Starting out with being here
and then being here with Francois.

FRANCOIS
And, let's be honest:
it was Maria who set this whole hurricane off
with her suspicions about Ariel and me.

[When we didn't notice,

Bob, a big scary-looking guy, entered,
and stands to one side.]

MARIA
I set it off?
I think you were the one who set off the hurricane.

FRANCOIS
I set off nothing. I was living my life as an innocent
person.

JONATHAN
But really, finally, mother,
to be honest
I'm grateful that you did it
because then I could see just what Ariel thinks of
me deep down
before I almost proposed to her.

FRANCOIS
It's very soon in life for you to know what she feels
deep down.

FRANK
It took me thirty years.

MARIA
For what?

FRANK
To discover how you feel about me deep down.

BOB
Excuse me.

FRANK
Yes?

BOB
I've brought the composter.

FRANK
The composter?
Did we order a composter?

MARIA
I don't remember ordering a composter.

BOB
Someone ordered a composter.

FRANK
I don't think so.

BOB
I have the order form right here.

MARIA
Begging your pardon, but
I don't think this is the perfect moment to....

BOB
The thing is
I have just brought this composter
on the back of my snowmobile
an hour out from the shop
and now it will be an hour back to the shop through
the snow
and I'll be needing someone to sign for the
composter

before I leave.

FRANCOIS
And yet, to be fair,
I'm not sure if....

EDMUND
No one wants a composter now!
This is the middle of winter!

BOB
I think there's someone here who can sign for it.
You could sign for it.

EDMUND
Yes. Fine. Of course.
I could sign for it.
Let me have it.

[Bob gives him the clipboard with the form to sign.]

You know,
there is no one here by this name.

BOB
What name?

EDMUND
Bevington.

MARIA
Oh, the Bevingtons live down the beach a few miles.

BOB
Do they?

MARIA
Yes. Don't they, Frank?

FRANK
A couple of miles, I think.
In the gray house.

MARIA
The white house.

FRANK
I would call it gray.

JONATHAN
Do you mean where David Bevington lives?

MARIA
Yes, dear, there's not another Bevington.

JONATHAN
That's the brownish house,
it's like three miles down.

MARIA
I don't think so.

JONATHAN
I know where David lives, mother.

FRANK
In any case:
[smiles in a friendly way]

Not far.

BOB
I went by there, and there was no one home.
So you folks can take the composter over to the Bevingtons
when they come back up in the summer.

EDMUND
Fine.

BOB
Just sign right here.

EDMUND
Fine. No problem.

BOB [while Edmund is signing]
I wasn't sure anyone would be here between Christmas and New Year's.
I took a chance.

EDMUND
Yes, yes, you did.

BOB
What are you folks doing here
if you don't mind my asking?

JONATHAN
Oh, you know, it's complicated.

BOB
I'm not stupid.

JONATHAN
It's just,
you know....a private matter.

[silence]

I came out with my friend Ariel
hoping for a time alone....
And then my family showed up,
and their friends
and now suddenly it seems
Ariel has had an affair with my mother's lover

[a gesture toward Francois]

BOB
Right.

JONATHAN
And I really don't understand how she could do this.

BOB
And with a man your mother's age.

JONATHAN
Almost my mother's age.

BOB
Right. People are not faithful, that's how it is.
You know what they say.

JONATHAN
No. No, I don't what they say.

BOB
What they say is
once you have your love,
you lose interest.

JONATHAN
Who says that?

BOB
Everyone says that.
Sappho.
Everyone.
I've done some reading about this, because
you know,

I've had some time.

And what you find is, in Greek,
what eros means is a desire for something that
is missing.
And, once it is no longer missing,
you no longer have the desire.
That's eros.

FRANK
That's completely stupid.

BOB
That's what the word means
in Greek.
What Plato said was
desire can only be for something that is lacking.
If you don't lack it,

you can't desire it.

MARIA
You mean a person can't love another person?

BOB
Can't keep loving another person.

EDMUND
I think that's true.

FRANCOIS
I've noticed that myself.

JONATHAN
I think that must be it.

BOB
And the Greeks thought:
people can't help themselves.
That's why people talk about falling in love,
because they didn't choose to step into love,
you never hear of someone who stepped into love,
they fell, they plunged, they lost themselves.

MARIA
I don't think the Greeks knew much about love.

BOB
Why do you say that?

MARIA
I've seen Greek plays, you know.
There's not a single one that's a love story.

BOB
Every single one of them is a love story.

MARIA
Not one.
They're all about killing your mother and killing your father.

BOB
Because the thing that starts everything is:
Helen
falls in love with Paris,
and he takes her
to Troy,
and then Helen's husband,
to get her back,
starts the Trojan war,
and then Agamemnon,
to get the favor of the gods for the war,
has to sacrifice his own daughter,
as a result of which Agamemnon's wife
Clytemnesta
kills him,
and their son Orestes
murders Clytemnestra -
all the murders and wreckage and ruin of Greece
comes from a love story.

MARIA
Really.

BOB
Why do people kill each other all the time

if it isn't because of love gone wrong
or hurt feelings
feeling someone was disrespected
or despised
or deprived of what should have been his
treated fairly
as a good person, given in return what he himself
gave
to the other person
then maybe it would be something bad would not
have happened.
Or you could say in a more general way
if society itself had provided
which is to say, been more generous,
which is to say, loving
maybe you would not be seeing certain social
behaviors.
You could say
economic exploitation itself is a lack of social love
where selfishness has made love difficult to give
or possessiveness or a fear of loss has overpowered
love
and when you see a person dying of poverty
of the lack of medical care
this is a symptom of perversion
of the withholding of love
or the positive imposition of sadistic impulses
and thus, as you can see,
it is not just the whips and chains of sadists
and masochists in nightclubs

that you might call perverse
but the practice of politics altogether
when it deprives people of the life-giving sustenance
they need.

JONATHAN
Oh, right, well, sure, OK, I can accept that.

FRANCOIS
This could be true.

BOB
This is how it is to be a human being.
You've heard of Jeffrey Dahmer.

JONATHAN
Sure.

BOB
That's how it is if love goes wrong.

JONATHAN (laughing easily)
I hope I'm not going to kill someone.

BOB
How do you know?

JONATHAN
I'm not that sort of person.

BOB
Maybe you don't know what sort of person you are
until you do something
and then you see what sort of person you are.

Right. Nice chatting.
But I'm going to have to get back to the shop.
I can't just be staying here socializing with you
people all day.

EDMUND
No.
Of course.
Nice chatting.

[Ariel has entered,
wearing a winter coat and scarf and knitted cap
and carrying her cross country skis.]

BOB
Enjoy that composter!

[he leaves]

ARIEL
I've called for a tow truck.

MARIA
A tow truck?

ARIEL
Because the car is stuck in the snow.

MARIA
But that's okay.
We don't need the car.

ARIEL
I'm leaving.
This is not fun for me.

I am not having a good time.
I don't feel happy.
So I am leaving.

FRANCOIS
Well, that's not a reason to leave.
That was never a reason to leave.
For anybody.

MARIA
Ariel, dear,
if we've been
somehow
to blame for your having a bad time
you know, we'll have a party or dinner
or cocktails

FRANK
Would you like a cocktail?

MARIA
Or we will all leave
and leave you and Jonathan alone here in the house
together
because we never meant to spoil your time together.

JONATHAN
We don't want to be together now.

MARIA
Don't be silly. Of course you do.

JONATHAN
We don't.

FRANK
I'm sure you do.

EDMUND
People always like to be together.

ARIEL
We never want to see one another again.

MARIA
Now then, I know Jonathan wants to see you again.
I speak as his mother.

JONATHAN
Don't speak as my mother, mother.
Ariel has spoken to me with such loathing
I hope I will never ever see her again.

ARIEL
And you have spoken to be with such
superiority
such loftiness
as though you were my father
reprimanding me
for what?
You're such a stupid dick.

JONATHAN
There.

MARIA
She doesn't mean it the way it sounds.

FRANCOIS
You know, your mother speaks to me this way all
the time.

FRANK
And to me.

FRANCOIS
She doesn't mean it really.
Well, she means it, of course,
but only for the moment
and then a moment later
she means something else
this is how it is to be a human being
we have feelings
they come and go
and when we are in love
we learn to weather it

JONATHAN
It's easy for you to say.

[everyone speaks at once]

FRANCOIS
No. No, it isn't.

FRANK
No.

EDMUND
It never has been.

MARIA
No, it's not easy.

FRANCOIS
But, it's the way it is.
You can't stop living
just because you run into a little obstacle along
your path.

And here, you see,
a moment ago,
everyone was suspicious of me
thinking I had somehow had some relationship
with Ariel in the past
thinking I am that sort of person
who would have some sort of illicit love affair
and now
poof
that's all in the past and forgotten.

[Doctor Jaqueline Benoit enters.]

JAQUELINE
I beg your pardon.
I am looking for Hilda Braunschweiger.

FRANK
And you are?

JAQUELINE
I am going to be called Doctor Jaqueline Benoit.
I had the phone call
that Ms. Braunschweiger has had the severe chill
and needs the doctor?

FRANK
You are a medical doctor?

JAQUELINE
Oh, yes.

MARIA
And you're making a house call?

JAQUELINE
A house call I don't know.

MARIA
You are coming to the house
and not having the patient come to your office.

JAQUELINE
Ah, because I am the doctor without walls
and I happen to be here
because the snow she is not having the other
doctors to be here.

FRANK
I see.

FRANCOIS
And you are visiting for the holiday?

JAQUELINE
Francois?

FRANCOIS
Yes?

JAQUELINE
You don't recognize me?

FRANCOIS
Ah!
Recognize you!
Recognize you!

Of course I recognize you!

Jaqueline!

JAQUELINE
I would hope so.
After this night in Zagreb.

FRANCOIS
Ah. Yes. Well.
[checking with Maria and the others]
That afternoon.

JAQUELINE
Yes, this afternoon and this night and this day.

FRANCOIS
The uncertainty of the political situation. No place
to spend the night.

JAQUELINE
I like this hotel.

FRANCOIS
Yes, I mean, of course, we finally found a hotel
which we had to share, with...
so many others, refugees.

MARIA
The room?

JAQUELINE
The hotel.

MARIA
You mean there were other guests in the hotel.

JAQUELINE
Yes. Of course.

MARIA
Are you saying the two of you spent the night together?

JAQUELINE
In Zagreb.

MARIA
When was this?

FRANCOIS JAQUELINE
Oh, long ago. This spring last time.

FRANCOIS
It seems so long ago.

MARIA
Last spring?

FRANCOIS
It couldn't have been.

JAQUELINE
And then your wife took you away.

MARIA
Your wife?

What wife?

JAQUELINE
He had to go with her
because, although no longer they were close
as the lovers
and had not to make love in years before -
as I think I can know,
because of how it was to be with us
this afternoon and this night and this day -
his wife, she was ill
and he was devoted to her.
Very nice. Very gentle.
How is she, Francois?

FRANCOIS
Ah, she has passed away.

MARIA
She has passed away?

JAQUELINE
I'm sorry to hear this.

FRANCOIS
Yes, well....

JAQUELINE
But, does this mean you are now free?
Because, I don't, excuse me,
I am not with thinking,
I don't mean just to jump like this at you.
I am only thinking, perhaps you need the friend.

FRANCOIS
Yes, indeed, I do.

DOCTOR
And because you did say,
one day, when you are free,
you want to be with me.

MARIA
You are a pig, Francois.

FRANCOIS
Yes, it's true.
I am afraid it's true.
I am a pig.
I can't understand it.

MARIA
And on top of that
telling her you had a wife.

FRANCOIS
Except that, in a way,
I did have a wife
I mean,
even if,
in an official sense
she was someone else's wife.

JAQUELINE
I beg your pardon?

MARIA
He doesn't have a wife.

FRANK
He has my wife.

JAQUELINE
I have been waiting for you, Francois.
Waiting and waiting for you.
I thought -
the way you care for me -
I never know a man like you.
From the moment we make love
my life she has never been the same.

MARIA
He is a bad person.

FRANCOIS
You know, I have never pretended to be other than
a bad person

MARIA
And you are.

How you are:
it is not funny
it is not charming

FRANK
It's not even French, necessarily.

EDMUND
Or male even.

MARIA
No one is amused.

EDMUND
People are not going to forgive you
for being the person you are.

JAQUELINE
I am....I don't know.
I feel air in the head.

[she sits]

FRANCOIS
No, yes, I am,
here, let me help you,
it is not funny
it is not funny to me
I am a tormented individual
a sick person
from birth probably
you would know about this, being a doctor,
but also you know the way I have been socialized
perhaps I don't know
probably I was raised too permissively
or not
or not
it may be I was raised to be hyper-masculine
and allowed to run and jump
and be rowdy
and even shove and wrestle
probably because there was recess
and there should not have been any recess.

I should have been forced to play with dolls

to bathe them and help them get dressed
I live a life of such confusion
sometimes I think I can't go on

MARIA
and then you do

FRANCOIS
and then I do and I regret it
because look at me
I am a wreck.

FRANK
No one feels sympathy for you, Francois.

FRANCOIS
Good. Good.
Everyone blames me.
And is this fair?
[to Maria]
Let's say it were you
let's say it would be a woman who did this
no one would think she is a pig

MARIA
I would never do this.

FRANCOIS
What?

MARIA
Have a fling with a woman in Zagreb.
Or a man.
This is not what women do

that's why they are not pigs.

FRANCOIS
Maybe it is not something you would do
but some woman might do it.

MARIA
No woman would do it.

FRANCOIS
How do you say no woman would do it?

JAQUELINE
I did it.

FRANCOIS
So you see.

MARIA
You are still a pig, Francois.

FRANK
I am ashamed to know you, Francois.

EDMUND
And yet, Frank,
let's not be the first one to cast a stone.

FRANK
Why do you say that?

MARIA
He is only saying:
because are you in such a position really to criticize
others?

FRANK
Are you criticizing me for criticizing him?
And who are you to talk of casting stones?

EDMUND
She is only saying,
let's not be too quick to judge.

FRANK
But you are not too quick to judge me?

EDMUND
What are you saying?
What does he mean?

MARIA
He means you are judging him.

EDMUND
I am only saying perhaps he shouldn't judge
Francois.

FRANK
And you are judging that I am judging him
and you judge me wrong for that.

JONATHAN
Always this bickering and bickering.

FRANCOIS
You will see
in a relationship that lasts
people bicker.

JONATHAN
Are you saying I know nothing about
how to conduct a long term relationship?

FRANCOIS
I am only saying that perhaps
you've not had one
and so possibly you don't know.

JONATHAN
I don't think you should be casting stones at me.

FRANCOIS
Good. Good.
So.
I am out of here.

JAQUELINE
I am out of here, too.
That's it to me.
No problem.
I know if I am not to be wanted.
I know if I am to be neglecting and ignoring.
I am not a person without a sense of my own worth
of myself.
I am to be out.

[they are all leaving at once,
all in different directions,
as, at the same time, they are all speaking at once:]

FRANK
So am I if it comes to that!

FRANCOIS
I've had enough!

JAQUELINE
Let the chilly woman suck it up!

MARIA
I am leaving, too, Francois,
and when I leave,
don't think I am coming back.

FRANCOIS
No, don't come back. Don't.

Because I am not coming back either!

FRANK
I am finished with trying and trying and trying
and no one cares!

ARIEL
This is a total nightmare!
And you bring me here to this place?
Why did you bring me here?

JONATHAN
I thought we were going to get married.

ARIEL
Jonathan, I would not marry you
if you were the last dildo on earth.

JONATHAN
Ariel! Ariel!

[he leaves in pursuit of Ariel]

MARIA
I am gone! I am gone!

I am gone!

[Everyone is gone except Edmund.

Francois returns with lingerie.

He has done nothing more than step off stage

and right back on.]

FRANCOIS
So.
It's nothing.
All this.
It will pass over.

EDMUND
What?

FRANCOIS
We have forgotten, that's all.
We have lost perspective.
We think
if only we will argue and argue and argue
someone will win
and then everything will be good.
But, obviously, this is absurd.
As my mother used to say,
I am sure your mother used to say,
honey will draw more flies than sugar.

[Francois starts to take off his clothes
and put on the lingerie.]

EDMUND
What is this, Francois?

FRANCOIS
A person wants to be seduced, that is all.
Because a person likes to be desired and flattered
and wooed
to feel your desire for her
or him.
Why
why do people get upset?
Because they think the other person doesn't love
them
or doesn't love them enough
or doesn't love them any more
or loves someone else.
Does a person want to yell and yell
and break up with their love?
No, of course not.
They want you to say: I love you
I love you
I have always loved you
and I always will
I love you with my whole heart
come to me
come to me
I love you.

EDMUND
Uh-huh.

FRANCOIS
And first
you want to get their attention
so you seduce them a little bit
with a look
a manner
this sort of thing
and then it melts their heart
and so you are back together again.

EDMUND
To you life is so simple.

FRANCOIS
Well, yes. It is.
We keep forgetting this.
But, what do you think?

EDMUND
If it were for me you were doing this,
I would want it a little more
racy somehow.

FRANCOIS
How do you mean?

EDMUND
A little striptease, maybe.

FRANCOIS
I can do that.

I can do that.

[he snaps his fingers
and music comes up

Dick's Holler by Clifford Jordan
from Atlantic Jazz, The Best of the Sixties

and he starts into a seductive dance;

he is dancing, stripping,
and flirting with Edmund,
dancing for Edmund

when Maria comes into the room
and stands looking at him]

MARIA
Francois!

[the music stops]

Now you are taking up with Edmund?!

And to think I was was coming back to forgive you!

FRANCOIS
Oh, thank god,
because
I love you, Maria.
I love you.
I love you to the moon and back.
I have always loved you
and I always will
come to me

come to me
I love you.

[she slaps him
and leaves]

Edmund!

Speak to her!
Tell her!

EDMUND
Tell her what?

FRANCOIS
Tell her I love her!

EDMUND
Are you crazy, Francois?
You are just some fucked up
repulsive old seducer.
This sort of thing
it's not even in fashion any more, Francois.

FRANCOIS
I love her, Edmund.
After all,
I love her.

[silence;

Edmund leaves in disgust;

Ariel enters to get the suitcase, or skis, that she
forgot]

ARIEL
I'm sorry.
I didn't know anyone was....
Anyone was....
Anyone was here in their lingerie.

I just came back to get my suitcase.

FRANCOIS
Oh,
I was just doing a striptease.

ARIEL
Why?

FRANCOIS
Just practicing my technique.

ARIEL
Are you a stripper?

FRANCOIS
Oh, no, no,
just thinking
if someone thought I were
sexy or appealing
or even funny
then perhaps
they would forgive me
and
you know.

ARIEL
No.

FRANCOIS
Probably it doesn't matter
because I think it's not working.

ARIEL
That could be a good thing.
People are animals, it's true,
but maybe they should try a little harder
also to be human beings.

FRANCOIS
This is my plan.
So far, I have always been tripped up.
But this is my plan, now,
to be a civilized animal.
But I think, who cares,
still, it's too late.
This time I've gone too far.

[Jonathan enters.]

ARIEL
I'm sure it's not too late.
I'm such an impulsive person.
I think you are, too.
Maybe we've both been too quick to give up
finding fault in the other and in ourselves
forgetting what we had in the beginning
how fun it was
what pure pleasure
how it lifted our hearts
how happy it made us feel

how it seemed even to give a point to our lives
how the whole world seemed filled with energy
and lightness and spark.

I gave myself to our love
in a way I'd never given myself to anyone or
anything before
and I felt finally in the center of my life
and at the center of the universe.
I knew now I had a life
and so I wasn't afraid even of dying any more
I wanted more and more of it
I wanted to live forever to have our love
but I was no longer afraid of anything.
Our love gave life to me
and I hope it goes on forever and ever.

JONATHAN
OK, it is true.

ARIEL
Yes!

FRANCOIS
What is true?

JONATHAN
You and Francois.

ARIEL
No!

JONATHAN
I don't ever want to see you again, Ariel.

FRANCOIS
Please....

JONATHAN
You're a filthy lying shit, Francois.

but now I see that Ariel is just a slut, too
worse than a slut
taking up with you
two human beings so despicable
it makes me want to vomit.

ARIEL
Jonathan....

JONATHAN
I can't believe I loved you
I thought you would be my whole life
I saw nothing else ahead of me
but you and our life together
and now it turns out
you've been sleeping with this creep
he's not even a person
he's just a loose phallus
going from bed to bed
trying to find a real life
and so it turns out
what?
you're just the same?
now how could I ever trust you again?
I thought you were an honest person
and a sensitive person and vulnerable

and now I see you're just a lying, disloyal, fickle, deceitful
woman.

ARIEL
You
are an ignorant shoot from the hip cowboy
with your boots in cowshit
like a cow puncher savage
thinking you are such hot stuff
rolling your cigarette with one hand at a full gallop
but in reality you are a baby
a baby dude ranch greenhorn dweeb
who knows nothing
nothing
nothing about whatever
nothing about life
nothing about women
nothing about men
nothing about horses
you are a guy that's all
you are just a guy
I could spit at you
[she spits]
I could spit at you and spit at you
[she spits and spits]
because what you are is a typical male
I'll say no more
a typical male
you are a
typical

male
which is to say a shithook
and a dickhead

JONATHAN
I wish you were dead.
Dead.

FRANCOIS
And yet, perhaps you are being just a little hasty....

JONATHAN
Dead.

[deafening music comes up -
a love song at full volume:

Jussi Bjorling singing " nessun dorma" from
Puccini's Turandot

Jonathan turns
and yells
and runs full tilt into a tree
and falls down

He picks himself up
a runs full tilt at another tree
and falls down.

He does this over and over.

Ariel, watching Jonathan do this,
picks up a coffee cup and hurls it offstage
with a crash.

Then she takes the saucer and hurls it off
in the opposite direction with a crash.

Then she picks up another cup or glass and does
the same
as Francois watches her.

Then, while she continues to hurl one item after
another

Francois picks up a glass
and he hurls it offstage with a crash.

And then, joining in with Ariel,
he takes another and another
and hurls them offstage
just as Ariel is doing.

Frank enters,
stops,
sees people are throwing things,
looks around for something to throw,
goes to the CD player,
takes a pile of CDs
and hurls or sails them one by one into the wings.

Edmund enters,
stops,
sees people are throwing things,
looks around for something to throw,
goes to the couch
and throws the pillows down again and again
(carefully, on the couch, so they don't get dirty,
picking one up and dusting it off if by accident

it fell to the floor,
and then throwing it again onto the couch).

By the time the music ends,
everyone is reeling from exhaustion
or collapsed on the floor -
or poised to hurl another dish.

Hilda enters.]

HILDA
People. People.
Come quick.
Maria has thrown herself into the lake
and drowned.

FRANK
And what?

HILDA
She has disappeared under the ice.
She is gone.
She is drowned.

FRANK
No.

FRANCOIS
Maria!

JONATHAN
Mother!

FRANK
God no, don't let it be true!

HILDA [speaking as others speak over her]
It's true.
She's gone so far under
or to the side
I can't see her.

FRANK
It's not too late.
Bring some rope.
Bring some ski poles.

FRANCOIS
I can swim! I can swim!

EDMUND
I'm coming, Frank!

ARIEL
Jonathan!

FRANK
Maria! Maria!

[he runs out,
followed by everyone else
with skis and ski poles and snowshoes.

Hilda hastens after them.]

Act Two

We hear an aria:
the full eleven minutes plus of
Cecilia Bartoli singing "gelido in ogni vena" from
Vivaldi's Farnace.

The whole house is draped in black.

White orchids to one side.

Seven chairs, covered in black, face front in a line.

Two tables,
one at each side,
with orchids and funeral cakes and drinks.

As the music continues,
Frank enters, dressed in black.
He checks the room.
He fixes an orchid.
He checks the room.
He sits, at last, deeply dejected.

Edmund enters, dressed in black.
He looks around the room.
He moves toward the line of chairs,
without thinking about it, to sit next to Frank;
he stops, thinks about it,
moves to the chair furthest from Frank.

Jonathan enters, dressed in black,
sits as far from the other two as he can.

Ariel enters, dressed in black,
sits as far from Jonathan as she can.

Bertha and Hilda enter together, both dressed in
black,
take two seats together.

A long silence.

At last, Frank speaks,
very quietly at first -
not making a speech
but just saying what he feels.

Because they are all sitting in a line,
they can't very well speak to one another
but speak front.]

FRANK
I suppose
the way that we could
honor Maria the most....

[silence, as he collects himself]

would be
to end the squabbling and the jealousies
that sent her out to the lake
to plunge
into the water

to plunge
under the ice

[silence]

the least we could do for her now
would be

to let our love for one another
find its way into our hearts again
in her name.

[long silence, as he collects himself]

Because
now we see that
without trust
the world falls apart
the whole world
and everyone in it
that the whole secret to life
is to be brave enough to trust
in another human being.

And we see
what harm it does
to be caught up with what we lack
rather than to treasure what we have.

And we think
if only what we have lost

[silence]

could come back.
This time it would be treasured.

[silence]

ARIEL
This is why people believe in heaven
because this is the second chance we have
if we believe in heaven.

EDMUND
Or in reincarnation.

ARIEL

Or in reincarnation.

Because the idea that you haven't got a second chance in life
is too unbearable.

FRANK
Yes.

[silence]

It is.

[Francois enters]

FRANCOIS
I apologize.
I'm sorry to be late.

FRANK
You're not late.
We haven't started.

EDMUND
The minister should be here any minute.

FRANCOIS
The truth is I
felt a little sheepish
feeling that
all of you blame me.

FRANK
No.

EDMUND

No, no, Francois.

JONATHAN
We don't blame you
any more than we blame ourselves.

FRANK
All the jealousies
all the imagined and real betrayals.

FRANCOIS
Real betrayals?

EDMUND
The fact that you did take up with Dr. Benoit.

FRANK
And the fact that I did take up with you, Edmund.

EDMUND
And, as far as that goes,
the fact that you betrayed me every day
going back to Maria again and again as you did.

FRANCOIS
Well, and the fact that Maria betrayed me.

[silence]

I beg your pardon.
Not that this is the moment to blame Maria for
anything.

Frank, I apologize to you.
Our jealousies, you know....

FRANK
I apologize to you, Francois.

FRANCOIS
No.

FRANK
Yes.
And I apologize to you, too, Edmund.

EDMUND
For what?

FRANK
For making you feel anxious all this time we've
been together
not knowing quite where you stood with me
being uncertain of my regard for you
I know how destructive that can be
and I see now
how I've let my anxieties
get in the way of the big things
the primary things.
I will never let you feel uncertain again, Edmund.

EDMUND
You owe me no apology, Frank.

JONATHAN
I owe you an apology, too, Ariel.

ARIEL
Yes, really, you do.

JONATHAN
I'm sorry.
I think, really, it's all my fault.
I think my mother did this
to put a stop to the mistake I was making with you.
I know probably she did it
because she was just sick of all the difficulties with
everyone
but I think
maybe she thought, too,
even if there was no hope for them
there was hope for us
starting out fresh
and she could save our love and our lives.

And I
I apologize
and I'm sorry, Ariel
and I wish you would forgive me
because I love you
and I treasure you
and I don't ever want to wreck my life again

ARIEL
I love you, Jonathan.

I love you, with all my heart.
I love your hands and your kneecaps and your hair
and your ears
and I love the way you are sweet when you are
sweet
and the way you fuck up

because even when you fuck up
and it makes me so mad
you are actually so incompetent at it
such a wild, untargeted loser that I love you
because I think the reason you are such a loser
is that your heart is good
and so you can't hit the bullseye
when you are acting like a nasty shit
so that people don't have to take it seriously
and they can just wait till you realize
how wrong you've been
and also right
also right
because I don't think you are a pathetic loser
that people love out of pity
or because they want to be with some weak
useless guy they can manipulate
you really are a winner
because of your heart
which is always there
and when you come around
we all see it
and see you always were a good human being.

HILDA
OK.
We can have a little memorial service now
and then
with the spring thaw
we can recover the body and have a proper funeral.

[silence at the brutal frankness of this]

FRANK
Yes.

ARIEL
When is the spring thaw in this part of the country?

HILDA
March, I would say.

EDMUND
March.

BERTHA
Early March or the middle of March.

HILDA
I remember when a friend of mine
went to Aspen
to go skiing over the New Year's holiday
and he drove up into the mountains in his rental
car
to see the heights
not a good time
to go driving up into the mountains in a car
and so, of course, he slipped off the road into a
ditch
and couldn't get it out again
and had to walk all the way back down the mountain
to find a tow truck
and by the time he got there it had started snowing
a real blizzard

and so the tow truck guy said
there was no way he was going up the mountain in
that snow
my friend, he said, would just have to wait for the
spring thaw
so my friend said,
right, when does the spring thaw come in this part
of the country
and the tow truck guy said,
July.

Luckily, luckily,
it comes here in March.

FRANK
I know how sad it is for a son to lose his mother,
Jonathan.
And, for me,
thinking about you now
I think about when I will die
and how I will miss you
and I think

how I have neglected you all these years
taken up with my career
and, let's be honest, with my love affairs
and even my golf game

EDMUND
What golf game?

FRANK
You don't think my golf game is any good?

EDMUND
I don't think you can say you really play golf I mean
when you go out now and then
maybe only once a month

FRANK
Not like you, possibly
with the, one might almost say,
the obsessive compulsive disorder you have about it

EDMUND
I am a player, Frank.

FRANK
I am a player, too.

EDMUND
You would be a player if you would come out with
me more often.
I beg you and beg you and you never do.

FRANK
I've had other things to do.
I have my family, you know.

JONATHAN
I'll miss you when you're gone, dad.
More, probably, than I miss you now.
Now, I just mostly wish you'd leave me alone.

FRANK
Yes, you do, and really, that breaks my heart
because I see that I am mortal
I won't live forever

and I think one day I'll be on my deathbed
I'll have a day or two to live
or maybe only hours
and you will come to be with me then
and we will both feel
we ran out of time
we thought we had all the time in the world
but we ran out of time
and now it's too late
we will never have those times together as father
and son
just relaxed times
not you trying to measure up to some goal I've set
or you think I set
not me trying to nudge you this way or that in your
life
but just to be together
to pass an afternoon or an evening together
many afternoons and evenings
and feel some sense of continuity
some sense of life going on even when it ends
because I live in you
I will live in you
and I will always wish I knew you
better than I do.

JONATHAN
This time I've been here
you've hardly spoken to me.

FRANK
Or you to me.

JONATHAN
No.

FRANK
And now, in my old age,
what consolations will I have
aside from cheap movie tickets and air fares?
Where will I go?
Where do I want to go?
I don't think I want to go to Phoenix over and over
again
and you get no discount for Paris.

HILDA
Still, there are compensations for declining powers
most of all, I think,
the sheer pleasure of luxuriating in old age.

EDMUND
If you are lucky enough not to be sick
and in pain.

FRANK
Sometimes it's hard to know
whether one would rather die in middle age or old
age.

EDMUND
Of course,
it's always better to die in middle age
than in youth.

BERTHA
And how sad it is

when you are older
to be deprived of the time to look back over your
life
as you never had while you were living it.
To relish it finally.

HILDA
Or, not just to live in the past
but to go on living to the end
to have more and more and more time
to keep going
never to get tired of it

BERTHA
to be released from the anxieties that, when you
were young,
held you back or clouded over the pleasures

HILDA
to have the weight lifted

BERTHA
and be able to wallow in each moment

HILDA
to enjoy the early morning and the long afternoons

BERTHA
and the sunsets.

HILDA
To be deprived of that by early death
is to be deprived of the dessert of life
of the after-dinner brandy and cigar.

Because, in old age,
we are not always sick or ruined altogether
but just some chunk has been taken out
you still have your knowledge of algebra
even if you can't remember a single song lyric
or your knowledge of the classics is still completely
intact
even while you breathe from a cannister of oxygen.
All the time I'm talking to some old guy
who can't remember who I am or where we are
and he has spit running out of the corner of his
mouth
and suddenly he's talking about Nietzsche
with perfect clarity
and still taking pleasure
in the possession of his consciousness of being
alive.

Because a person loves life
that's the truth of it.

ARIEL
It seems to me especially sad
for a woman to die in the prime of her life
to me she seemed still so vital and young
with so much more life ahead of her
to die just when her children were raised
and finally she could live for herself
do all the things she wanted to do
this is the most tragic age for a woman to die
after she has given all her life to others

and she is about to have her own life
and then she never does

JONATHAN
Last night I dreamed
my mother and I were in a white,
sun-filled summer house together,
and my mother was at the top of the stairs,
and I was at the bottom looking up at her,
and she said to me all of a sudden:
do you remember always to hold onto the bannister
when you go up and down stairs?
And I reassured her that I did,
even though I didn't.
Good, she said,
and yet, she didn't remember herself,
because one day she was carrying an armful of
tulips
in the upstairs hallway,
and, even though she had lived in the house for
thirty-five years,
she forgot to pay attention,
she let her mind wander for a moment,
and she walked right out through an open window
and fell to her death.

[Ariel speaks now partly to Jonathan,
partly to the others.]

ARIEL
When my mother died I dreamed
she was in an airplane

a small plane
a Piper Cub or some other little plane
like a mosquito
and she was taking off and landing
taking off and landing
going up to heaven
and coming back again to earth
and she could come and go
just as she wished
there was no finality to it
she came back to me again and again.

For the first year after she died
I dreamed of her all the time.
I was so grateful for my dreams.
And so grateful to my mother
for coming to me in my dreams.
And now I don't dream of her much anymore.
Very rarely.
She's leaving me at last.

[Jonathan takes her hand.

Bob enters.]

BOB
Excuse me.
I don't mean to intrude
if you are having a private family moment.

FRANK
Ah. The compost man.
Yes, indeed, as it happens

we are having a memorial service for my wife who

just passed away.

BOB
Right. OK.
I'm here to conduct the service.

FRANK
You?

BOB
You see, the minister is in Barbados,
and I often serve as deacon,
and so
I've come in his place.

Where is the deceased?

FRANK
Ah. The deceased.

EDMUND
She's in the lake.
Her body is in the lake.
She drowned in the lake,
and because she is down under the ice
we can't find her
so we thought we would have a little memorial
service now
and then in the spring,
after the thaw,
we can have a proper burial service.

BOB
Right.
Excellent.
I'm glad you're not going to have her cremated.
So often people think that would be a nice idea
and just this last summer
a fellow's wife died
and she wanted to have her ashes scattered over
Long Island Sound
so he got a pilot to take him up in a private plane
but when he opened the cannister with the ashes
they all just blew back into the plane
so he more or less inhaled his wife.

EDMUND
No. We won't be doing that.

BOB
Right. Excellent.

Your wife fell into the lake.

FRANK
She jumped in on purpose.

BOB
Ah. A suicide.

EDMUND
Yes.

BOB
Still, we don't judge people for these things.
Because a person can come into the world

different from all other people
and we don't know where such a person has come
from
like fruit flies, like worms in cheese,
they come from nowhere,
like the universe itself
which, in the beginning,
was nothing but chaos
and out of that chaos a mass was formed
just as cheese is made out of milk
and worms appeared in the cheese
and these were the angels
and among the angels was also God
he too having been created out of the cheese at the
same time
and all the creatures
of all kinds
as a result of which we have today
the inhabitants of the islands of Nacumera
who have the heads of dogs
and yet are reasonable people with good
understanding
and the pigmies
who are beautiful and graceful because of their
smallness
and they get married when they are six months old
and have children when they are two or three years
old
and do not live more than six or seven years
and they battle against the birds in their country

and often are taken and eaten by the birds.

EDMUND
Indeed.

BOB
And we don't judge these people
because this is how they are
just like you and me.

EDMUND
Yes, indeed.

BOB
We don't judge them
just as I am not judging you
and you are not judging me.
Live and let live
this was God's intention
to love all the creatures of the earth
and try not to kill them or hurt them.

EDMUND
No.

BOB
And if you can't help yourself
never mind then, that's your nature
because it was how you were made
and you are going to want to try to do better next
time.

EDMUND
Yes. Indeed.

BOB
I'll be leading you in some prayers
but I wondered if any of you has anything you'd
like to say.
A memorial service, customarily,
has some memories if you'd like to mention them.

[silence]

FRANK
I remember when I met Maria
our first date
I don't remember who arranged it
a blind date
and I picked her up at a little hotel where she was
staying
when she first came to New York
and she came running down the stairs
to meet me in the lobby
there was no elevator
and we talked there for a moment
and then we saw
water running down the stairs
amazing it was
a little waterfall
cascading down the stairs
and then Maria said, Oh,
I left the bathtub running!
And the water just flooded the lobby
before they got it turned off.
So of course she was kicked out of the hotel

and I told her she could come and stay with me
so she did.

FRANCOIS
She was always a little absent-minded.

FRANK
Caught up in the moment.

FRANCOIS
Exactly.

FRANK
Living in the present.

FRANCOIS
Exactly.

When I first met Maria
it was in the lobby of a theatre.
A friend of mine had said
oh, you're coming to see whatever it was
this evening, that's good
because there is a woman named Maria
who wants to meet you.
And so, when I got to the theatre and I saw my
friend
I went over and he said this is Maria
and I said, oh, would you like to have a drink after
the performance?
And she looked a little shocked and said
no, I don't think so.
And so I said, how about dinner tomorrow?

And she seemed almost offended
and said, no, no, I don't think so.
And all the time
this friend of mine was standing behind her
and making faces and sort of waving his arms
but I didn't know what he meant
and, ordinarily I would not have been so forward
with a woman
but after all she was the one who wanted to meet me
so I said
then how about lunch the next day or dinner
or lunch the day after that or tea
or breakfast the following day
so that finally she said she would have lunch with
me
on the following Friday
and I said good, perfect, good,
and she excused herself to say hello to someone
else
and after she had gone
my friend said to me,
that was the wrong Maria.

But, of course, it wasn't at all.

EDMUND
I remember when -this was a few years ago
when women wore panty hose -
and Maria and Frank and I went to a casino together
and I was wearing my loafers without socks
and, for some reason, the guy at the door decided

to pick on me
and he said I couldn't come into the casino without
socks
and I said that's completely demented
because look at all the women you have in the
casino without socks
and it sort of got ugly really fast
and so Maria took my arm
and led me away from what was getting to be really
nasty
and told me to wait for her for a minute
and she went into the women's room and took off
her panty hose
and came out and gave them to me
and told me to put them on right over my shoes
and my pants
which I did
because I was always happy to do whatever she told
me
and then she took me back to the door of the casino
and said to the guy
there, now he's wearing socks
so there was nothing the guy could do but let us in.

HILDA
All right, all right,
these are lovely memories
but it seems a little easy
to be cozily consoling yourselves like this
as though the only thing that matters is how sad
you feel

when what you did was to drive a woman to
distraction
with all your bad behavior
bad, childish behavior
and these memories are not going to bring her back
here was a wonderful woman
and none of you appreciated her
none of you got past your own petty little feelings
to understand here was a life worth honoring and
esteeming
worth keeping from all harm
keeping alive with you forever and ever
because none of you will ever know another person
as vital as she was

you should spend the rest of your lives doing
penance now
mourning her death
and chastising yourselves for your self-centeredness
and your pettiness
these little, little emotions that have such big
consequences
that cost other people their very lives on earth
in the olden days you would have worn ashes and
sack cloth
and a good thing it would have been.

FRANK
It's true. What you say is true.

FRANCOIS
Very true.

FRANK
There's no bottom to it.

HILDA
I think this is the time for everyone to rend their garments.

FRANK
Rend our garments?

HILDA
Yes, rend your garments.
Show your grief.
Never mind your lovely clothes.
You have lost the woman you love.
Rend your garments.
This is a ritual that was done in ancient times.

BOB
Yes, we've done that, too, in some of our services.
People seem to like it.
They feel better after they've done it.
I guess the ancients knew what works.

EDMUND
I don't think I'm going to rend my garments.

ARIEL
I don't know how to rend a garment.

FRANK
I'm going to rend my garments.

JONATHAN
I'm going to rend my garments, too.

EDMUND
Fine then, I'm going to rend my garments, too.

FRANCOIS
Let's all rend our garments.

ARIEL
I'm rending my garments.

HILDA
I'll show you how.

[she takes hold of a piece of her dress
and, the very instant she rends it,
and everyone tears their clothes to shreds
[they all have on bright, flowered, colorful
underwear]

music comes up at full, deafening volume:
O mio babbino caro from Gianni Schicchi:

Edmund sings:
O mio babbino caro
Mi piace e bello, bello;
Vo'andare in Porta Rosa
a comperar l'anello!

Everyone joins him in singing:
Si, si, ci voglio andare!
e se l'amassi andaro,
andrei sul Ponte Vecchio
Ma per buttarmi in Arno!

as Maria enters -unseen by the others -

and, finally,
Maria sings the very last phrase of the aria,
at full volume
and with immense passion:
Mi struggo e mi tormento!
O Dio, vorrei morir!

Silence.]

FRANK
Maria!

FRANCOIS
Maria!
Is it really you?

FRANK
Is it true?

EDMUND
Is it some sort of hoax?

JONATHAN
Is this some horrible trick?

FRANK
Maria.
You're alive.
You really are alive.

FRANCOIS
It's really you!

FRANK
Thank God, you're alive.

Oh, Maria, what happened?

FRANCOIS
How did you get out?

[Everyone goes to Maria to kiss her
and hug her.]

FRANK
We thought you were gone forever.
Thank God you've come back.

JONATHAN
We looked for you and looked for you and looked
for you
and we thought we would never find you.

FRANCOIS
I should have known you would find a way.

BOB
Is this the deceased, then?

FRANK
How could we have given up?
I told you we should have kept looking for her!
How could we have given up?
Oh, thank God you're alright.

ARIEL
How did you get dry?

EDMUND
Did you just come out of the lake?

ARIEL
You've had time to change?

MARIA
I never was in the lake!
Hilda only said I was to see how you would feel
if I were dead.

FRANK
Hilda?

EDMUND
After we were so nice to you when you fell in
you thought this was a good trick to play on us?

MARIA
Because every single one of you
was so consumed by jealousy and suspicion
you were ruining your lives
forgetting how lucky you are
each one of you
to have found someone who cares for you so
completely
this thing that people live for
and some never find ever in their lives
each one of you already has it
and then you would throw it away
and it would be gone forever
and you would die alone
and what would have been the point?
But none of you would stop
even for a moment

to consider what you really had
until you realized
oh
I could die
and it would be over
and now suddenly I see what was possible for me
as long as I was alive
so now
maybe you can thank god for your good luck
for what you have
and savor it
before it's too late.

FRANCOIS
This was a cheap trick.
How can you just jerk us around?

MARIA
Francois, you have jerked so many people around.

FRANCOIS
Not on purpose.
Never on purpose.

MARIA
All the time on purpose!

JONATHAN
Mother, how could you do this?

EDMUND
It was very sly, I have to admit.

FRANK [gently, not accusingly]
You gave us a scare
you broke our hearts
all of us
you plunged us into thoughts of the end of our
own lives.

FRANCOIS
I tell you what, Maria:
now I will never trust you again.
So
I am out of here.
Forget it.
I am out of here.

[he leaves]

MARIA
Francois!

JONATHAN
I don't understand how you could do a thing like
this.
You've never tricked me like this.
How can you do this?

[Francois returns]

FRANCOIS
If you want to know who feels betrayed now
I'll tell you:
I feel betrayed!
Everyone feels betrayed by you!

You think you can frighten me like this?
I thought you were dead!
So, now, you have what you want!
No one will bother you anymore
because no one will ever live in the same house
with you again!

[he leaves again]

MARIA
Francois!

JONATHAN
And neither will I, this is not my house any more.
This is not how you treat your own child
so that he can't count on anyone any more
or ever learn to trust another person
if he can't trust his own mother!

BOB
Maria, it may be that you can't just play with people
like this
because other people are people, too.
They have feelings, too, just as you do.
They thought they never could go on with their
lives.
They thought they would live forever in sorrow.

FRANK [again, gently, not accusingly]
I thought I would end my own life.
But it doesn't matter.
Nothing matters
as long as you are alive.

[Francois returns]

FRANCOIS
No one is ever even going to speak to you again.
I am going to tell everyone I know what you have done
and no one will want to be your friend anymore!

MARIA
What are you saying
I have to kill myself again to get your attention?

[silence]

The next time I die it will be the real thing
this is your chance right now
if you don't take it, it's gone forever.

ARIEL
We are glad to see you back.

MARIA
Thank you.

FRANCOIS
You are right, you are right of course
what is this remorse and anger
when we could be feeling relief
and joy!
Because you are alive again!
And this is a happy time!

[music;

Francois instantly pulls his shorts down to expose

his butt;
looks at Hilda;
she pulls her shorts down to expose her butt;
and the two of them dance
a sort of fraudulent flamenco dance,
moving toward one another

while we hear the Buena Vista Social Club's
El Cuarto De Tula

Everyone else pulls their shorts down to expose
their butts,
and they, too, join in the dance.

The dance transforms into a big celebratory
Dionysian dance number
until, at last,
one by one,
they sit exhausted in the chairs,

and the two tables come in from the sides
to form a banquet table at which they sit,

and we begin to hear fireworks in the distance.]

HILDA
And now we can have our party.
Bertha and I have been planning a Viking feast
for New Year's.

[some of the guests pick up party hats from the
table
and put them on

Music for the Royal Fireworks from Handel
Greatest Hits
plays through the following scene

FRANK
I would like to propose a toast

[colorful confetti rains down]

to Hilda
who has never given up on life
who has, in fact, insisted on it
and who has saved us all from drowning
and brought us all back to life with her.

[firecrackers;
and the sound of fireworks
becomes louder, more present]

HILDA
And to all of you.
May you live as long as I have
and get to be half as smart.

[music]

EDMUND
I would like to offer a toast
to the end of squabbling
the end of jealousy
the end of suspicions
to the new times of gratitude
for what we have.

[all raise their glasses]

FRANCOIS
I will drink to that absolutely.
I will drink and drink to that.
Because I am grateful to you, Maria,
for being alive.
That's all.
You don't need to do anything else
if only you are alive
every morning I will thank God for that

FRANK
And so will I.

MARIA
And I will drink to you, Francois,
and I will never distrust you again
even though I know
you are not to be trusted
because I love you.

FRANK
Oh!

MARIA
I love you, too, Frank.
But I realized while I was gone,
if I am going to die,
I need to die with Francois.

FRANCOIS
So, OK, it's good. OK.

I am going to die with you.

MARIA
But first I am going to take you to the other room
and knock you down
and have my way with you.

FRANCOIS
So. OK. Good.
What could be wrong with that?

[she takes him by the hand
and they leave]

FRANK
Maria!

[he gets up to follow Maria,

stops,

watches her go with Francois,

turns back to the table,

sits, his head in his hands;

Edmund watches him for a moment.]

EDMUND
I had a dream
that I finally agreed to let you kill me, Frank.

FRANK
Oh, Edmund.

EDMUND
I took off all my clothes
and you went into the kitchen and came back with
the butcher knife
and you stabbed me all over my body.
78 wounds.
And then you left.
and I put on my white bathrobe
and lay down on the deck
so that the blood would run down between the
wooden slats.
And I closed my eyes and waited.
But there wasn't any blood.
I opened the robe to look at my wounds
and they were all gaping wide but no blood was
coming out.
And then people started arriving for dinner.
and they just stepped over me on their way into the
house
and no one noticed me.
So then I closed my eyes again and waited.
and then I stood up and jumped up and down to
get the blood running
but still no blood came out.
The maitre d' was getting impatient.
He said if I wasn't going to die, I should do
something useful
so I started seating people in the main dining room
and handing out menus
but then one lady said to me,

you better get over to blah blah hospital and see
doctor blah blah
he's the only one who can get rid of those scars.
And I thought: my god, she's right,
if I live, I don't want to have these scars
so I ran out into the streets to get a taxi
but there were no cabs in the streets
and I was panicked
so I started running and screaming for help
and then I fell face first onto the pavement
and I couldn't get up
and that was when I knew that it had worked
that you had finally killed me.

[Edmund picks up his suitcase and ice skates

and leaves]

BOB
Hey, hold up! I'll drive you!

[Frank turns to see Edmund is gone.]

BERTHA
Well!
So much for your Viking party!

HILDA
As swift as a Viking raid!

BERTHA
These people should show a little more appreciation
for all the trouble you've gone to.

HILDA
I know they feel it in their hearts.

BERTHA
I think they should be showing you a little more
outward recognition.

HILDA
Now, now...

BERTHA
A little more gratitude.

HILDA
Come, Bertha, you're getting grouchy staying up
this late.
These young people can stay up till all hours if they
like.
But it's past our bedtime.
Come, come, I'm putting you to bed.
Say goodnight to these nice young people.
Happy New Year to you, Jonathan,
and to you, Ariel.

BERTHA
Happy New Year.
Happy New Year.

ARIEL
Thank you.
And to you.

[As Hilda and Bertha leave, they speak.]

BERTHA
I am not grouchy.

HILDA
Bertha, you were born grouchy
you live in a snit
and you will die in a huff.

BERTHA
I never heard such a thing.

[they are gone]

FRANK
You think if you had your life to live over again
you could make it turn out right;
but then, for some of us, it turns out to be exactly
the same
no matter how many chances we get.

[he puts his head in his hands]

JONATHAN
Ariel.

ARIEL
Yes.

JONATHAN
Do you still love me?

ARIEL
I love you again.

[They kiss,

while the music and the fireworks

and the rain of confetti continue

and the lights fade on the couple

and on Frank, with his head in his hands.]

A NOTE ON THE TEXT:
Wintertime was deeply affected by reading Anne Carson's Eros the Bittersweet.

FIRE ISLAND

This play is written to be performed on stage,
as a film, and on the internet.

First, here is an indication of one way it could be
done on stage, And, after this, is a suggestion of
one way it can be done on the internet.

For the stage,
there is a big screen filling the entire back wall.
The screen will be greatly obscured by set pieces,
but around the corners of the set pieces,
and for the entirety of the play
can be seen a projected Hollywood romance,
perhaps Casablanca or some other film in the
public domain.

There is another large screen on the stage,
and two small television sets.

It could be that one of the television sets has another movie on
for the entirety of the play,
or it shows us the beach for the whole of the play,
or it goes from beach to movie to golf tournament, etc.

At the opening of the play, on the large onstage screen,
we see a movie of the first scene of the play (see the dialogue below).

It takes place on the ferry going to Fire Island
and follows these two characters as they get off the ferry
and walk along the boardwalk
to the summer house where most of the play will take place.

Just inside the theatre door,
the two actors are picked up, as they enter, by a live videographer
who follows them onstage,
filming them (and following them) as they walk onstage
and finish the scene.

There is a second couple in the living room ,
and they pick up with the second scene
as the first couple passes through the room-
the woman going off, as she says, to get a cup of coffee,

the man standing, uncertainly for a moment,
and then taking his suitcase to another room.

And the second couple gives way to a third couple
coming in from the beach.

And, at the end of the third couple's scene,
the woman from the third couple sits down in the
living room,
and watches the fourth couple do their scene on
the television.

And then the videographer is filming, live,
the fifth couple in the bedroom
and that film is shown on the large onstage screen.

And that gives way to the sixth couple live onstage.

And the seventh couple might simply be overheard
as voiceovers
while the camera pans the beach.

So we have then, for example:

A couple walking on the beach.
Another couple on the beach.
A couple having drinks on the porch.
A couple in the ocean waves.
A couple in a bar.
Another couple on the beach.
A couple at dinner.
A couple on the porch in the evening.
A couple in bed together.
Another couple in bed together?

And so forth.
Some on stage, some on television, some on the
bigger screen.

We see some couples we have seen before
in the background of the new couples scenes.

And, as we go along,
we return to some of the couples,
for a second or third scene.

In this way, the scenes tumble on, one after another,
in the house, outside the house, on the beach,
offstage -in a bedroom, for example,
and sometimes in what is frankly seen as a dressing
room.

The last scene will then be filmed
so that we see the last couple leave the house,
after their weekend on Fire Island,
walk along the boardwalk,
and get back on the ferry.

FOR THE FILM:

The film wants to feel like a single, continuous
tracking shot,
moving from couple to couple without a break.
An inexpensive, handheld, digital film.

FOR THE INTERNET:

Once these scenes have been filmed,
they can be put on the internet

in such a way that we see what are the first and
last scenes
that frame the event as a whole,

but the other scenes can be called up at will, at
random,

sometimes simultaneously on split screens
so that, among other things,
we can listen to one scene, while we watch another.

For the internet, too,
animations, popups, scene and character lists (for
navigation)
and other features can be added,
and, with the dialogue shown on the screen,
or with new dialogue they write themselves,
people can also film their own boy/girl, boy/boy,
girl/girl scenes-with the little camera eye on their
imacs or on their cell phones
and put them into the play.

Or they can join in a scene already filmed,
So that they dub themselves in for the dialogue
With one of the actors or actresses in the film.

And then, too, there are the random scenes
That come in any order,
Not because they are part of any particular story
But because they are part of the whole story,
And we know what they mean:
1. We see a woman walking on the beach weeping,
   while we hear a love song.

2. Or we see her walk into the ocean while we hear a love song.

3. We see a woman throwing three hundred plates and glasses against a wall.

4. We see a door in its frame-no room, no building, just a door in a free-standing frame, and a guy slams it, then another guy comes along and slams it, then a woman slams it, then a guy slams it over and over and over, then a guy looks at a woman, and steps through the door, slamming it behind him, and so forth.

5. A guy has a wooden box on the porch; he breaks one wine bottle after another by throwing it into the box-two dozen wine bottles-and then he sticks his head down into the box.

6. A woman lies on her back, seemingly comatose, a TV on her stomach.

7. A woman in a nice black dress Comes into the living room,
   Picks up the floor lamp and dances with it to a love song.

8. A woman in bikini underwear runs through the living room and out,
   Runs back through the living room and out,
   Back through the living room and out,
   Back through the living room and out onto the porch,
   down the path to the beach,
   while Yesterday plays.

9. A woman lifts her dress up above her head

hiding her upper body entirely
exposing herself from the waist down
and takes a long, slow exit from the living room.

10. A woman stands looking at a man who throws himself repeatedly to the floor.
Finally she throws herself to the floor along with him.
But at last she leaves,
leaving him to go on until he is exhausted.

11. Guys on the beach go into a football huddle-while the football lies in the middle of the huddle.
Then they all grapple violently in the huddle with the ball and fall down-and just that is the football play

12. 2 guys jump up and down
up and down
up and down
mostly harmoniously, and happily, not competitively.

13. A bunch of guys sit on plastic chairs on a lawn
Or on the beach, Looking out at the water,
Listening to deafening music.
A woman walks among the guys,
yelling about something, but the deafening music drowns her out.

14. A guy in a clown outfit stops a woman on the beach,
not letting her pass, gesturing at his cheek until she finally puckers up to kiss his cheek and he

turns his head and kisses her full on the mouth.
15. A guy on the beach in a wet suit with suspenders
    holding a wash tub around his waist
    And a shower over his head
    carrying a placard saying: Don Quixote.
16. A clown on his hands and knees barking at a dog
17. An Asian woman appears in the living room
    in a chinky/junky outfit looking like one of the
    dancers from the Strange Mushroom company.
    She looks at herself in a full-length mirror.
    And then she leaves.
    She returns a few moments later in a red shirt,
    white undies
    with a pillow in her arms
    and turns abruptly and leaves at once.
    She returns wearing a white shirt and tie and
    glasses
    like an office worker -
    as though, all this time,
    she has been trying out identities that will be
    acceptable.
    Finally she returns for the last time
    this time only in white underpants.
18. 3 naked people at a dinner table
    -and one woman at the table in evening clothes:
    a snapshot of weekend society.
19. A long piano solo under the stars.
    A vast, empty, dark space full of heartache.
    ....and so forth.

Of course, for the stage version,

these performance pieces can be seen on the
television screens,
or they can be done live in the intervals between
the couples scenes.

Or not.

MUSIC:

For music throughout the piece,
as background songs,
and, sometimes, as songs for a couple to dance by,
in the living room or on the beach,
or to stroll on the beach,
certainly for an opening song
while we are on the ferry
and at the end, when we are on the ferry again,
one good possibility is all the songs by one person:
the incredibly deep-voiced throat singer from the
Russian Federation of Tuva,
Albert Kuvezin and Yat-Kha
doing covers of
Love Will Tear Us Apart,
Ramblin Man,
Her Eyes Are a Blue Million Miles
When the Levee Breaks
and Play With Fire.

Or not.

1. Lydia and Nikos
Nikos and Lydia
are talking as they arrive
and get settled.

NIKOS
I thought,
I've always liked you, Lydia
seeing you with your sisters
sometimes in the summers
when our families would get together at the beach.
I thought you were fun, and funny
and really good at volleyball

LYDIA
Volleyball?

NIKOS
which I thought showed you have a
well,
a natural grace
and beauty
and a lot of energy.

LYDIA
Oh.

NIKOS
And it's not that I thought I fell in love with you at
the time
or that I've been like a stalker or something in the
background
all these years.

LYDIA
No, I never....

NIKOS
But really, over the years,

I've thought back from time to time
how good it felt just to be around you.

LYDIA
Oh.

NIKOS
And so I thought: well, maybe this is an okay way
to have a marriage

LYDIA
A marriage.

NIKOS
to start out
not in a romantic way, but
as a friendship

LYDIA
Oh.

NIKOS
because I admire you

and I thought perhaps this might grow
into something deeper
and longer lasting

LYDIA
Oh.

NIKOS
but maybe this isn't quite the thing you want
and really I don't want to force myself on you
you should be free to choose

I mean: obviously.

LYDIA
Thank you.

NIKOS
Although I think I should say
what began as friendship for me
and a sort of distant, even inattentive regard
has grown into a passion already

LYDIA
A passion.

NIKOS
I don't know how
or where it came from, or when
but somehow the more I felt this admiration
and, well, pleasure in you

LYDIA
Pleasure.

NIKOS
seeing you become the person that you are
I think a thoughtful person and smart
and it seems to me funny and warm

LYDIA
Funny.

NIKOS
and passionate, I mean about the things
I heard you talk about in school

a movie or playing the piano
I saw you one night at a cafe by the harbor
drinking almond nectar
and I saw that happiness made you raucous.
And I myself don't want to have a relationship
that's cool or distant
I want a love really that's all-consuming
that consumes my whole life

LYDIA
Your whole life.

NIKOS
and the longer the sense of you has lived with me
the more it has grown into a longing for you
so I wish you'd consider
maybe not marriage
because it's true you hardly know me
but a kind of courtship

LYDIA
A courtship.

NIKOS
or, maybe you'd just I don't know
go sailing with me or see a movie

LYDIA
Gee, Nikos,
you seem to talk a lot.

NIKOS
I talk too much.
I'm sorry.

LYDIA
Sometimes it seems to me
men get all caught up
in what they're doing
and they forget to take a moment
and look around
and see what effect they're having
on other people.

NIKOS
That's true.

LYDIA
They get on a roll.

NIKOS
I do that sometimes.
I wish I didn't.
But I get started on a sentence,
and that leads to another sentence,
and then, the first thing I know,
I'm just trying to work it through,
the logic of it,
follow it through to the end
because I think,
if I stop,
or if I don't get through to the end
before someone interrupts me
they won't understand what I'm saying
and what I'm saying isn't necessarily wrong-
it might be, but not necessarily,
and if it is, I'll be glad to be corrected,

or change my mind-
but if I get stopped along the way
I get confused
I don't remember where I was
or how to get back to the end of what I was saying.

LYDIA
I understand.

NIKOS
And I think sometimes I scare people
because of it
they think I'm so, like determined
just barging ahead-
not really a sensitive person,
whereas, in truth,
I am.

LYDIA
I know.

I'm getting a cup of coffee, Nikos.

NIKOS
Now?

[she puts a hand reassuringly on his arm -
she's genuinely friendly and warm towards him]

LYDIA
I'll be right back.

[he is left alone

to his amazement he overhears two other people

having a conversation on almost the same subject
he has just been having]

2. Henry and Yvette
[they speak with French or Spanish accents]

HENRY
I wonder:
would you marry me
or
would you have a coffee with me
and think of having a conversation
that would lead to marriage?

YVETTE
Oh.
Well,
a coffee with you
I would have a coffee with you.

HENRY
You are free now?

YVETTE
Free now? No, well, no
right now
I am busy.

HENRY
OK then maybe later this evening?

YVETTE
Well, later this evening also I am busy.

HENRY
Or late supper.
Or breakfast tomorrow
or lunch or tea in the afternoon
or a movie
or dinner the day after
Thursday for lunch
or Friday dinner
or perhaps you would go for the weekend with me
to my parents' home in Provence
or we could stop along the way
and find a little place for ourselves
to be alone.

YVETTE
I don't think I can be alone.

HENRY
With me?
Or by yourself?
You don't like to be alone by yourself?

YVETTE
No, I mean with you this weekend.

HENRY
Oh.
Or then just we could
have coffee over and over again
every day
until we get to know one another
and we have the passage of the seasons

in the cafe
we could celebrate our anniversary
and then perhaps you would forget
that you are not married to me
and we can have a child.

YVETTE
A child?

HENRY
Because
don't you think
after we have been together for a year
it will be time to start to think of these things?

YVETTE
We haven't been together for a day.

HENRY
You know, I have known many women.
I mean, I don't mean to say....

YVETTE
No.

HENRY
I mean just
you know
my mother, my grandmother
my sisters
and also women I have known romantically
and then, too, friends,
and even merely acquaintances

but you know
in life
one meets many people
and it seems to me
we know so much of another person
in the first few moments we meet
not from what a person says alone
but from the way they hold their head
how they listen
what they do with their hand as they speak
or when they are silent
and years later
when these two people break up
they say
I should have known from the beginning
in truth
I did know from the beginning
I saw it in her, or in him
the moment we met
but I tried to repress the knowledge
because it wasn't useful at the time
because,
for whatever reason
I just wanted to go to bed with her as fast as I could
or I was lonely
and so I pretended I didn't notice
even though I did
exactly the person she was from the first moment
I knew
and so it is with you

and I think probably it is the same for you with me
we know one another
right now from the first moment
we know so much about one another in just this
brief time
and we have known many people
and for myself
I can tell
you are one in a million
and I want to marry you
I want to marry you
and have children with you
and grow old together
so I am begging you
just have a coffee with me.

YVETTE
OK.

HENRY
When will you do this?

YVETTE
Right now.

HENRY
Oh.
Oh, good.
Good.

[he kisses her hand]

Good.
Good.

[Wilson rushes in.]
3. Wilson and Susan

WILSON
How could you just suddenly: disappear?

SUSAN
I didn't.

WILSON
I thought you did.
And I thought you loved me.

SUSAN
Well, I do love you.

WILSON
Yes, you love me,
but you don't love me in that way.

SUSAN
I never pretended to love you in that way.

WILSON
I can't go on in life
without being loved in that way.

SUSAN
A lot of people are never loved in that way.

WILSON
How can you tell
if you are really alive
if you're never loved in that way?

SUSAN
What do you mean: in that way?

WILSON
Unless I thought you were crazy for me
so crazy for me you couldn't stand it
you just had to kiss me
you just had to knock me down and kiss me
because you couldn't stand it
that you laughed at my jokes
or thought I was so cool
or like said really intelligent things that made you
think
maybe not all of those things
but even just any one of them
just one of them

[Silence.]

You see what I mean, not even one.

SUSAN
I'm sorry.

WILSON
Why did you live with me, then?

SUSAN
I thought I loved you
but I guess I didn't know what love was.
I liked you in a way
not much
but in some ways

or at least in the ways I thought guys could
be likeable
and the rest of it I thought maybe that's just
how guys are
and as time went on maybe it wouldn't matter so
much
but then I find it does matter
I can't help myself
some stuff you do
I just can't get over it
and the stuff I liked:
that I thought you were a responsible person
and mature
solid and dependable
all those turned out not to be true at all
so what am I left with?

WILSON
It's not your fault.

SUSAN
No, it's not.

WILSON
Or maybe it is
that you weren't thinking very clearly
or being very focused when you made your choice
and a lot of people were depending on that choice
being really clear
or at least I was

SUSAN
I know.

I'm sorry.

WILSON
Being sorry doesn't cut it somehow.
I know people always say they're sorry
and probably they are
and I don't think it means nothing
I'm sure it means something
and it's essential for people to feel it
and to say it
in order for life to go on at all
and yet
the truth is
it doesn't cut it.
I'm sorry: but it doesn't.

SUSAN
I'm sorry.

WILSON
Is that somehow now
supposed to cut it?

[Wilson storms out.]

4. Constantine and Thyona

CONSTANTINE
What do you think?
You think you live in a world nowadays where
you can throw out a promise
just because you don't feel like keeping it?

Just because
drugs are rife
gambling is legal
medicine is euthanasia
birth is abortion
homosexuality is the norm
pornography is piped into everybody's home on
the internet
now you think you can do whatever you want
whenever you want to do it
no matter what the law might say?

I don't accept that.

Sometimes I like to lie down at night
with my arms around someone
and KNOW she is there for me
know this gives her pleasure -
my arms around her
her back to me
my stomach pressed against her back
my face buried in her hair
one hand on her stomach
feeling at peace.

That's my plan
to have that.
I'll have my bride.
If I have to have her arms tied behind her back
and dragged to me
I'll have her back.

What is it you women want
you want to be strung up with hoods and gags and
blindfolds
stretched out on a board with weights on your chest
you want me to sew your legs to the bed
and pour gasoline on you
and light you on fire
is that what I have to do to keep you?

The future is going to happen, Thyona,
whether you like it or not.
You say, you don't want to be taken against your
will.
People are taken against their will every day.
Do you want tomorrow to come?
Do you want to live in the future?
Never mind. You can't stop the clock.
Tomorrow will take today by force
whether you like it or not.
Time itself is an act of rape.
Life is rape.
No one asks to be born.
No one asks to die.
We are all taken by force, all the time.
You make the best of it.
You do what you have to do.

5. Edmund and Herbert

EDMUND
I think you are lying to me, Herbert.

You are always lying to me
because you wish something would be true
but it isn't.
You are a weak spineless person, Herbert,
feckless, feeble and ineffective.

But I love you like a cicada.

HERBERT
A cicada?

EDMUND
Yes.

HERBERT
Like a grasshopper you mean?

EDMUND
Do you know what a cicada is?

HERBERT
I thought I did.

EDMUND
There was a time long ago, in prehistoric times
when cicadas were human beings
back before the Muses were born.
And then when the Muses were born
and song came into being
some of these human creatures were so taken by
the pleasure of it
that they sang and sang and sang.
And they forgot to eat or drink
they just sang and sang

and so,
before they knew it,
they died.

And from those human creatures a new species
came into being
the cicadas
and they were given this special gift from the
Muses:
that from the time they are born
they need no nourishment
they just sing continuously
caught forever in the pleasure of the moment
without eating or drinking
until they die.

This is the story of love.
If you stay there forever in that place
you die of it.

That's why people
can't stay in love.

But that's how I've loved you.
And how I love you now.
And how I always will.

6. Phil the Trucker and His Girl

PHIL, THE TRUCKER
I look at you and I think
if it wouldn't be wrong

I'd like to make love with you on a pool table.

HIS GIRL
It wouldn't be wrong if you'd let me handcuff you
to the pockets.

PHIL, THE TRUCKER
You could do that.

HIS GIRL
What I think about is
I'd like to have sex with you in the parking lot
behind the Exxon station
near that diner on the Malibu highway
you know the one?

PHIL, THE TRUCKER
Near that road up into the canyon.

HIS GIRL
That's the one.

PHIL, THE TRUCKER
That would be pretty public.

HIS GIRL
I'd like to have the whole world see
you want me so much
you can't wait.
I'd like to have the whole world see
you're not ashamed of me.

PHIL, THE TRUCKER
Why would I be ashamed of you?

HIS GIRL
I feel ashamed myself.

PHIL, THE TRUCKER
For what reason?

HIS GIRL
Who knows?
Every fifteen minutes I feel ashamed of myself at least once.
And humiliated.
For no reason.
It just comes back to me over and over again.
Do you ever feel that way?

PHIL, THE TRUCKER
Every fifteen minutes I feel worried.

HIS GIRL
Do you feel you want to hurt someone?

PHIL, THE TRUCKER
No.

HIS GIRL
Do you feel you want to get even?

PHIL, THE TRUCKER
No.

HIS GIRL
That's good.
Do you feel you want to bite something?

PHIL, THE TRUCKER
I don't think so.
Maybe I feel that.

HIS GIRL
Do you feel you want to take off all your clothes?

PHIL, THE TRUCKER
No.
I usually don't feel that.

HIS GIRL
Do you feel you want more money?

PHIL, THE TRUCKER
Oh, sure. Everybody feels that.

[Hiroko comes up to Catherine]

7. Hiroko and Catherine
HIROKO
I'm glad to see you again.

CATHERINE
So you say.
And yet
I don't know how it could be true.

HIROKO
How could it not be true?

CATHERINE
Because if you were glad to see me
you would never have left me.

HIROKO
Of course I would.

CATHERINE
No, because
if you love someone
you don't leave them.
You hold onto them for dear life
you hold onto them forever
unless you are a stupid person
which I don't think you are
so
what else can I think
except you never really loved me
I was just another one of your flings along the way
whereas I loved you
I knew
if you love someone
you don't let them go

HIROKO
And yet you did.

CATHERINE
I never did.

HIROKO
You said:
if one day you are going to leave me
then go now
don't just keep tormenting me.

CATHERINE
And so?

JACQUEINE
And so.
It's not that I left you.

CATHERINE
Excuse me.
I didn't leave you.
And yet, you are not with me.
What else happened?

HIROKO
It turned out
we were at different points in our lives
we couldn't go on.

CATHERINE
I could have gone on.

HIROKO
Shall we talk about something else?

CATHERINE
I see
in the world
people have wars and they die
entire countries come to an end
Etienne has died of cancer

HIROKO
I didn't know.

CATHERINE
How could you?
And yet
there it is.
And one day I will die
and so will you.
And yet
you could leave me.
I don't understand.
I will never understand
how it is if you have only one life to live
and you find your own true love
the person all your life you were meant to find
and your only job then was to cherish that person
and care for that person
and never let go
but it turns out
you can still think
for some reason
because this or that
you end it
you end it forever
you end it for the only life you will ever live on
earth.
Maybe if you would be reincarnated
and you could come back to life again and again a
dozen times
then this would make sense
to throw away your only chance for love in this life
because you would have another chance in
another life

but when this is your only chance
how can this make sense?

Do you think
there will ever be a time
when we could get back together?

HIROKO
No.

CATHERINE
Not ever?

HIROKO
No.

CATHERINE
Not ever at all
even ever?

HIROKO
No.

CATHERINE
And yet
this is so hard for me to accept.

More than anything
I love to lie in bed with you at night
and look at your naked back
and stroke your back slowly
from your neck to your coccyx
and let my fingers fan out
and drift over your smooth buttock

and slip slowly down along your thigh
to your sweet knee
only to return again
coming up the back of your thigh
hesitating a moment
to let my fingers rest in the sweet valley
at the very top of your thigh, just below your
buttock
and so slowly up along the small of your back
to your shoulder blade
and then to let your hair tickle my face
as I put my lips to your shoulder
and kiss you and kiss you and kiss you forever
this is what I call heaven
and what I hope will last forever

[Hiroko stands to leave]

HIROKO
I love you, Catherine.
I have never loved anyone in my life as I have loved
you
and I know I never will.
But we cannot be together.

[she leaves;
Catherine watches her go.]

8. Harold and Edith

Harold lies stretched out over several chairs.

After a few moments, Edith enters.]

EDITH
Shove up.

HAROLD [awakened from sleeping -still half-asleep, disoriented]
What?

EDITH
Shove up I said shove up.

HAROLD
What what?

EDITH
I want to sit down here.

HAROLD
Goddam it to hell, this is my God Damn place.
Can't you see I am sleeping here?

EDITH
This is not your God Damn place.
This is a common place
and I said:
[shrieking]
shove up!!!

HAROLD [shouting]
Can't you see
I am trying to sleep in peace?

EDITH
You want peace?

You want peace?
Go someplace else.

HAROLD
I did go someplace else.
This is where I went.

EDITH
I am going to explain this to you:
I am not the sort of person who looks at a man and thinks
oh, I could take him on
make a project out of him
fix him up
he looks okay to me
not too disgusting
I am going to reason with the sonofabitch.
No.
This is not who I am.
I am the sort of person who says shove up
or
[she starts trying to kick him]
I will kick you black and blue,
because I am tired of walking around!

HAROLD
Okay, okay, sit.

[he makes room for her]

EDITH
Thank you.

HAROLD
Do we know each other?

EDITH
No. No, we do not.

[she rummages through her stuff,
brings out a bottle]

Sherry?

HAROLD
What?

EDITH
Are you hard of hearing?

HAROLD
What?

EDITH
Can't you hear too well?

HAROLD [shouting]
What does that have to do with it?
I don't enjoy the opera any more, if that's what you
mean.
Or the symphony.
I used to go to Ravinia.
Do you know Ravinia?

EDITH
Ravinia.

HAROLD
Outdoors, in the summertime

every Friday night.
Fritz Reiner conducting.
You remember Fritz Reiner?

EDITH
Of course I remember Fritz Reiner.

HAROLD
That was lovely.
You know, lying out on the lawn listening to the music.
Mozart, all those fellows.
Like the Grand Canyon, you know,
a marvel of nature, that's all,
a complete breakthrough of the divine
or whatever, you know,
if you believe in that sort of thing.

EDITH
I don't.

HAROLD
Well, then, a breakthrough of the human.
But that's all gone
now that I can't hear a thing
you know there's a lot you can't enjoy any more.
When you get down to it, at my age,
I don't see so well either.

EDITH
Well, it's the end of an era.

HAROLD
That's for sure.

The end of a way of life.

EDITH
An entire way of life.

HAROLD
The end of poetry.

EDITH
Of the book itself.

HAROLD
Yes, well....

EDITH
Don't go gentle into that good night!

HAROLD
No. No. Right you are.

EDITH
Would you like a little nip of sherry?

HAROLD
Well.
Yes.
Okay.
Thank you.
Very kind of you.

9. Riff: The Boys

GEORGE [speaking to Joseph]
You know, you'll be wanting to go slow with girls

because

STEVE
Because you can scare a girl

GEORGE
You can scare anyone really.

STEVE
You can scare anyone.

GEORGE
And you don't want always
to be looking at women out the window

STEVE
The passersby on the sidewalk.

GEORGE
Because this can give a bad impression.

STEVE
You can scare a person.

PHIL
Do you ever take a girl home with you?

JOSEPH
Yes.

STEVE
And what do you do?

JOSEPH
Well, usually,
we will sit in the kitchen.

GEORGE
Yes?

JOSEPH
We will have tea usually.

STEVE
Tea?

PHIL
That's all?

JOSEPH
And I will open the window, usually,
so the birds can fly in
and eat crumbs from the kitchen table.

GEORGE
Eat crumbs.

JOSEPH
Yes.

PHIL
During the summer.

JOSEPH
Yes, well,
yes.

GEORGE
During the winter?

JOSEPH
Well. Yes.

GEORGE
I see.

JOSEPH
People like this usually.

STEVE
And then they leave?

JOSEPH
Yes. Well, by then it will be late afternoon.
So it's time to leave.

GEORGE
Yes, well.

PHIL
Tea and crumbs.

GEORGE
Tea and crumbs.

PHIL
Still, I like an herbal tea.

GEORGE
A peppermint tea.

PHIL
Or a tisane.

GEORGE
Something made with roots and berries.

[Joseph, ever a voyeur,
watches them as they continue the conversation.]

STEVE
I would say
probably
I would have to say
licorice root
that would be my favorite root
because it contains a
thick astringent mucilage
with a little aroma
which is a very good pectoral.

PHIL
A pectoral?

STEVE
Very good for illnesses of the chest and lungs.

PHIL
Ah.

STEVE
And that happens to be
my own personal
preoccupation.

PHIL
I see.

STEVE
Whereas I don't know
for you....

PHIL
For me it would be

the hawthorn
which used to be used always
to decorate the front door on May Day

STEVE
Oh, well
but of course
also it was said to invite death indoors.

PHIL
No.

STEVE
Yes.

PHIL
No.

STEVE
I am afraid so.
I mean, excuse me, but
I am an herbalist.

PHIL
Still.

STEVE
No. There is no getting around it.

GEORGE
I would have to say
my favorite herb
would be the common quince.

STEVE
Indeed?

GEORGE
Oh, yes,
because for two reasons
you know
it was once thought to be
the forbidden fruit of the Garden of Eden.

STEVE
I knew that, yes.

GEORGE
And so it was served
at wedding feasts in ancient Rome.

STEVE
Of course.

PHIL
Of course.

GEORGE
So, to me,
it is the sexiest herb.

STEVE
Fruit.

GEORGE
I beg your pardon?

STEVE
Fruit. It is a fruit.

Not an herb.

GEORGE
Oh yes, fruit.
I thought we could mention either herbs or fruits.

STEVE
Well, the conversation was about herbs.

GEORGE
And I brought the conversation around
to include fruits.

STEVE
If you are not going to stick to the point
I'm afraid
this is not my kind of conversation.

[he leaves;

the others look around
and, one by one, feeling uncomfortable,
they decide to leave, too]

10. Riff: The Girls

OLYMPIA
Now you see, there are men who are kind and
decent.

THYONA
You think you found this man's good side.
Men don't have a good side.

OLYMPIA
I've known men who have a good side, Thyona.
I've known men you could sit with after dinner
in front of the fireplace
and just listen to the way he speaks
and hear the gentleness in his way of speaking
and the carefulness
I've known men who think,
oh,
a woman,
I'd like to take care of her
not in any way that he thinks he is superior and has
control
but in the way that he understands
a woman is a different sort of person
and precious because of that
vulnerable in certain ways because of that
in ways that he isn't
although he might be vulnerable in other ways
because of his stuff that he has
and that he treasures what a woman has
and thinks, oh, if only I could be close to her
and feel what she feels
and see the world as she sees it
how much richer my life would be
and so, because of that, he thinks,
oh, a woman,
I can really respect her
and love her
for who she really is

THYONA
I know a man who will say I want to take care of
you
because he means he wants to use you for a while
and while he's using you
so you don't notice what he's doing
he'll take care of you as if you were a new car
before he decides to trade you in.

OLYMPIA
I've known men like that, too.
But not all men are necessarily the same.
Sometimes you can hear the whole man just in his
voice
how deep it is or how frightened
where it stops to think
and how complex and supple and sure it is
you can hear the strength in it
and you can know that you're safe

THYONA
The male
the male is a biological accident
an incomplete female
the product of a damaged gene
a half-dead lump of flesh
trapped in a twilight zone somewhere between
apes and humans
always looking obsessively for some woman

OLYMPIA
That's maybe a little bit extreme.

THYONA
any woman
because he thinks if he can make some connection
with a woman
that will make him a whole human being!
But it won't. It never will.

Boy babies should be flushed down the toilet
at birth.

11. Phil the Trucker and His Girl 2

THE TRUCKER'S GIRL
The woman next door
is having an affair with an orchestra conductor in
Cincinnati.

PHIL, THE TRUCKER
Does Cincinnati have an orchestra?

THE TRUCKER'S GIRL
I guess it does.

PHIL, THE TRUCKER
Does her husband know?

THE TRUCKER'S GIRL
He doesn't know.
She just flies off to Cincinnati from time to time
when her husband is away on business
or the conductor comes to Denver.

PHIL, THE TRUCKER
How did they meet?

THE TRUCKER'S GIRL
On an airplane.

PHIL, THE TRUCKER
What does she do?

THE TRUCKER'S GIRL
I don't know.
She flies around a lot.

PHIL, THE TRUCKER
Is she a stewardess?

THE TRUCKER'S GIRL
Oh, right.
She's a stewardess.

PHIL, THE TRUCKER
No wonder she can just go wherever she wants.

THE TRUCKER'S GIRL
Right.

PHIL, THE TRUCKER
It's a perfect job if you want to have love affairs.

THE TRUCKER'S GIRL
Right.

PHIL, THE TRUCKER
Do you think all stewardesses are having love affairs?

THE TRUCKER'S GIRL
Well, most of them probably.

PHIL, THE TRUCKER
Why not?

THE TRUCKER'S GIRL
Exactly.

PHIL, THE TRUCKER
Would you, if you were a stewardess?

THE TRUCKER'S GIRL
Yes, I think I would.

PHIL, THE TRUCKER
So would I.

THE TRUCKER'S GIRL
I have to pee.

PHIL, THE TRUCKER
What?

THE TRUCKER'S GIRL
I have to pee.
Would you wait here?

PHIL, THE TRUCKER
Oh. Sure.

[She leaves;
everyone stops what they are doing,
turn to look, and just stand around waiting for her
to come back;
we hear a flush from offstage;
finally she returns.]

THE TRUCKER'S GIRL
Times have changed.

[Everyone else resumes what they were doing.]

PHIL, THE TRUCKER
Since when?

THE TRUCKER'S GIRL
Since, oh, I don't know.

PHIL, THE TRUCKER
I don't think they have.

THE TRUCKER'S GIRL
Of course they have.

PHIL, THE TRUCKER
Well, of course they have
in the sense that now you have electric lights and
so forth
the internet
whatnot,
but otherwise I don't think times have changed.

THE TRUCKER'S GIRL
I think they have.

PHIL, THE TRUCKER
Compared to what?

THE TRUCKER'S GIRL
My grandmother.

PHIL, THE TRUCKER
You wouldn't know.

THE TRUCKER'S GIRL
That's true.
I wouldn't know.
Maybe that's what changed.
But in Russia you know
they didn't have love affairs for years
all during the communists.

PHIL, THE TRUCKER
How do you know?

THE TRUCKER'S GIRL
There was a study.
They didn't even have sex with their husbands and wives
not much.

PHIL, THE TRUCKER
Why not?

THE TRUCKER'S GIRL
They didn't feel like it.

PHIL, THE TRUCKER
Are they having sex now?

THE TRUCKER'S GIRL
Now! Well, sure. I suppose they are.
You know, things have changed in Russia.

12. Riff: Ariel Ranks on Cowboys

ARIEL
You
are an ignorant shoot from the hip cowboy
with your boots in cowshit
like a cow puncher savage
thinking you are such hot stuff
rolling your cigarette with one hand at a full gallop
but in reality you are a baby
a baby dude ranch greenhorn dweeb
who knows nothing
nothing
nothing about whatever
nothing about life
nothing about women
nothing about men
nothing about horses
you are a guy that's all
you are just a guy
I could spit at you
[she spits]
I could spit at you and spit at you
[she spits and spits]
because what you are is a typical male
I'll say no more
a typical male
you are a
typical
male
which is to say a shithook
and a dickhead

13. Riff: Personal Ads
[she picks up a magazine,
turns some pages to the back of the magazine
and reads]

Very Pretty, Stylish, Gay White Female-40-
something
seeking pretty, white, sweet, intelligent,
feminine wife, 35-45
I am a hopeless romantic
very fit, socially outgoing,
yet shy at other times.
I am mentally strong
yet emotionally tender.
I wear dresses/high heels by day
and jeans/sneakers at night.
I love excitement and spontaneity
yet balance and security.
I am financially stable and I do not look gay-
neither should you.
I am looking for a woman capable of emotional
intimacy
and committed to a partnership-
and not just after 5 PM.
I have flexible working hours
and believe weekdays were made for play, not just
work.
If you have worked on your relationship skills
and you are what I am looking for,
be prepared to meet a woman
with a generous heart, quick mind, good sense of

humor
and lots of integrity.

[she looks up from the magazine,
thinks for a moment
and then says]

I could do that.

[she returns to the magazine
and reads]

Distinguished-Looking, Successful Man-
Company president, grey hair, tall,
sense of humor.
Two residences. Variety of interests
including music, horses, sailing, etc.
and just "hanging out."
Interested in meeting woman in her 30s or early
40s,
to share good times and friendship.

[she looks up from the magazine,
thinks for a moment
and then says]

I could do that.

[she returns to the magazine
and reads]

Warm, Loving, Happy
Accomplished Professional-
very youthful, active, 55

fit, fun, full of life and love
bright, kind, sensitive,
communicative and involved,
seeks fine-valued, accomplished soul mate
to share love, laughter, family, and friends.

[she looks up from the magazine,
thinks for a moment
and then says]

I could do that.

14. Riff: Bella on the Scooter

BELLA
I had a man once
I was walking along the Apia Antica
and he came along on his motor scooter
and offered me a ride.
A skinny, ugly fellow with dark hair and big ears
and skin so sleek and smooth
I wanted to put my hands on it.
I got on the back of his motor scooter
and ten minutes later
we were in bed together at his mother's house
and I married him
and we had our boys.
All his life he worked
giving the gift of his labor to me
and to our children
he died of a heart attack

while he was out among the trees
harvesting the olives

and
if he came along now
I would get on the scooter again just like the first
time.

15. Riff: Frank on Faithfulness

FRANK
You know, one doesn't want to seize on any little
thing
some doubt one has of another's love
or faithfulness
and blow it up.
Otherwise there's no end to it.
There's something every day you can make a case
out of
if you choose.

JONATHAN
Unless it's clear someone is being unfaithful to you
and then you don't want to wander around oblivious
to the fact that you are being betrayed behind your
back.

FRANK
Still, as a grownup
one has to let the little things pass
even if sometimes some little rumor might possibly
be true

one has to let it pass for the sake of a larger love.

JONATHAN
If sometimes some rumor might be true?

FRANK
I'm not saying whether it is or it isn't.
I'm only saying
as man to man
you keep your eye on the goal line
you don't let yourself get caught up
in the details along the way.

JONATHAN
Unless, in fact, you can easily hear in the other person's voice
that she hates you.
As I could hear when Ariel spoke to me.
And then things are clear enough.

FRANK
I didn't hear that.

JONATHAN
Did you hear the way she spoke to me?

FRANK
No.

JONATHAN
The contempt in her voice.

FRANK
No.

JONATHAN
The scorn.

FRANCOIS
I didn't notice it.

FRANK
No.

FRANCOIS
This jealousy and suspicion,
it's like a rising tide,
it could swamp all boats.

JONATHAN
Did you hear her say:
"I'm not going to spend my life
defending myself against wild talk."

FRANCOIS
Perhaps it was a little wild.

JONATHAN
The sneering.
The derision in her voice.

FRANK
I didn't notice it.

JONATHAN
I did.

FRANCOIS
Still, seizing on these things -
sometimes women speak this way

even if in this case she didn't
sometimes they do
possibly sometimes we deserve it I don't know
but one lets it pass
water off a dog's back
if one wants to change the mood
and move on toward making love.

16. Riff: Bob on Fruit flies

BILL
She jumped in on purpose.

BOB
Ah. A suicide.

BILL
Yes.

BOB
Still, we don't judge people for these things.
Because a person can come into the world
different from all other people
and we don't know where such a person has come
from
like fruit flies, like worms in cheese,
they come from nowhere,
like the universe itself
which, in the beginning,
was nothing but chaos
and out of that chaos a mass was formed
just as cheese is made out of milk

and worms appeared in the cheese
and these were the angels
and among the angels was also God
he too having been created out of the cheese at the
same time
and all the creatures
of all kinds
as a result of which we have today
the inhabitants of the islands of Nacumera
who have the heads of dogs
and yet are reasonable people with good
understanding
and the pigmies
who are beautiful and graceful because of their
smallness
and they get married when they are six months old
and have children when they are two or three years
old
and do not live more than six or seven years
and they battle against the birds in their country
and often are taken and eaten by the birds.

BILL
Indeed.

BOB
And we don't judge these people
because this is how they are
just like you and me.

BILL
Yes, indeed.

BOB
We don't judge them
just as I am not judging you
and you are not judging me.
Live and let live
this was God's intention
to love all the creatures of the earth
and try not to kill them or hurt them.

17. Riff: Willy on Marriage and Red Meat

WILLY
What is the point of marriage
any more these days anyway?

MARIA
I'm sorry?

WILLY
Do they think something is going to change
because they've had a wedding?

And then everybody has the same boring thing,
with the same boring speeches,
the same boring white dress,
the same boring food.
I would rather go to a funeral than a wedding.
At a wedding
everyone is supposed to have the greatest day of
their lives
and they never do.
At a funeral no one expects to have a wonderful day

and so usually it turns out to be really nice.

why was this idea of marriage ever invented?
because women
because they have menstrual periods
are subject to chronic shortages of iron in their
systems
and so they require constant infusions of mcat
but because they were not hunters
they were never hunters
they had to find a way to manipulate men
with sexual favors
into bringing home blood-soaked dinners every
night
and if they were good at it
to marry them
to have a steady supply of meat

18. Lydia and Nikos 2

LYDIA
Do you know about dreams?

NIKOS
Well, I have dreams.

LYDIA
But do you know what they mean?

NIKOS
I don't know. Maybe.

LYDIA
I had this dream
I was going to a wedding
of these old friends of mine
and part of the wedding -uh, sort of event -
was an enormous pond that they had built,
and I was late getting to the wedding
so I got someone to airlift me in,
and I dove into the pond but,
when I landed in the water,
the walls of the pond collapsed and it drained out
and 1500 fish died,
and everyone was looking for survivors
but I had to leave to take Yeltsin to the Museum of
Modern Art,
because I had to get to the gym.

So, when I took him in to one of the exhibits
and turned around to hug him goodbye,
he turned to my mother and said,
"Wow, look at that Julian Schnabel bridge."
There was an enormous sterling silver bridge
designed by Julian Schnabel.
So I walked my mother into the water to say
goodbye to her,
and this immense 25-story high tidal wave crashed
over me
and threw me up over the Julian Schnabel bridge
and then I was completely alone in the middle of
the ocean
until I realized:

I had the cell phone tucked into my undies.
So I phoned Olympia to come and get me,
and she said, oh, perfect, I'll send Chopin-
which is the name of her dog-
I'll send Chopin over in the car,
and then would you take him for a walk
and leave the car on 8th avenue?

What do you think of that?

NIKOS
Well,
I think things happen so suddenly sometimes.

LYDIA
Sometimes people don't want to fall in love.
Because when you love someone
it's too late to set conditions.
You can't say
I'll love you if you do this
or I'll love you if you change that
because you can't help yourself
and then you have to live
with whoever it is you fall in love with
however they are
and just put up with the difficulties you've made
for yourself
because true love has no conditions.
That's why it's so awful to fall in love.

19. Wilson and Susan 2

WILSON [confronting Susan]
So
it turns out
you come to me
to be with me
and then
as soon as you feel reassured that I love you
you go back to your husband
and then if you talk to me on the phone
and I seem to be slipping away from you
if I seem anxious or uncertain
then you come back to me and make love with me
and stay with me
until you know you have me again
I can't help myself loving you
and then you go back to your husband again
so it turns out
the only way I can keep you is by making you feel
anxious
keeping you on edge
making you feel I'm about to drop you
so the way to have you
is to reject you
and if I don't reject you
then I don't have you
we are in a relationship that is sick
where you show love by showing aversion
you show aversion by showing love
so that you live a backwards life

and the one person you want to love and cherish
and show how much you care
is the one person you will drive away by doing any
of those things
how can we go on like this?
this is insane
this will make us both insane
this is how people go insane!

[He storms out.]

BECKER
I think I know how he feels myself.
I thought you cared for me, too.

SUSAN
I did care for you.
There was something about you
I don't even know what it was that just hit me
I couldn't help myself
but then it turns out
it was like a summer storm
it passed as quickly as it came
and then it was over.

BECKER
Maybe it wasn't over for me.

SUSAN
I'm sorry.

BECKER
I don't think you can just drop someone like that

and just say I'm sorry.

SUSAN
I didn't just say I'm sorry
I am sorry.

BECKER
This is why some people call women fickle.

SUSAN
I don't think it has anything to do with being fickle.
How it is for women:
Women feel what they feel when they feel it
and then when they don't feel it any more they
don't feel it.
Unlike a man
who won't know what he feels when he feels it
and then later on
he'll realize how he felt
and so he'll talk himself into feeling it again
when he doesn't feel it
because he thinks he should be consistent about
the positions he takes
and stick to them
so a man always thinks he feels things he doesn't feel
and so he never really knows how he feels at all.

BECKER
That could be true.

SUSAN
Of course it's true.
Pretty soon

you're going to thank god you had such a narrow
escape
you're going to feel lucky I dumped you

BECKER
I'm never going to feel that.

SUSAN
Maybe not.

BECKER
I think you must be a sort of a tease
or worse
some kind of seducer and dumper kind of person
who is just a loose cannon
cutting a swath through men
leaving them wrecked all around you
what is that all about?

[She speaks, with a mouth full of cake,
eating as she speaks,
with greater and greater animation as she goes on,
till she is yelling through a mouth full of cake.]

SUSAN
Maybe that would be about something
if it were in any way true
but it is not in any way true
I'm a person who is looking for true love
like anyone else
except the difference is
I am trying not to be afraid of my feelings
and censor things

and lie and lie and lie all the time
pretending I feel like this or that
going with some guy because I couldn't be sure
any more
how I felt about him
because he had some things I liked and other
things I didn't
and trying to talk myself into not caring about the
things I cared about
and caring about the things I didn't care about
because I've done that a lot in the past
so I am trying to let my feelings lead me through
life
And
feelings are feelings
they come and go.
So probably I'm just as disoriented as you are
and left in the lurch
suddenly dropped
or thrown down the stairs
it's not as though this is not a struggle for me too
but the one thing you can be sure of is
if ever I am sure of how I feel
in a way that is the kind of feeling that I know
will last
then when that time comes
if it so happens that I do tell you I love you
then you can be sure of it.

20. Yvette and Henry 2

YVETTE
You know I like to cook

HENRY
Yes

YVETTE
And I like to make apricot confiture

HENRY
Yes

YVETTE
And I straighten up
but not right away
and usually I live in a mess
but then I straighten up later on
only it's not always straightened up.

HENRY
Right.

YVETTE
I do dishes, and I do laundry,
but I'm not good at really cleaning.

HENRY
Unh-hunh.

YVETTE
So that's how it is if you live with me
that's how it will be
that's all.

I just wanted, if we're going to be together, you know,
for everything to be clear.

HENRY
Right.

YVETTE
So you understand about laundry and dishes
and not straightening up
and there are no surprises
like you're not suddenly going to discover
oh, she doesn't straighten up
this will never work out
because I can't stand a mess
I'm sorry I wish I could
I wish I could just rise above it
but chaos makes me crazy
I just fall apart
and I can't go on living with you.

HENRY
Like that.

YVETTE
Right. That's not how it is for me.
Because, moving in with you,
this is a big deal for me,
and I don't want there to be any misunderstandings
because this is a big move for me
and I don't think
after I do this

that there will be any going back
I mean, if a year from now you were to say
oh, you never straighten up
I don't think I can live with that
the point is
I think I'd shoot you.

HENRY
Right.

YVETTE
That's how it is for me.

HENRY
That's it?

YVETTE
Yes.

HENRY
That's all.

YVETTE
Yes. I don't think there's anything else. I think that's everything.

HENRY
The truth is
I can do the laundry, too, and I do dishes.

YVETTE
Oh.

HENRY
So, I think everything's going to be OK.

YVETTE
Oh. Good. Good. That's good then.

HENRY
Right.
Plus, I cook, too.

YVETTE
You cook, too.

HENRY
Right.

YVETTE
Oh.

HENRY
Plus, I love you like crazy.

YVETTE
Oh,
you do.
Oh, good.
Good.
That's good then.
I can accept that.

21. Riff: Maria and Bob on the Greeks

MARIA
I don't think the Greeks knew much about love.

BOB
Why do you say that?

MARIA
I've seen Greek plays, you know.
There's not a single one that's a love story.

BOB
Every single one of them is a love story.

MARIA
Not one.
They're all about killing your mother and killing your father.

BOB
Because the thing that starts everything is:
Helen
falls in love with Paris,
and he takes her
to Troy,
and then Helen's husband,
to get her back,
starts the Trojan war,
and then Agamemnon,
to get the favor of the gods for the war,
has to sacrifice his own daughter,
as a result of which Agamemnon's wife
Clytemnesta
kills him,
and their son Orestes
murders Clytemnestra -
all the murders and wreckage and ruin of Greece
comes from a love story.

MARIA
Really.

BOB
Why do people kill each other all the time
if it isn't because of love gone wrong
or hurt feelings
feeling someone was disrespected
or despised
or deprived of what should have been his
treated fairly
as a good person, given in return what he himself
gave
to the other person
then maybe it would be something bad would not
have happened.
Or you could say in a more general way
if society itself had provided
which is to say, been more generous,
which is to say, loving
maybe you would not be seeing certain social
behaviors.
You could say
economic exploitation itself is a lack of social love
where selfishness has made love difficult to give
or possessiveness or a fear of loss has overpowered
love
and when you see a person dying of poverty
of the lack of medical care
this is a symptom of perversion
of the withholding of love

or the positive imposition of sadistic impulses
and thus, as you can see,
it is not just the whips and chains of sadists
and masochists in nightclubs
that you might call perverse
but the practice of politics altogether
when it deprives people of the life-giving sustenance
they need.

JONATHAN
Oh, right, well, sure, OK, I can accept that.

FRANCOIS
This could be true.

BOB
This is how it is to be a human being.
You've heard of Jeffrey Dahmer.

JONATHAN
Sure.

BOB
That's how it is if love goes wrong.

JONATHAN
(laughing easily)
I hope I'm not going to kill someone.

BOB
How do you know?

JONATHAN
I'm not that sort of person.

BOB
Maybe you don't know what sort of person you are
until you do something
and then you see what sort of person you are.

22. Riff: Forgiveness

WILLIAM
Do you think forgiveness is possible?

JOHN
Uh, primarily, uh, uh, the, uh, the...primarily the
question is does man have the power to forgive
himself. And he does. That's essentially it. I mean
if you forgive yourself, and you absolve yourself
of all, uh, of all wrongdoing in an incident, then
you're forgiven. Who cares what other people
think, because uh...

WILLIAM
Was this a process you had to go through over a
period of time.
Did you have to think about it?

JOHN
Well, no. Not until I was reading the Aquarian
gospel did I, did I strike upon, you know I had
almost had ends meet because I had certain uh
you know to-be-or-not-to-be reflections about of
course what I did. And uh,

WILLIAM
I'm sorry, what was that?

JOHN
Triple murder. Sister, husband. Sister, husband, and a nephew, my nephew. And uh, you know, uh, manic depressive.

WILLIAM
Do you mind my asking what instruments did you use?
What were the instruments?

JOHN
It was a knife. It was a knife.

WILLIAM
Knife?

JOHN
Yes.

WILLIAM
So then, the three of them were all...

JOHN
Ssssss...

(points to slitting his throat)

like that.

WILLIAM
So, uh, do you think that as time goes by, this episode will just become part of your past, or has it already...

JOHN
It has already become part of my past.

WILLIAM

Has already become part of your past. No sleepless nights? No...

JOHN

Aw, no. In the first three or four years there was a couple of nights where I would stay up thinking about how I did it, you know. And what they said... they told me later there were so many stab wounds in my sister and I said no, that's not true at all, you know. So I think I had a little blackout during the murders, but uh...

WILLIAM

I'm sorry, they said there were many stab wounds....

JOHN

Well, uh, they said there was something like thirty stab wounds in my sister, and I remember distinctly I just cut her throat once. That was all, you know, and I don't know where the thirty stab wounds came from. So that might have been some kind of blackout thing. You know, I was trying to re- re- re- uh, re- uh, uh, resurrect the uh, the crime -my initial steps, etc. You know, and uh, and uh, I took, as a matter of fact, it came right out of the, I was starting the New Testament at the time, matter of fact I'm about the only person you'll ever meet that went to, to do a triple murder with a Bible in his, in his pocket, and, and, listening to a radio. I had delusions of grandeur with the radio. Uh, I had a red shirt on that was symbolic of, of some lines in Revelation, in the, in the New Testament. Uh I had a red motor...as a matter of fact, I think it was chapter 6 something, verses 3, 4, or 5, or something where uh it was a man, it was a man. On a red horse. And, and, a man on a red horse came out, and uh, and uh uh, and he was given a knife, and unto him was given the power to kill and destroy. And I actually thought I was this person. And I thought that my red horse was this red Harley Davidson I had. And I wore...it was just, you know, it was kind of a symbolic type of thing. And and and uh, you know, uh after the murders I thought the nephew was, was the, was a new devil or something, you know. This, this is pretty bizarre now that I think back on it. I thought he was a new devil and uh, uh. I mean basically I love my sister, there's no question about that. But at times my sister hadn't come through uh for me. You know and I was in another, one of these manic attacks. And uh, and uh, uh, uh, you know, uh, I was just uh, I was just you know, I mean I was fed up with all this you know one day they treat me good and then they tell all these other people that I was a maniac and watch out for me and etc. and like that. And uh, uh, so I went to them that night to tell them I was all in trouble again, you know, and could they put me up for the night, you know, and they told me to take a hike and uh so uh, believing that I had the power to kill, uh you know, that was that for them. You know. I mean when family turns you out, that's a real blow. You know. But uh, back to the original subject of forgiveness. If I forgive myself I'm forgiven. You know that's essentially the answer. I'm the captain of my own ship. I run my own ship. Nobody can crawl in my ship unless they get permission. I just (he nods) "over there." You know. "I'm forgiven." You know. Ha-ha. You know. (Laughs.) It's as simple as that. You know. You're your own priest, you're your own leader, you're your own captain. You know. You run your own show, a lot of people know that.

NOD
What do you think of the soaps?

JOHN
What?

NOD
The soaps.

JOHN
You mean the daytimes?

NOD
Right.

JOHN
They're OK.

NOD
I think they're wonderful. I think the clothes could be better, and they could use some comic relief, you know, but otherwise I think they're wonderful.

Although, of course, I guess they could use some more fantasy. You know. In times like these, we need a little more "I wanna be," and not so much "I am."

JOHN
Uh-huh.

NOD
I think it's incredible how much excellence you see in the scenes.

JOHN
Uh-huh.

NOD
Although I think they could have more minority representation.
And I think they should move faster. You know, they should have shorter stories -beginning, middle, end, like that, and not just have the same story go on for a year or something. I mean they get lost in the past, they don't quite catch up with the times. You know, I like to see some stuff going on, I don't just want to watch my next-door neighbors.

Do you think they're too believable?

JOHN
No.

WILLIAM
Yes, I do. That's what I would say.

NOD
I'm a little tired of seeing spouses coming back
from the dead all the time and plots with missing
babies. I think that's a little too obvious.

JOHN
To me, my only complaint would be that most
shows are overly lit.

NOD
Too bright.

JOHN
Exactly.

23. Harold and Edith 2

EDITH
The truth is
I'm not a baby.

HAROLD
No.

EDITH
I've had a whole life
I've had other relationships in my lifetime
and other things, not even relationships
and people I've cared about

HAROLD
Yes, indeed.
So you've said.

EDITH
cared about deeply
people, in fact, I thought I loved
but it wasn't as though I looked at them
and felt at once I had to cry
because I felt such closeness

HAROLD
Empathy.

EDITH
Empathy.
Exactly.
Immediate empathy.
I looked at you
I almost fell on the floor.

HAROLD
Things happen so suddenly sometimes.

EDITH
Do you believe in love at first sight?

HAROLD
No.

EDITH
Neither do I.
And yet there it is:
I'd just like to kiss you.

HAROLD
Oh.

EDITH
I think for me it took so long to be able to love
another person
such a long time to grow up
get rid of all my self-involvement
all my worrying whether or not I measured up

HAROLD
Yes.

EDITH
or on the other hand
the feeling that perhaps other people were just
getting in my way
wondering if they were what I wanted
or what I deserved
didn't I deserve more than this
to be happier
is this all there is

HAROLD
Right.

EDITH
Or I thought
I need to postpone gratification
and so I did
and I got so good at it
I forgot how to seize the moment

HAROLD
breaking hearts along the way if someone else was
capable of love

at that earlier age when you weren't

EDITH
exactly
and now I think: what's the point of living a long time
if not to become tolerant of other people's idiosyncrasies

HAROLD
Or imperfections.

EDITH
you know damn well you're not going to find the perfect mate

HAROLD
someone you always agree with or even like

EDITH
and now you know that
you should be able to get along with someone who's in the same ball park

HAROLD
a human being

EDITH
another human being

HAROLD
because we are lonely people

EDITH
we like a little companionship

HAROLD
just a cup of tea with another person
what's the big deal

EDITH
you don't need a lot

HAROLD
you'd settle for very little

EDITH
very very little when it comes down to it

HAROLD
very little
and that would feel good

EDITH
a little hello, good morning, how are you today

HAROLD
I'm going to the park
OK, have a nice time
I'll see you there for lunch

EDITH
can I bring you anything

HAROLD
a sandwich in a bag?

EDITH
no problem
I'll have lunch with you in the park

HAROLD
we'll have a picnic
and afterwards
I tell you a few lines of poetry I remember
from when I was a kid in school
what I had to memorize

EDITH
and after that a nap or godknows whatall

HAROLD
and to bed

EDITH
you don't even have to touch each other
sure, what
a little touch wouldn't be bad

HAROLD
you don't have to be Don Juan
have some perfect technique

EDITH
just a touch, simple as that

HAROLD
an intimate touch?

EDITH
fine. nice. so much the better.

HAROLD
that's all: just a touch
that feels good

EDITH
OK, goodnight, that's all

HAROLD
I'd go for that.

EDITH
I'd like that.

HAROLD
I'd like that just fine.

EDITH
I'd call that a happy life

HAROLD
as happy as it needs to get for me

EDITH
Sometimes in life
you just get one chance.
Romeo and Juliet
They meet, they fall in love, they die.
That's the truth of life
you have one great love
You're born, you die
in between, if you're lucky
you have one great love
not two, not three,
just one.
It can last for years or for a moment
and then
it can be years later or a moment later

you die
and that's how it is to be human
that's what the great poets and dramatists have
known
you see Romeo and Juliet
you think: how young they were
they didn't know
there's more than one pebble on the beach
but no.
There's only one pebble on the beach.
Sometimes not even one.

24. Catherine and Hiroko 2

CATHERINE
I thought
how it was for us
you knew I loved you.

HIROKO
This is what you always said.

CATHERINE
This is what I meant.

HIROKO
And yet
whenever I was sad
you just
withdrew.

CATHERINE
I didn't think I did.

I thought I tried to help
or sometimes I put my arms around you
but sometimes it seemed
you needed space
or you felt if I just consoled you
I was condescending toward you
or if I tried to cajole you out of it
you thought I was dismissive of how you felt
or, so
then I would stand back
to give you the space you needed.

HIROKO
Yes, you would withdraw.
So that I felt
you had no empathy for me.

CATHERINE
But I did.
I did.

HIROKO
When I was with Henry
if I was sad or upset
he would just say
oh, I'm so sorry
and put his arms around me
and kiss me.

CATHERINE
You wish I would be like Henry.

HIROKO
No.

CATHERINE
You wish you were with Henry again.

HIROKO
No.

CATHERINE
I don't understand.

HIROKO
You don't understand anything I say.

CATHERINE
What are you saying?

HIROKO
I am saying
you could just say
Hiroko,
I pity you.
I pity you, Hiroko.

CATHERINE
I pity you, Hiroko.

HIROKO
You see,
it's not so hard.

CATHERINE
That's it?

HIROKO
That's all I need.
I don't need to be taken out to La Coupole
or some other restaurant
or for you to buy me little dresses
or take me to the oceanside
I just need to know
when I am sad
you pity me

CATHERINE
I pity you, Hiroko.
I pity you.
I pity you.

HIROKO
I love you, Catherine.

25. Riff: the Stars

ALLEN
The way the stars are, with your naked eyes you can't see much.

SUSAN
Oh.
No. Unless you know a lot.

ALLEN
But even looking at the stars,
I would rather say the night sky,
you see two kinds of things...3 or 4 kinds of things.

SUSAN
You see planets, you see stars, you see meteorites,
you can see aircrafts ...
all these things...

ALLEN
so it's a great show
the way the planets appear and dance around,
we follow it all the time
and we have on our bulletin boards in the back ...
and we have a chart of the whole thing,
and people record that stuff...
because we know these motions very well.
It's the foundation probably of qualitative science.

SUSAN
The early work of people trying to understand...

ALLEN
first just day and night,
then the seasons
and then the stars and then the planets...
there are different things that go back tens of
thousands of years,
older than written history.

SUSAN
Right.

ALLEN
There is a great deal more space than time, you
know.

SUSAN
No.

ALLEN
Yes.
And this is because the signals we can get
all come in at the speed of light...

SUSAN
that's really fast.

ALLEN
Yes. And they cover a great distance.
So it doesn't take them much time to cover a lot of
distance -
that's how you get more space than time in the
universe.

SUSAN
Right.
Right.

26. Lydia and Nikos 3

LYDIA
You know
I've been thinking about it
and it turns out
I do love you

NIKOS
You do?

LYDIA
Yes.

NIKOS
How could that be?

LYDIA
I look at you
and I think you're sweet.

NIKOS
Oh, sweet.

LYDIA
and good-natured.

NIKOS
Good-natured.

LYDIA
Yes.

NIKOS
You do?

LYDIA
Yes, I really do.
And I think
if you think a person's agreeable and warmhearted
then I think there's something there you can't
explain
that gives you real
delight.

NIKOS
Oh.

LYDIA
I find
you give delight to me.

NIKOS
Oh. Well.
That's what I'd hope for more than anything.

LYDIA
So would I.

NIKOS
And you're not sorry about it?

LYDIA
How do you mean?

NIKOS
That you find delight in someone
who doesn't seem to you in any other way
desirable
who doesn't perhaps have those qualities
that you can count on
for, you know, the solid, long-term kind of thing.

LYDIA
I would just take delight long-term.

NIKOS
Oh.

So would I.

THE END

Made in the USA
Middletown, DE
17 March 2018